STENDHAL
ON LOVE

TRANSLATED BY
PHILIP SIDNEY WOOLF AND
CECIL N. SIDNEY WOOLF

WITH DECORATIVE DRAWINGS BY
ROBERT GRECO

The Peter Pauper Press
MOUNT VERNON · NEW YORK

A Note on Stendhal

STENDHAL was born in 1783, when the old France was dying, and died in 1842, when the new France was not yet born. Stendhal was the pen-name of Henri Beyle, whose life was spent in an era of wars and political ferment; his own career was a series of journeys and campaigns, assignments to foreign posts, and returns to Paris.

Like his times, he was torn between the old and the new, a creature of unsettled ferment, with many contradictory impulses. Though an ardent liberal and Bonapartist, he relished the old courtly days, when a decadent aristocracy had the leisure to explore and savor the nuances of feeling. He shared the current romantic sentimentality, and the vogue of the Medieval, but he also had the modern scientific urge to locate, isolate, and describe the facts of truth without any sentimentality whatever. He was a poor painter and a good soldier. His happiest years were spent in the aristocratic salons of Milan, where everyone cultivated the graces, but when he wrote his books he consciously avoided all graces, and sought to convey only his exact meanings, with no secondary pleasure in the sound of words.

In his own lifetime he was an "unsuccessful" author. Balzac appreciated him, and specially praised the present book; but even so his great novels went largely unread. Stendhal himself (in the following preface) blamed this indifference on the then current interest in politics, and neglect of passion, in France.

For some years after his death, this indifference to Stendhal persisted; but in 1853 a new edition of his works was published at the urging of a few admirers, and in the following year the great and influential Sainte-Beuve focussed the attention of the literary world upon him. Modern readers have taken Stendhal to their hearts, for, with all his contradictions, he was largely a creature of modern times, and a forerunner of that school which describes not so much the actions as the meanings of our lives.

Preface to the Edition of 1842

I COME to beg indulgence of the reader for the peculiar form of this *Physiology of Love*. It is twenty-eight years since the turmoil, which followed the fall of Napoleon, deprived me of my position. Two years earlier chance threw me, immediately after the horrors of the retreat from Russia, into the midst of a charming town, where I had the enchanting prospect of passing the rest of my days. In happy Lombardy, at Milan, at Venice, the great, or rather only, business of life is pleasure. No attention, there, to the deeds and movements of your neighbor; hardly a troubled thought for what is to happen to you. If a man notice the existence of his neighbor, it does not enter his head to hate him. Take away from the occupations of a French provincial town jealousy — and what is left? The absence, the impossibility of that cruel jealousy forms the surest part of that happiness, which draws all the provincials to Paris.

Following the masked balls of the Carnival, which in 1820 was more brilliant than usual, the noise of five or six completely reckless proceedings occupied the society of Milan an entire month; although they are used over there to things which in France would pass for incredible. The fear of ridicule would in this country paralyze such fantastic actions: only to speak of them I need great courage.

One evening people were discussing profoundly the effects and the causes of these extravagances, at the house of the charming Mme. Pietra Grua, who happened, extraordinarily enough, not to be mixed up with these escapades. The thought came to me that perhaps in less than a year I should have nothing left of all those strange facts, and of the causes alleged for them, but a recollection, on which I could not depend. I got hold of a concert program, and wrote a few words on it in pencil. A game of faro was suggested: we were thirty seated round a card-table, but the conversation was so animated that people forgot to play. Towards the close of the evening came in Col. Scotti, one of the most charming men in the Italian army: he was asked for his quantum of circumstances relative to the curious facts with which we were busy, and, indeed, his story of certain things, which chance had confided to his knowledge, gave them an entirely new aspect. I took up my concert program and added these new circumstances.

This collection of particulars on Love was continued in the same way, with pencil and odd scraps of paper, snatched up in the salons, where I heard the anecdotes told. Soon I looked for a common rule by which to recognize different degrees in them. Two months later fear of being taken for a Carbonaro made me return to Paris — only for a *few months I hoped, but never again have I seen Milan, where I had passed seven years.*

6 *Pining with boredom at Paris, I conceived the idea of occupying myself again with the charming country from which fear had driven me. I strung together my scraps of paper and presented the book to a publisher. But soon a difficulty was raised: the printer declared that it was impossible to work from notes written in pencil and I could see that he found such copy beneath his dignity. The printer's young apprentice, who brought me back my notes, seemed quite ashamed of the more than doubtful compliment, which had been put into his mouth: He knew how to write and I dictated to him my pencil notes.*

I understood, too, that discretion required me to change the proper names, and, above all, abridge the anecdotes. Although no one reads in Milan, the book, if ever it reached there, might have seemed a piece of wicked mischief.

So I brought out an ill-fated volume. I have the courage to own that I despised at that period elegance in style. I saw the young apprentice wholly taken up with avoiding sentence-endings that were unmusical and odd sounds in the arrangement of words. In return, he made throughout no scruple of changing details of fact, difficult to express: Voltaire himself is afraid of things which are difficult to tell.

The Essay on Love had no claim to merit except the number of the fine shades of feeling, which I begged the reader to verify among his memories, if he were happy enough to have any. But in all this there was something much worse: I was then, as ever, very inexperienced in the department of literature, and the publisher, to whom I had presented the MS., printed it on bad paper and in an absurd format. In fact a month later, when I asked him for news of the book — "On peut dire qu'il est sacré," he said, "For no one comes near it."

It had never even crossed my mind to solicit articles in the papers: such a thing would have seemed to me an ignominy. And yet no work was in more pressing need of recommendation to the patience of the reader. Under the menace of becoming unintelligible at the very outset, it was necessary to bring the public to accept the new word "crystallization," suggested as a lively expression for that collection of strange fancies, which we weave round our idea of the loved one, as true and even indubitable realities.

At that time wholly absorbed in my love for the least details, which I had lately observed in the Italy of my dreams, I avoided with care every concession, every amenity of style, which might have rendered the Essay on Love less peculiarly fantastic in the eyes of men of letters.

Further, I was not flattering to the public. Literature at that time, all defaced by our great and recent misfortunes, seemed to have no other interest than the consolation of our unhappy pride: it used to rhyme "gloire" with "victoire," "guerriers" with "lauriers," etc. The true circumstances of the situations, which it pretends to treat, seem never to have any attraction for the tedious literature of that period: it looks for nothing but an opportunity of complimenting that people, enslaved to fashion, whom a great man had called a great nation, forgetting that they were only great on condition that their leader was himself.

As the result of my ignorance of the exigencies of the humblest success, I found no more than seventeen readers between 1822 and 1833: it is doubtful whether the Essay on Love has been understood after twenty years of existence by a hundred connoisseurs. A few have had the patience to observe the various phases of this disease in the people infected with it in their circle; for we must speak of it as a disease, in order to understand that passion which in the last thirty years our fear of ridicule has taken so much trouble to hide — it is this way which sometimes leads to its cure.

Now and now only, after half a century of revolutions, engrossing one after another our whole attention, now and now only after five complete changes in the form and the tendencies of our government, does the revolution just begin to show itself in our way of living. Love, or that which commonly appropriates Love's name and fills its place, was all-powerful in the France of Louis XV. Colonels were created by the ladies of the court; and that court was nothing less than the fairest place in the kingdom. Fifty years after, the court is no more; and the gift of a license to sell tobacco in the meanest provincial town is beyond the power of the most surely established ladies of the reigning bourgeoisie or of the pouting nobility.

It must be owned, women are out of fashion. In our brilliant salons the young men of twenty affect not to address them; they much prefer to stand round the noisy talker dealing, in a provincial accent, with the question of the right to vote, and to try and slip in their own little word. The rich youths, who, to keep up a show of the good-fellowship of past times, take a pride in seeming frivolous, prefer to talk horses and play high in the circles where women are excluded. The deadly indifference which seems to preside over the relations of young men and the women of five-and-twenty, for whose presence society has to thank the boredom of marriage, will bring, perhaps, a few wise spirits to accept this scrupulously exact description of the successive phases of the malady called Love.

Seeing the terrible change which has plunged us into the stagnation of to-day, and makes unintelligible to us the society of 1778, such as we find it in the letters of Diderot to Mlle. Voland, his mistress, or in *the Memoirs of Madame d'Epinay, a man might ask the question, which of our successive governments has killed in us the faculty of enjoying ourselves, and drawn us nearer to the gloomiest people on the face of the earth? The only passable thing which that people have invented — parliament and the honesty of their parties — we are unable even to copy. In return, the stupidest of their gloomy conceptions, the spirit of dignity, has come among us to take the place of our French gaiety, which is to be found now only in the five hundred balls in the outskirts of Paris or in the south of France, beyond Bordeaux.*

But which of our successive governments has cost us the fearful misfortune of anglicization? Must we accuse that energetic govern-ment of 1793, which prevented the foreigners from coming to pitch their camp in Montmartre — that government which in a few years will seem heroic in our eyes and forms a worthy prelude to that, which under Napoleon, went forth to carry our name into all the capitals of Europe?

We shall pass over the well-meaning stupidity of the Directoire, *illustrated by the talents of Carnot and the immortal campaign of 1796-1797 in Italy.*

The corruption of the court of Barras still recalled something of the gaiety of the old order; the graces of Madame Bonaparte proved that we had no aptitude at that time for the churlishness and charnel-house of the English.

The profound respect, which despite the jealousy of the Faubourg Saint-Germain, we could not but feel for the First Consul's method of government, and the men whose superior merit adorned the society of Paris — such as the Cretets and the Darus — relieves the Empire of the burden of responsibility for the remarkable change which has been effected, in the first half of the nineteenth century, in the character of the French.

Unnecessary to carry my investigation further: the reader will reflect and be quite able to draw his own conclusions.

An Essay on Love

Of Love

M Y aim is to comprehend that passion, of which every sincere development has a character of beauty.

There are four kinds of love.

1. Passion-love — that of the Portuguese nun, of Héloïse for Abelard, of Captain de Vesel, of Sergeant de Cento.

2. Gallant love — that which ruled in Paris towards 1760, to be found in the memoirs and novels of the period, in Crébillon, Lauzun, Duclos, Marmontel, Chamfort, Mme. d'Epinay, etc. 'Tis a picture in which everything, to the very shadows, should be rose-color, in which may enter nothing disagreeable under any pretext whatsoever, at the cost of a lapse of etiquette, of good taste, of refinement, etc. A man of breeding foresees all the ways of acting, that he is likely to adopt or meet with in the different phases of this love. True love is often less refined; for that in which there is no pas-

sion and nothing unforeseen, has always a store of ready wit: the latter is a cold and pretty miniature, the former a picture by the Carracci. Passion-love carries us away in defiance of all our interests, gallant love manages always to respect them. True, if we take from this poor love its vanity, there is very little left: once stripped, it is like a tottering convalescent, scarcely able to drag himself along.

3. Physical love. Out hunting — a fresh, pretty country girl crosses your path and escapes into the wood. Everyone knows the love founded on this kind of pleasure: and all begin that way at sixteen, however parched and unhappy the character.

4. Vanity-love. The vast majority of men, especially in France, desire and have a fashionable woman, in the same way as a man gets a fine horse, as something which the luxury of a young man demands. Their vanity more or less flattered, more or less piqued, gives birth to transports of feelings. Sometimes there is also physical love, but by no means always: often there is not so much as physical pleasure. A duchess is never more than thirty for a bourgeois, said the Duchesse de Chaulnes, and those admitted to the Court of that just man, King Louis of Holland, recall with amusement a pretty woman from the Hague, who could not help finding any man charming who was Duke or Prince. But true to the principle of monarchy, as soon as a Prince arrived at Court, the Duke was dismissed: she was, as it were, the decoration of the diplomatic body.

The happiest case of this uninspiring relationship is that in which to physical pleasure is added habit. In that case store of memories makes it resemble love a little; there is the pique of self-esteem and sadness on being left; then, romance forces upon us its ideas and we believe that we are in love and melancholy, for vanity aspires to credit itself with a great passion. This, at least, is certain that, whatever kind of love be the source of pleasure, as soon as the soul is stirred, the pleasure is keen and its memory alluring, and in this passion, contrary to most of the others, the memory of our losses seems always to exceed the bounds of what we can hope for in the future.

Sometimes, in vanity-love habit or despair of finding better produces a kind of friendship, of all kinds the least pleasant: it prides itself on its security, etc.[1]

Physical pleasure, being of our nature, is known to everybody, but it takes no more than a subordinate position in the eyes of tender and passionate souls. If they raise a laugh in the *salons*, if often they are made unhappy in the intrigues of society, in return the pleasure which they feel must remain always inaccessible to those hearts, whose beat only vanity and gold can quicken. A few virtuous and sensitive women have scarcely a conception of physical pleasures: they have so rarely risked them, if one may use the expression, and even then the transports of passion-love caused bodily pleasure almost to be forgotten.

There are men victims and instruments of diabolical pride, of a pride in the style of Alfieri. Those people who, perhaps, are cruel because, like Nero, judging all men after the pattern of their own heart, they are always atremble — such people, I say, can attain physical pleasure only in so far as it is accompanied by the greatest possible exercise of pride, in so far, that is to say, as they practice cruelties on the companion of their pleasures. Hence the horrors of *Justine*. At any rate such men have no sense of security.

To conclude, instead of distinguishing four different forms of love, we can easily admit eight or ten shades of difference. Perhaps mankind has as many ways of feeling as of seeing; but these differences of nomenclature alter in no degree the judgments which follow. Subject to the same laws, all forms of love, which can be seen here below, have their birth, life and death or ascend to immortality.[2]

[1] Well-known dialogue of Pont de Veyle with Madame du Deffant, at the fireside.

[2] This book is a free translation of an Italian MS. of M. Lisio Visconti, a young man of the highest distinction, who died recently at Volterra, the place of his birth. The day of his sudden death he gave the translator permission to publish his Essay on Love, if means were found to shape it to a decorous form. Castel Fiorentino, June 10th, 1819.

14 THIS is what takes places in the soul: —

    1. Admiration.

    2. A voice within says: "What pleasure to kiss, to be kissed."

    3. Hope.

We study her perfections: this is the moment at which a woman should yield to realize the greatest possible physical pleasure. In the case even of the most reserved women, their eyes redden at the moment when hope is conceived: the passion is so strong, the pleasure so keen, that it betrays itself by striking signs.

    4. Love is born.

To love — that is to have pleasure in seeing, touching, feeling, through all the senses and as near as possible, an object to be loved and that loves us.

    5. The first crystallization begins.

The lover delights in decking with a thousand perfections the woman of whose love he is sure: he dwells on all the details of his happiness with a satisfaction that is boundless. He is simply magnifying a superb bounty just fallen to him from heaven, — he has no knowledge of it but the assurance of its possession.

Leave the mind of a lover to its natural movements for twenty-four hours, and this is what you will find.

At the salt mines of Salzburg a branch stripped of its leaves by winter is thrown into the abandoned depths of the mine; taken out two or three months later it is covered with brilliant crystals; the smallest twigs, those no stouter than the leg of a sparrow, are arrayed with an infinity of sparkling, dazzling diamonds; it is impossible to recognize the original branch.

I call crystallization the operation of the mind which, from everything which is presented to it, draws the conclusion that there are new perfections in the object of its love.

A traveller speaks of the freshness of the orange groves at Genoa, on the sea coast, during the scorching days of summer. —What pleasure to enjoy that freshness with her!

One of your friends breaks his arm in the hunting-field. — How sweet to be nursed by a woman you love! To be always with her, to see every moment her love for you, would make pain almost a blessing: and starting from the broken arm of your friend, you conclude with the absolute conviction of the angelic goodness of your mistress. In a word, it is enough to think of a perfection in order to see it in that which you love.

This phenomenon, which I venture to call crystallization, is the product of human nature, which commands us to enjoy and sends warm blood rushing to our brain; it springs from the conviction that the pleasures of love increase with the perfections of its object, and from the idea: "She is mine." The savage has no time to go beyond the first step. He is delighted, but his mental activity is employed in following the flying deer in the forest, and with the flesh with which he must as soon as possible repair his forces, or fall beneath the axe of his enemy.

At the other pole of civilization, I have no doubt that a sensitive woman may come to the point of feeling no physical pleasure but with the man she loves.[1] It is the opposite with the savage. But among civilized peoples, woman has leisure at her disposal, while the savage is so pressed with necessary occupations that he is forced to treat his female as a beast of burden. If the females of many animals are more fortunate, it is because the subsistence of the males is more assured.

But let us leave the backwoods again for Paris. A man of passion sees all perfections in that which he loves. And yet his attention may still be distracted; for the soul has its surfeit of all that is uniform, even of perfect bliss.[2]

[1] If this peculiarity is not observed in the case of man, the reason is that on his side there is no modesty to be for a moment sacrificed.

[2] That is to say, that the same tone of existence can give but one instant of perfect happiness; but with a man of passion, his mood changes ten times a day.

This is what happens to distract his attention: —

6. Birth of Doubt.

After ten or twelve glances, or some other series of actions, which can last as well several days as one moment, hopes are first given and later confirmed. The lover, recovered from his first surprise and, accustomed to his happiness or guided by theory, which, always based on the most frequent cases, must only take light women into account — the lover, I say, demands more positive proofs and wishes to press his good fortune.

He is parried with indifference,[1] coldness, even anger, if he show too much assurance — in France a shade of irony, which seems to say: "You are not quite as far as you think."

A woman behaves in this way, either because she wakes up from a moment of intoxication, and obeys the word of modesty, which she trembles to have infringed, or simply through prudence or coquetry.

The lover comes to doubt of the happiness, to which he looked forward: he scans more narrowly the reasons that he fancied he had for hope.

He would like to fall back upon the other pleasures of life, and finds them annihilated. He is seized with the fear of a terrible disaster, and at the same time with a profound preoccupation.

7. Second crystallization.

Here begins the second crystallization, which forms diamonds out of the proofs of the idea — "She loves me."

The night which follows the birth of doubts, every quarter of an hour, after a moment of fearful unhappiness, the lover says to himself — "Yes, she loves me" — and crystallization has its turn, discovering new charms. Then doubt with haggard eye grapples him and brings him to a standstill,

---

[1] The *coup de foudre* (thunderbolt from the blue), as it was called in the novels of the seventeenth century, which disposes of the fate of the hero and his mistress, is a movement of the soul, which for having been abused by a host of scribblers, is experienced none the less in real life. It comes from the impossibility of this defensive manœuvre. The woman who loves finds too much happiness in the sentiment, which she feels, to carry through successful deception: tired of prudence, she neglects all precaution and yields blindly to the passion of loving. Diffidence makes the *coup de foudre* impossible.

blank. His heart forgets to beat — "But does she love me?" he says to himself. Between these alternatives, agonizing and rapturous, the poor lover feels in his very soul: "She would give me pleasures, which she alone can give me and no one else."

It is the palpability of this truth, this path on the extreme edge of a terrible abyss and within touch, on the other hand, of perfect happiness, which gives so great a superiority to the second crystallization over the first.

The lover wanders from moment to moment between these three ideas: —

1. She has every perfection.
2. She loves me.
3. What means of obtaining the greatest proof of her love?

The most agonizing moment of love, still young, is when it sees the false reasoning it has made, and must destroy a whole span of crystallization.

Doubt is the natural outcome of crystallization.

Of Hope

A VERY small degree of hope is enough to cause the birth of love.

In the course of events hope may fail — love is none the less born. With a firm, daring and impetuous character, and in an imagination developed by the troubles of life, the degree of hope may be smaller: it can come sooner to an end, without killing love.

If a lover has had troubles, if he is of a tender, thoughtful character, if he despairs of other women, and if his admiration is intense for her whom he loves, no ordinary pleasure will succeed in distracting him from the second crystallization. He will prefer to dream of the most doubtful chance of pleasing her one day, than to accept from an ordinary woman all she could lavish.

The woman whom he loves would have to kill his hope at that period, and (note carefully, not later) in some inhuman manner, and overwhelm him with those marks of patent contempt, which make it impossible for him to appear again in public.

Far longer delays between all these periods are compatible with the birth of love.

It demands much more hope and much more substantial hope, in the case of the cold, the phlegmatic and the prudent. The same is true of people no longer young.

It is the second crystallization which ensures love's duration, for then every moment makes it clear that the question is — be loved or die. Long months of love have turned into habit this conviction of our every moment — how find means to support the thought of loving no more? The stronger the character the less is it subject to inconstancy.

This second crystallization is almost entirely absent from the passions inspired by women who yield too soon.

After the crystallizations have worked — especially the second, which is far the stronger — the branch is no longer to be recognized by indifferent eyes, for: —

1. It is adorned with perfections which they do not see.

2. It is adorned with perfections which for them are not perfections at all.

The perfection of certain charms, mentioned to him by an old friend of his love, and a certain hint of liveliness noticed in her eye, are a diamond in the crystallization[1] of Del Rosso. These ideas, conceived during the evening, keep him dreaming all the night.

An unexpected answer, which makes me see more clearly a tender, generous, ardent, or, as it is popularly called,

[1] I have called this essay a book of Ideology. My object was to indicate that, though it is called "Love," it is not a novel and still less diverting like a novel. I apologize to philosophers for having taken the word Ideology: I certainly did not intend to usurp a title which is the right of another. If Ideology is a detailed description of ideas and all the parts which can compose ideas, the present book is a detailed description of all the feelings which can compose the passion called Love. Proceeding, I draw certain consequences from this description: for example, the manner of love's cure. I know no word to say in Greek "discourse on ideas." I might have had a word invented by one of my learned friends, but I am already vexed enough at having to adopt the new word crystallization, and,

romantic[1] soul, preferring to the happiness of kings the simple pleasures of a walk with the loved one at midnight in a lonely wood, gives me food for dreams[2] for a whole night.

Let him call my mistress a prude: I shall call his a whore.

The Seven Stages of Love

IN a soul completely detached — a girl living in a lonely castle in the depth of the country—the slightest astonishment may bring on a slight admiration, and, if the faintest hope intervene, cause the birth of love and crystallization.

In this case love delights, to begin with, just as a diversion.

Surprise and hope are strongly supported by the need, felt at the age of sixteen, of love and sadness. It is well

if this essay finds readers, it is quite possible that they will not allow my new word to pass. To avoid it, I own, would have been the work of literary talent: I tried, but without success. Without this word, which expresses, according to me, the principal phenomenon of that madness called Love — madness, however, which procures for man the greatest pleasures which it is given to the beings of his species to taste on earth — without the use of this word, which it were necessary to replace at every step by a paraphrase of considerable length, the description, which I give of what passes in the head and the heart of a man in love, would have become obscure, heavy and tedious, even for me who am the author: what would it have been for the reader?

I invite, therefore, the reader, whose feelings the word crystallization shocks too much, to close the book. To be read by many forms no part of my prayers — happily, no doubt, for me. I should love dearly to give great pleasure to thirty or forty people of Paris, whom I shall never see, but for whom, without knowing, I have a blind affection. Some young Madame Roland, for example, reading her book in secret and precious quickly hiding it, at the least noise, in the drawers of her father's bench — her father the engraver of watches. A soul like that of Madame Roland will forgive me, I hope, not only the word crystallization, used to express that act of madness which makes us perceive every beauty, every kind of perfection, in the woman whom we begin to love, but also several too daring ellipses besides. The reader has only to take a pencil and write between the lines the five or six words which are missing.

[1] All his actions had at first in my eyes that heavenly air, which makes of a man a being apart, and differentiates him from all others. I thought that I could read in his eyes that thirst for a happiness more sublime, that unavowed melancholy, which yearns for something better than we find here below, and which in all the trials that fortune and revolution can bring upon a romantic soul,

> ... still prompts the celestial sight
> For which we wish to live or dare to die.

(Last letter of Bianca to her mother. Forlì, 1817.)

[2] It is in order to abridge and to be able to paint the interior of the soul, that the author, using the formula of the first person, alleges several feelings to which he is a stranger: personally, he never had any which would be worth quoting.

known that the restlessness of that age is a thirst for love, and a peculiarity of thirst is not to be extremely fastidious about the kind of draught that fortune offers.

Let us recapitulate the seven stages of love. They are: —

1. Admiration.
2. What pleasure, etc.
3. Hope.
4. Love is born.
5. First crystallization.
6. Doubt appears.
7. Second crystallization.

Between Nos. 1 and 2 may pass one year. One month between Nos. 2 and 3; but if hope does not make haste in coming, No. 2 is insensibly resigned as a source of unhappiness. A twinkling of the eye between Nos. 3 and 4.

There is no interval between Nos. 4 and 5. The sequence can only be broken by intimate intercourse.

Some days may pass between Nos. 5 and 6, according to the degree to which the character is impetuous and used to risk, but between Nos. 6 and 7 there is no interval.

The Power of Love

MAN is not free to avoid doing that which gives him more pleasure to do than all other possible actions.[1]

Love is like the fever, it is born and spends itself without the slightest intervention of the will. That is one of the principal differences between gallant-love and passion-love. And you cannot give yourself credit for the fair qualities in what you really love, any more than for a happy chance.

Further, love is of all ages: observe the passion of Madame du Deffant for the graceless Horace Walpole. A more recent and more pleasing example is perhaps still remembered in Paris.

[1] As regards crime, it belongs to good education to inspire remorse, which foreseen, acts as a counterbalance.

In proof of great passions I admit only those of their consequences, which are exposed to ridicule: timidity, for example, proves love. I am not speaking of the bashfulness of the enfranchised schoolboy.

The Crystals of Salzburg

CRYSTALLIZATION scarcely ceases at all during love. This is its history: so long as all is well between the lover and the loved, there is crystallization by imaginary solution; it is only imagination which makes him sure that such and such perfection exists in the woman he loves. But after intimate intercourse, fears are continually coming to life, to be allayed only by more real solutions. Thus his happiness is only uniform in its source. Each day has a different bloom.

If the loved one yields to the passion, which she shares, and falls into the enormous error of killing fear by the eagerness of her transports,[1] crystallization ceases for an instant; but when love loses some of its eagerness, that is to say some of its fears, it acquires the charm of entire abandon, of confidence without limits: a sense of sweet familiarity comes to take the edge from all the pains of life, and give to fruition another kind of interest.

Are you deserted? — Crystallization begins again; and every glance of admiration, the sight of every happiness which she can give you, and of which you thought no longer, leads up to this agonizing reflection: "That happiness, that charm, I shall meet it no more. It is lost and the fault is mine!" You may look for happiness in sensations of another kind. Your heart refuses to feel them. Imagination depicts for you well enough the physical situation, mounts you well enough on a fast hunter in Devonshire woods.[2] But

[1] Diane de Poitiers, in the *Princesse de Clèves*, by Mme. de Lafayette.

[2] If you could imagine being happy in that position, crystallization would have deferred to your mistress the exclusive privilege of giving you that happiness.

you feel quite certain that there you would find no pleasure. It is the optical illusion produced by a pistol shot.

Gaming has also its crystallization, provoked by the use of the sum of money to be won.

The hazards of Court life, so regretted by the nobility, under the name of Legitimists, attached themselves so dearly only by the crystallization they provoked. No courtier existed who did not dream of the rapid fortune of a Luynes or a Lauzun, no charming woman who did not see in prospect the duchy of Madame de Polignac. No rationalist government can give back that crystallization. Nothing is so *anti-imagination* as the government of the United States of America. We have noticed that to their neighbors, the savages, crystallization is almost unknown. The Romans scarcely had an idea of it, and discovered it only for physical love.

Hate has its crystallization: as soon as it is possible to hope for revenge, hate begins again.

If every creed, in which there is absurdity and inconsequence, tends to place at the head of the party the people who are most absurd, that is one more of the effects of crystallization. Even in mathematics (observe the Newtonians in 1740) crystallization goes on in the mind, which cannot keep before it at every moment every part of the demonstration of that which it believes.

In proof, see the destiny of the great German philosophers, whose immortality, proclaimed so often, never manages to last longer than thirty or forty years.

It is the impossibility of fathoming the "why?" of our feelings, which makes the most reasonable man a fanatic in music.

In face of certain contradictions it is not possible to be convinced at will that we are right.

Birth of Love in the Two Sexes

WOMEN attach themselves by the favors they dispense. As nineteen-twentieths of their ordinary dreams are relative to love, after intimate intercourse these day-dreams group themselves round a single object; they have to justify a course so extraordinary, so decisive, so contrary to all the habits of modesty. Men have no such task; and, besides, the imagination of women has time to work in detail upon the sweetness of such moments.

As love casts doubts upon things the best proved, the woman who, before she gave herself, was perfectly sure that her lover was a man above the crowd, no sooner thinks she has nothing left to refuse him, than she is all fears lest he was only trying to put one more woman on his list.

Then, and then only appears the second crystallization, which being hand in hand with fear, is far the stronger.[1]

Yesterday a queen, to-day she sees herself a slave. This state of soul and mind is encouraged in a woman by the nervous intoxication resulting from pleasures, which are just so much keener as they are more rare. Besides, a woman before her embroidery frame — insipid work which only occupies the hand — is thinking about her lover; while he is galloping with his squadron over the plain, where leading one wrong movement would bring him under arrest.

I should think, therefore, that the second crystallization must be far stronger in the case of women, because theirs are more vivid fears; their vanity and honor are compromised; distraction at least is more difficult.

A woman cannot be guided by the habit of being reasonable, which I, Man, working at things cold and reasonable for six hours every day, contract at my office perforce. Even outside love, women are inclined to abandon themselves to their imagination and habitual high spirits: faults, there-

---

[1] This second crystallization is wanting in light women, who are far away from all these romantic ideas.

fore, in the object of their love ought more rapidly to disappear. Women prefer emotion to reason — that is plain: in virtue of the futility of our customs, none of the affairs of the family fall on their shoulders, so that reason is of no use to them and they never find it of any practical good.

On the contrary, to them it is always harmful; for the only object of its appearance is to scold them for the pleasures of yesterday, or forbid them others for to-morrow.

Give over to your wife the management of your dealings with the bailiffs of two of your farms — I wager the accounts will be kept better than by you, and then, sorry tyrant, you will have the *right* at least to complain, since to make yourself loved you do not possess the talent. As soon as women enter on general reasonings, they are unconsciously making love. But in matters of detail they take pride in being stricter and more exact than men. Half the small trading is put into the hands of women, who acquit themselves of it better than their husbands. It is a well-known maxim that, if you are speaking business with a woman, you cannot be too serious.

This is because they are at all times and in all places greedy of emotion. — Observe the pleasures of burial rites in Scotland.

Imagination and Experience

This was her favored fairy realm, and here she erected her aerial palaces — Bride of Lammermoor, Chap. III

A GIRL of eighteen has not enough crystallization in her power, forms desires too limited by her narrow experiences of the things of life, to be in a position to love with as much passion as a woman of twenty-eight.

This evening I was exposing this doctrine to a clever woman, who maintains the contrary. "A girl's imagination being chilled by no disagreeable experience, and the prime of youth burning with all its force, any man can be the motive upon which she creates a ravishing image. Every time that she meets her lover, she will enjoy, not what he is in reality, but that image of delight which she has created for herself.

"Later, she is by this lover and by all men disillusioned, experience of the dark reality has lessened in her the power of crystallization, mistrust has clipped the wings of imagination. At the instance of no man on earth, were he a very prodigy, could she form so irresistible an image: she could love no more with the same fire of her first youth. And as in love it is only the illusion formed by ourselves which we enjoy, never can the image, which she may create herself at twenty-eight, have the brilliance and the loftiness on which first love was built at sixteen: the second will always seem of a degenerate species."

"No, madam. Evidently it is the presence of mistrust, absent at sixteen, which must give to this second love a different color. In early youth love is like an immense stream, which sweeps all before it in its course, and we feel that we cannot resist it. Now at twenty-eight a gentle heart knows itself: it knows that, if it is still to find some happiness in life, from love it must be claimed; and this poor, torn heart becomes the seat of a fearful struggle between love and mistrust. Crystallization proceeds gradually; but the crystallization, which emerges triumphant from this terrible proof, in which the soul in all its movements never loses sight of the most awful danger, is a thousand times more brilliant and more solid than crystallization at sixteen, in which everything, by right of age, is gaiety and happiness."

"In this way love should be less gay and more passionate."[1]

This conversation (Bologna, 9 March, 1820), bringing into doubt a point which seemed to me so clear, makes me believe more and more, that a man can say practically nothing with any sense on that which happens in the inmost heart of a woman of feeling: as to a coquet it is different — *we* also have senses and vanity.

---

[1] Epicurus said that discrimination is necessary to participation in pleasure.

26 The disparity between the birth of love in the two sexes would seem to come from the nature of their hopes, which are different. One attacks, the other defends; one asks, the other refuses; one is daring, the other timid.

The man reflects: "Can I please her? Will she love me?"

The woman: "When he says he loves me, isn't it for sport? Is his a solid character? Can he answer to himself for the length of his attachments?" Thus it is that many women regard and treat a young man of twenty-three as a child. If he has gone through six campaigns, he finds everything different — he is a young hero.

On the man's side, hope depends simply on the actions of that which he loves — nothing easier to interpret. On the side of woman, hope must rest on moral considerations — very difficult rightly to appreciate.

Most men demand such a proof of love, as to their mind dissipates all doubts; women are not so fortunate as to be able to find such a proof. And there is in life this trouble for lovers — that what makes the security and happiness of one, makes the danger and almost the humiliation of the other.

In love, men run the risk of the secret torture of the soul — women expose themselves to the scoffs of the public; they are more timid, and, besides, for them public opinion means much more. — "Sois considérée, il le faut."[1]

They have not that sure means of ours of mastering public opinion by risking for an instant their life.

Women, then, must naturally be far more mistrustful. In virtue of their habits, all the mental movements, which form periods in the birth of love, are in their case more mild, more timid, more gradual and less decided. There is therefore a greater disposition to constancy; they will less easily withdraw from a crystallization once begun.

A woman, seeing her lover, reflects with rapidity, or yields to the happiness of loving — happiness from which

[1] Remember the maxim of Beaumarchais: "Nature has said to woman: 'Be fair if you can, wise if you wish, but be *esteemed* — you must.' No admiration in France without *esteem* — equally no love."

she is recalled in a disagreeable manner, if he make the least attack; for at the call to arms all pleasures must be abandoned. The lover's part is simpler — he looks in the eyes of the woman he loves; a single smile can raise him to the zenith of happiness, and he looks continually for it.[1] The length of the siege humiliates a man; on the contrary it makes a woman's glory.

A woman is capable of loving and, for an entire year, not saying more than ten or twelve words to the man whom she loves. At the bottom of her heart she keeps note how often she has seen him — twice she went with him to the theatre, twice she sat near him at dinner, three times he bowed to her out walking. One evening during some game he kissed her hand: since then she allows no one to kiss it under any pretext, at the risk even of seeming peculiar.

In a man, Léonore remarked to me, such conduct would be called a feminine way of love.

Feeling and Expression

I MAKE every possible effort to be dry. I would impose silence upon my heart, which feels that it has much to say. When I think that I have noted a truth, I always tremble lest I have written only a sigh.

The Role of Beauty

IN proof of crystallization I shall content myself with recalling the following anecdote. A young woman hears that Edward, her relation, who is to return from the Army, is a youth of great distinction; she is assured that he loves

---

[1] Quando leggemmo il disiato riso
Esser baciato da cotanto amante,
Costui che mai da me non fia diviso,
La bocca mi bacciò tutto tremante.
Dante, *Inf.*, Cant. V.

["When we read how the desired smile was kissed by such a lover, he, who never from me shall be divided, on my mouth kissed me all trembling."]

her on her reputation; but he will want probably to see her, before making a proposal and asking her of her parents. She notices a young stranger at church, she hears him called Edward, she thinks of nothing but him — she is in love with him. Eight days later the real Edward arrives; he is not the Edward of church. She turns pale, will be unhappy for ever, if she is forced to marry him.

That is what the poor of understanding call an example of the senselessness of love.

A man of generosity lavishes the most delicate benefits upon a girl in distress. No one could have more virtues, and love was about to be born; but he wears a shabby hat, and she notices that he is awkward in the saddle. The girl confesses with a sigh that she cannot return the warm feelings, which he evidently has for her.

A man pays his attentions to a lady of the greatest respectability. She hears that this gentleman has had physical troubles of a comical nature: she finds him intolerable. And yet she had no intention of giving herself to him, and these secret troubles in no way blighted his understanding or amiability. It is simply that crystallization was made impossible.

In order that a human being may delight in deifying an object to be loved, be it taken from the Ardennes forest or picked up at a Bal de Coulon, that it seems to him perfect is the first necessity — perfect by no means in every relation, but in every relation in which it is seen at the time. Perfect in all respects it will seem only after several days of the second crystallization. The reason is simple — then it is enough to have the idea of a perfection in order to see it in the object of our love.

Beauty is only thus far necessary to the birth of love — ugliness must not form an obstacle. The lover soon comes to find his mistress beautiful, such as she is, without thinking of ideal beauty.

The features which make up the ideally beautiful would promise, if he could see them, a quantity of happiness, if

I may use the expression, which I would express by the number one; whereas the features of his mistress, such as they are, promise him one thousand units of happiness.

Before the birth of love beauty is necessary as advertisement: it predisposes us towards that passion by means of the praises, which we hear given to the object of our future love. Very eager admiration makes the smallest hope decisive.

In gallant-love, and perhaps in passion-love during the first five minutes, a woman, considering a possible lover, gives more weight to the way in which he is seen by other women, than to the way in which she sees him herself.

Hence the success of princes and officers.[1] The pretty women of the Court of old King Louis XIV were in love with that sovereign.

Great care should be taken not to offer facilities to hope, before it is certain that admiration is there. It might give rise to dullness, which makes love for ever impossible, and which, at any rate, is only to be cured by the sting of wounded pride.

No one feels sympathy for the simpleton, nor for a smile which is always there; hence the necessity in society of a veneer of rakishness — that is, the privileged manner. From too debased a plant we scorn to gather even a smile. In love, our vanity disdains a victory which is too easy; and in all matters man is not given to magnifying the value of an offering.

---

[1] Those who remarked in the countenance of this young hero a dissolute audacity mixed with extreme haughtiness and indifference to the feelings of others, could not yet deny to his countenance that sort of comeliness, which belongs to an open set of features well formed by nature, modelled by art to the usual rules of courtesy, yet so far frank and honest that they seemed as if they disclaimed to conceal the natural working of the soul. Such an expression is often mistaken for manly frankness, when in truth it arises from the reckless indifference of a libertine disposition, conscious of superiority of birth and wealth, or of some other adventitious advantage totally unconnected with personal merit. — *Ivanhoe*, Chap. VIII

Beauty and Pleasure

30 CRYSTALLIZATION having once begun, we enjoy with delight each new beauty discovered in that which we
love.

But what is beauty? It is the appearance of an aptitude
for giving you pleasure.

The pleasures of all individuals are different and often
opposed to one another; which explains very well how that,
which is beauty for one individual, is ugliness for another.
(Conclusive example of Del Rosso and Lisio, 1st January,
1820.)

The right way to discover the nature of beauty is to look
for the nature of the pleasures of each individual. Del
Rosso, for example, needs a woman who allows a certain
boldness of movement, and who by her smiles authorizes
considerable license; a woman who at each instant holds
physical pleasures before his imagination, and who excites
in him the power of pleasing, while giving him at the same
time the means of displaying it.

Apparently, by love Del Rosso understands physical love,
and Lisio passion-love. Obviously they are not likely to
agree about the word beauty.[1]

The beauty then, discovered by you, being the appearance of an aptitude for giving you pleasure, and pleasure
being different from pleasure as man from man, the crystallization formed in the head of each individual must bear
the color of that individual's pleasures.

A man's crystallization of his mistress, or her *beauty*, is
no other thing than the collection of all the satisfactions of
all the desires, which he can have felt successively at her
instance.

---

[1] *My Beauty*, promise of a character useful to *my* soul, is above the attraction
of the senses; that attraction is only one particular kind of attraction. 1815.

More about Crystallization

WHY do we enjoy with delight each new beauty, discovered in that which we love?

It is because each new beauty gives the full and entire satisfaction of a desire. You wish your mistress gentle — she is gentle; and then you wish her proud like Emilie in Corneille, and although these qualities are probably incompatible, instantly she appears with the soul of a Roman. That is the moral reason which makes love the strongest of the passions. In all others, desires must accommodate themselves to cold realities; here it is realities which model themselves spontaneously upon desires. Of all the passions, therefore, it is in love that violent desires find the greatest satisfaction.

There are certain general conditions of happiness, whose influence extends over every fulfilment of particular desires: — 1. She seems to belong to you, for you only can make her happy.

2. She is the judge of your worth. This condition was very important at the gallant and chivalrous Courts of Francis I and Henry II, and at the elegant Court of Louis XV. Under a constitutional and rationalist government women lose this range of influence entirely.

3. For a romantic heart — The loftier her soul, the more sublime will be the pleasures that await her in your arms, and the more purified of the dross of all vulgar considerations. The majority of young Frenchmen are, at eighteen, disciples of Rousseau; for them this condition of happiness is important.

In the midst of operations so apt to mislead our desire of happiness, there is no keeping cool.

For, the moment he is in love, the steadiest man sees no object such as it is. His own advantages he minimizes, and magnifies the smallest favors of the loved one. Fears and hopes take at once a tinge of the romantic. (Wayward.) He no longer attributes anything to chance; he loses the perception of probability; in its effect upon his happiness a thing imagined is a thing existent.[1]

A terrible symptom that you are losing your head: — you think of some little thing which is difficult to make out; you see it white, and interpret that in favor of your love; a moment later you notice that actually it is black, and still you find it conclusively favorable to your love.

Then indeed the soul, a prey to mortal uncertainties, feels keenly the need of a friend. But there is no friend for the lover. The Court knew that; and it is the source of the only kind of indiscretion which a woman of delicacy might forgive.

Of the First Step

THAT which is most surprising in the passion of love is the first step — the extravagance of the change, which comes over a man's brain.

The fashionable world, with its brilliant parties, is of service to love in favoring this first step.

It begins by changing simple admiration into (a) tender admiration (b) — what pleasure to kiss her, etc.

In a *salon* lit by thousands of candles a fast waltz throws a fever upon young hearts, eclipses timidity, swells the consciousness of power — in fact, gives them the daring to love. For to see a lovable object is not enough: on the contrary, the fact that it is extremely lovable discourages a gentle soul — he must see it, if not in love with him,[2] at least despoiled of its majesty. Who takes it into his head to become the paramour of a queen unless the advances are from her?[3]

[1] There is a physical cause — a mad impulse, a rush of blood to the brain, a disorder in the nerves and in the cerebral center. Observe the transitory courage of stags and the spiritual state of a soprano. Physiology, in 1922, will give us a description of the physical side of this phenomenon. I recommend this to the attention of Dr. Edwards.

[2] Hence the possibility of passions of artificial origin — those of Benedict and of Beatrice (Shakespeare).

[3] Cf. the fortunes of Struensee in Brown's *Northern Courts*, 3 vols., 1819.

Thus nothing is more favorable to the birth of love than a life of irksome solitude, broken now and again by a long-desired ball. This is the plan of wise mothers who have daughters.

The real fashionable world, such as was found at the Court of France,[1] and which since 1780[2] I think, exists no more, was unfavorable to love, because it made the solitude and the leisure, indispensable to the work of crystallization, almost impossible.

Court life gives the habit of observing and making a great number of subtle distinctions, and the subtlest distinction may be the beginning of an admiration and of a passion.[3]

When the troubles of love are mixed with those of another kind (the troubles of vanity — if your mistress offend your proper pride, your sense of honor or personal dignity — troubles of health, money and political persecution, etc.), it is only in appearance that love is increased by these annoyances. Occupying the imagination otherwise, they prevent crystallization in love still hopeful, and in happy love the birth of little doubts. When these misfortunes have departed, the sweetness and the folly of love return.

Observe that misfortunes favor the birth of love in light and unsensitive characters, and that, after it is born, misfortunes, which existed before, are favorable to it; in as much as the imagination, recoiling from the gloomy impressions offered by all the other circumstances of life, throws itself wholly into the work of crystallization.

[1] See the letters of Madame du Deffant, Mademoiselle de Lespinasse, Bezenval, Lauzun, the Memoirs of Madame d'Epinay, the *Dictionnaire des Etiquettes* of Madame de Genlis, the Memoirs of Danjeau and Horace Walpole.

[2] Unless, perhaps, at the Court of Petersburg.

[3] See Saint-Simon and Werther. However gentle and delicate are the solitary, their soul is distracted, and part of their imagination is busy in foreseeing the world of men. Force of character is one of the charms which most readily seduces the truly feminine heart. Hence the success of serious young officers. Women well know how to make the distinction between force of character and the violence of those movements of passion, the possibility of which they feel strongly in their own hearts. The most distinguished women are sometimes duped by a little charlatanism in this matter. It can be used without fear, as soon as crystallization is seen to have begun.

Memory and Crystallization

34 THE following point, which will be disputed, I offer only
to those — shall I say unhappy enough? — to have loved
with passion during long years, and loved in the face of
invincible obstacles: —

The sight of all that is extremely beautiful in nature and
in art recalls, with the swiftness of lightning, the memory
of that which we love. It is by the process of the jewelled
branch in the mines of Salzburg, that everything in the
world which is beautiful and lofty contributes to the beauty
of that which we love, and that forthwith a sudden glimpse
of delight fills the eyes with tears.

In this way, love and the love of beauty give life mutually
to one another.

One of life's miseries is that the happiness of seeing and
talking to the object of our love leaves no distinct memories
behind. The soul, it seems, is too troubled by its emotions
for that which causes or accompanies them to impress it.
The soul and its sensations are one and the same. It is perhaps because these pleasures cannot be used up by voluntary recollection, that they return again and again with
such force, as soon as ever some object comes to drag us
from day-dreams devoted to the woman we love, and by
some new connection[1] to bring her still more vividly to our
memory.

A dry old architect used to meet her in society every evening. Following a natural impulse, and without paying
attention to what I was saying to her, I one day sang his
praises in a sentimental and pompous strain, which made
her laugh at me. I had not the strength to say to her: "He
sees you every evening."

So powerful is this sensation that it extends even to the
person of my enemy, who is always at her side. When I see
her, she reminds me of Leonore so much, that at the time
I cannot hate her, however much I try.

[1] Scents.

It looks as if, by a curious whim of the heart, the charm, which the woman we love can communicate, were greater than that which she herself possesses. The vision of that distant city, where we saw her a moment,[1] throws us into dreams sweeter and more profound than would her very presence. It is the effect of harsh treatment.

The day-dreams of love cannot be scrutinized. I have observed that I can re-read a good novel every three years with the same pleasure. It gives me feelings akin to the kind of emotional taste, which dominates me at the moment, or if my feelings are *nil*, makes for variety in my ideas. Also, I can listen with pleasure to the same music, but, in this, memory must not intrude. The imagination should be affected and nothing else; if, at the twentieth representation, an opera gives more pleasure, it is either because the music is better understood, or because it also brings back the feeling it gave at the first.

As to new lights, which a novel may throw upon our knowledge of the human heart, I still remember clearly the old ones, and am pleased even to find them noted in the margin. But this kind of pleasure pertains to the novels, in so far as they advance me in the knowledge of man, and not in the least to day-dreaming — the veritable pleasure of novels. Such day-dreaming is inscrutable. To watch it is for the present to kill it, for you fall into a philosophical analysis of pleasure; and it is killing it still more certainly for the future, for nothing is surer to paralyze the imagination than the appeal to memory. If I find in the margin a note, depicting my feelings on reading *Old Mortality* three years ago in Florence, I am plunged immediately into the history of my life, into an estimate of the degree of happiness at the two epochs, in short, into the deepest problems of philosophy — and then good-bye for a long season to the unchecked play of tender feelings.

---

[1] Nessun maggior dolore
Che ricordarsi del tempo felice
Nella miseria. — Dante, *Inferno*, V (Francesca).

[No greater sorrow than to remember happy times in misery.]

Every great poet with a lively imagination is timid, he is afraid of men, that is to say, for the interruptions and troubles with which they can invade the delight of his dreams. He fears for his concentration. Men come along with their gross interests to drag him from the gardens of Armida, and force him into a fetid slough: only by irritating him can they fix his attention on themselves. It is this habit of feeding his soul upon touching dreams and this horror of the vulgar which draws a great artist so near to love.

The more of the great artist a man has in him, the more must he wish for titles and honors as a bulwark.

The End of Crystallization

SUDDENLY in the midst of the most violent and the most thwarted passion come moments, when a man believes that he is in love no longer — as it were a spring of fresh water in the middle of the sea. To think of his mistress is no longer very much pleasure, and, although he is worn-out by the severity of her treatment, the fact that everything in life has lost its interest is a still greater misery. After a manner of existence which, fitful though it was, gave to all nature a new aspect, passionate and absorbing, now follows the dreariest and most despondent void.

It may be that your last visit to the woman, whom you love, left you in a situation, from which, once before, your imagination had gathered the full harvest of sensation. For example, after a period of coldness, she has treated you less badly, letting you conceive exactly the same degree of hope and by the same external signs as on a previous occasion — all this perhaps unconsciously. Imagination picks up memory and its sinister warnings by the way, and instantly crystallization[1] ceases.

[1] First, I am advised to cut out this word; next, if I fail in this for want of literary power, to repeat again and again that I mean by crystallization a certain fever in the imagination, which transforms past recognition what is, as often as

The Influence of Music

In a small port, the name of which I forget, near Perpignan, 25th February, 1822.[1]

THIS evening I have just found out that music, when it is perfect, puts the heart into the same state as it enjoys in the presence of the loved one — that is to say, it gives seemingly the keenest happiness existing on the face of the earth.

If this were so for all men, there would be no more favorable incentive to love.

But I had already remarked at Naples last year that perfect music, like perfect pantomime, makes me think of that which is at the moment the object of my dreams, and that the ideas, which it suggests to me, are excellent: at Naples, it was on the means of arming the Greeks.

Now this evening I cannot deceive myself — I have the misfortune *of being too great an admirer of milady L.*[2]

And perhaps the perfect music, which I have had the luck to hear again, after two or three months of privation, although going nightly to the Opera, has simply had the effect, which I recognized long ago — I mean that of producing lively thoughts on what is already in the heart.

March 4th — eight days later.

I dare neither erase nor approve the preceding observation. Certain it is that, as I wrote it, I read it in my heart. If to-day I bring it into question, it is because I have lost the memory of what I saw at that time.

The habit of hearing music and dreaming its dreams disposes towards love. A sad and gentle air, provided it is not too dramatic, so that the imagination is forced to dwell on the action, is a direct stimulant to dreams of love and a

not, a quite ordinary object, and makes of it a thing apart. A man who looks to excite this fever in souls, which know no other path but vanity to reach their happiness, must tie his necktie well and constantly give his attention to a thousand details, which preclude all possibility of unrestraint. Society women own to the effect, denying at the same time or not seeing the cause.

[1] Copied from the diary of Lisio.

[2] [Written thus in English by Stendhal.]

delight for gentle and unhappy souls: for example, the drawn-out passage on the clarinet at the beginning of the quartet in *Bianca and Faliero*, and the recitative of La Camporesi towards the middle of the quartet.

A lover at peace with his mistress enjoys to distraction Rossini's famous duet in *Armida and Rinaldo*, depicting so justly the little doubts of happy love and the moments of delight which follow its reconciliations. It seems to him that the instrumental part, which comes in the middle of the duet, at the moment when Rinaldo wishes to fly, and represents in such an amazing way the conflict of the passions, has a physical influence upon his heart and touches it in reality. On this subject I dare not say what I feel; I should pass for a madman among people of the north.

Beauty Dethroned by Love

ALBERIC meets in a box at the theatre a woman more beautiful than his mistress (I beg to be allowed here a mathematical valuation) — that is to say, her features promise three units of happiness instead of two, supposing the quantity of happiness given by perfect beauty to be expressed by the number four.

Is it surprising that he prefers the features of his mistress, which promise a hundred units of happiness *for him?* Even the minor defects of her face, a small-pox mark, for example, touch the heart of the man who loves, and, when he observes them even in another woman, set him dreaming far away. What, then, when he sees them in his mistress? Why, he has felt a thousand sentiments in presence of that small-pox mark, sentiments for the most part sweet, and all of the greatest interest; and now, such as they are, they are evoked afresh with incredible vividness by the sight of this sign, even in the face of another woman.

If ugliness thus comes to be preferred and loved, it is because in this case ugliness is beauty. A man was passionately in love with a woman, very thin and scarred with small-pox: death bereft him of her. At Rome, three years after, he makes friends with two women, one more lovely than the day, the other thin, scarred with small-pox, and thereby, if you will, quite ugly.[1] There he is, at the end of a week, in love with the ugly one — and this week he employs in effacing her ugliness with his memories; and with a very pardonable coquetry the lesser beauty did not fail to help him in the operation with a slight whip-up of the pulse.[2] A man meets a woman and is offended by her ugliness; soon, if she is unpretentious, her expression makes him forget the defect of her features; he finds her amiable — he conceives that one could love her. A week later he has hopes; another week and they are taken from him; another and he's mad.

Limitations of Beauty

A<small>N</small> analogy is to be seen at the theatre in the reception of the public's favorite actors: the spectators are no longer conscious of the beauty or ugliness which the actors have in reality. Lekain, for all his remarkable ugliness, had a harvest of broken hearts — Garrick also. There are several reasons for this; the principal being that it was no longer the actual beauty of their features or their ways which people saw, but emphatically that which imagination was long since used to lend them, as a return for, and in memory of, all the pleasure they had given it. Why, take a comedian — his face alone raises a laugh as he first walks on.

A girl going for the first time to the Français would perhaps feel some antipathy to Lekain during the first scene;

---

[1] Beauty is only the promise of happiness. The happiness of a Greek was different to that of a Frenchman of 1822. See the eyes of the Medici Venus and compare them with the eyes of the Magdalen of Pordenone (in the possession of M. de Sommariva.)

[2] If one is sure of the love of a woman, one examines to see if she is more or less beautiful; if one is uncertain of her heart, there is no time to think of her face.

but soon he was making her weep or shiver — and how resist him as Tancrède[1] or Orosmane?

If his ugliness were still a little visible to her eyes, the fervor of an entire audience, and the nervous effect produced upon a young heart,[2] soon managed to eclipse it. If anything was still heard about his ugliness, it was mere talk; but not a word of it — Lekain's lady enthusiasts could be heard to exclaim "He's lovely!"

Remember that beauty is the expression of character, or, put differently, of moral habits, and that consequently it is exempt from all passion. Now it is passion that we want. Beauty can only supply us with probabilities about a woman, and probabilities, moreover, based on her capacity for self-possession; while the glances of your mistress with her small-pox scars are a delightful reality, which destroys all the probabilities in the world.

Limitations of Beauty

A WOMAN of quick fancy and tender heart, but timid and cautious in her sensibility, who the day after she appears in society, passes in review a thousand times nervously and painfully all that she may have said or given hint of — such a woman, I say, grows easily used to want of beauty in a man: it is hardly an obstacle in rousing her affection.

It is really on the same principle that you care next to nothing for the degree of beauty in a mistress, whom you adore and who repays you with harshness. You have very

[1] See Madame de Staël in *Delphine*, I think; there you have the artifice of plain women.

[2] I should be inclined to attribute to this nervous sympathy the prodigious and incomprehensible effect of fashionable music. (Sympathy at Dresden for Rossini, 1821.) As soon as it is out of fashion, it becomes no worse for that, and yet it ceases to have any effect upon perfectly ingenuous girls. Perhaps it used to please them, as also stimulating young men to fervor.

Madame de Sévigné says to her daughter (Letter 202, May 6, 1672): "Lully surpassed himself in his royal music; that beautiful *Miserere* was still further enlarged: there was a *Libera* at which all eyes were full of tears."

It is as impossible to doubt the truth of this effect, as to refuse wit or refinement to Madame de Sévigné. Lully's music, which charmed her, would make us run away at present; in her day, his music encouraged crystallization — it makes it impossible in ours.

nearly stopped crystallizing her beauty, and when your *friend in need* tells you that she isn't pretty, you are almost ready to agree. Then he thinks he has made great way.

My friend, brave Captain Trab, described to me this evening his feelings on seeing Mirabeau once upon a time. No one looking upon that great man felt a disagreeable sensation in the eyes — that is to say, found him ugly. People were carried away by his thundering words; they fixed their attention, they delighted in fixing their attention, only on what was beautiful in his face. As he had practically no beautiful features (in the sense of sculpturesque or picturesque beauty) they minded only what beauty he had of another kind, the beauty of expression.[1]

While attention was blind to all traces of ugliness, picturesquely speaking, it fastened on the smallest passable details with fervor — for example, the beauty of his vast head of hair. If he had had horns, people would have thought them lovely.[2]

[1] That is the advantage of being *à la mode*. Putting aside the defects of a face which are already familiar, and no longer have any effect upon the imagination, the public take hold of one of the three following ideas of beauty: —
   (1) The people — of the idea of wealth.
   (2) The upper classes — of the idea of elegance, material or moral.
   (3) The Court — of the idea: "My object is to please the women."
Almost all take hold of a mixture of all three. The happiness attached to the idea of riches is linked to a refinement in the pleasure which the idea of elegance suggests, and the whole comes into touch with love. In one way or another the imagination is led on by novelty. It is possible in this way to be interested in a very ugly man without thinking of his ugliness,* and in good time his ugliness becomes beauty. At Vienna, in 1788, Madame Viganò, a dancer and *the* woman of the moment, was with child — very soon the ladies took to wearing little *Ventres à la Viganò*. For the same reason reversed, nothing more fearful than a fashion out of date! Bad taste is a confusion of fashion, which lives only by change, with the lasting beauty produced by such and such a government, guided by such and such a climate. A building in fashion to-day, in ten years will be out of fashion. It will be less displeasing in two hundred years, when its fashionable day will be forgotten. Lovers are quite mad to think about their dress; a woman has other things to do, when seeing the object of her love, than to bother about his get-up; we look at our lover, we do not examine him, says Rousseau. If this examination takes place, we are dealing with gallant-love and not passion-love. The brilliance of beauty is almost offensive in the object of our love; it is none of our business to see her beautiful, we want her tender and languishing. Adornment has effect in love only upon girls, who are so rigidly guarded in their parents' house, that they often lose their hearts through their eyes. (L.'s words. September 15, 1820.)
  * Le petit Germain, *Mémoires de Grammont.*

[2] For their polish or their size or their form! In this way, or by the combination of sentiments (see above, the small-pox scars) a woman in love grows used to the faults of her lover. The Russian Princess C. has actually become used to a man who literally has no nose. The picture of his courage, of his pistol loaded

The appearance every evening of a pretty dancer forces a little interest from those poor souls, blasé or bereft of imagination, who adorn the balcony of the opera. By her graceful movements, daring and strange, she awakens their physical love and procures them perhaps the only crystallization of which they are still capable. This is the way by which a young scarecrow, who in the street would not have been honored with a glance, least of all from people the worse for wear, has only to appear frequently on the stage, and she manages to get herself handsomely supported. Geoffroy used to say that the theater is the pedestal of woman. The more notorious and the more dilapidated a dancer, the more she is worth; hence the green-room proverb: "Some get sold at a price who wouldn't be taken as a gift." These women steal part of their passions from their lovers, and are very susceptible of love from pique.

How manage not to connect generous or lovable sentiments with the face of an actress, in whose features there is nothing repugnant, whom for two hours every evening we see expressing the most noble feelings, and whom otherwise we do not know? When at last you succeed in being received by her, her features recall such pleasing feelings, that the entire reality which surrounds her, however little nobility it may sometimes possess, is instantly invested with romantic and touching colors.

"Devotee, in the days of my youth, of that boring French tragedy,[1] whenever I had the luck of supping with Mlle. Olivier, I found myself every other moment overbrimming with respect, in the belief that I was speaking to a queen; and really I have never been quite sure whether, in her case, I had fallen in love with a queen or a pretty tart."

---

to kill himself in despair at his misfortune, and pity for the bitter calamity, enhanced by the idea that he will recover and is beginning to recover, are the forces which have worked this miracle. The poor fellow with his wound must appear not to think of his misfortune. (Berlin, 1807)

[1] Improper expression copied from the Memoirs of my friend, the late Baron de Bottmer. It is by the same trick that Feramorz pleases Lalla-Rookh. See that charming poem.

The Unimportance of Beauty

PERHAPS men who are not susceptible to the feelings of passion-love are those most keenly sensitive to the effects of beauty: that at least is the strongest impression which such men can receive of women.

He who has felt his heart beating at a distant glimpse of the white satin hat of the woman he loves, is quite amazed by the chill left upon him by the approach of the greatest beauty in the world. He may even have a qualm of distress, to observe the excitement of others.

Extremely lovely women cause less surprise the second day. 'Tis a great misfortune, it discourages crystallization. Their merit being obvious to all and public property, they are bound to reckon more fools in the list of their lovers than princes, millionaires, etc.[1]

Love at First Sight

IMAGINATIVE souls are sensitive and also mistrustful, even the most ingenuous,[2] — I maintain. They may be suspicious without knowing it: they have had so many disappointments in life. Thus everything set-out and official, when a man is first introduced, scares the imagination and drives away the possibility of crystallization; the romantic is then, on the contrary, love's triumph.

Nothing simpler — for in the supreme astonishment, which keeps the thoughts busy for long upon something out of the ordinary, is already half the mental exercise necessary to crystallization.

---

[1] It is quite clear that the author is neither prince nor millionaire. I wanted to steal that sally from the reader.

[2] *The Bride of Lammermoor*, Miss Ashton.

A man who has lived finds in his memory numberless examples of "affairs," and his only trouble is to make his choice. But if he wishes to write, he no longer knows where to look for support. The anecdotes of the particular circles he has lived in are unknown to the public, and it would require an immense number of pages to recount them with the necessary circumstantiality. I quote for that reason from generally-known novels, but the ideas which I submit to the reader I do not ground upon such empty fictions, calculated for the most part with an eye to the picturesque rather than the true effect.

I will quote the beginning of the Amours of Séraphine (*Gil Blas,* Book IV, Chap. X). It is Don Fernando who tells the story of his flight, when pursued by the agents of the Inquisition. . . .

After crossing several walks I came to a drawing-room, the door of which was also left open. I entered, and when I had observed all its magnificence . . . One side of the room a door stood ajar; I partly opened it and saw a suite of apartments whereof only the furthest was lighted. "What is to be done now?" I asked myself. . . . I could not resist my curiosity. . . . Advancing boldly, I went through all the rooms and reached one where there was a light — to wit, a taper upon a marble table in a silver-gilt candlestick. . . . But soon afterwards, casting my eyes upon a bed, the curtains of which were partly drawn on account of the heat, I perceived an object which at once engrossed my attention: a young lady, fast asleep in spite of the noise of the thunder, which had just been bursting forth. I softly drew near her. My mind was suddenly troubled at the sight. Whilst I feasted my eyes with the pleasure of beholding her, she awoke.

Imagine her surprise at seeing in her room at midnight a man who was an utter stranger to her! She trembled on beholding me and shrieked aloud. . . . I took pains to reassure her and throwing myself on my knees before her, said — "Madam, have no fear." She called her women . . . Grown a little braver by his (an old servant's) presence, she haughtily asked me who I was, etc. etc."[1]

There is an introduction not easily to be forgotten! On the other hand, could there be anything sillier in our customs of to-day than the official, and at the same time almost sentimental, introduction of the young wooer to his future wife: such legal prostitution goes so far as to be almost offensive to modesty.

"I have just been present this afternoon, February 17th, 1790," says Chamfort, "at a so-called family function. That is to say, men of respectable reputation and a decent company were congratulating on her good fortune Mlle. de Marille, a young person of beauty, wit and virtue, who is to be favored with becoming the wife of M. R — an unhealthy dotard, repulsive, dishonest, and mad, but rich: she has seen him for the third time to-day, when signing

[1] [Translation of Henri van Laun.]

the contract. If anything characterizes an age of infamy, it is the jubilation on an occasion like this, it is the folly of such joy and — looking ahead — the sanctimonious cruelty, with which the same society will heap contempt without reserve upon the pettiest imprudence of a poor young woman in love."

Ceremony of all kinds, being in its essence something affected and set-out beforehand, in which the point is to act "properly," paralyzes the imagination and leaves it awake only to that which is opposed to the object of the ceremony, e.g. something comical — whence the magic effect of the slightest joke. A poor girl, struggling against nervousness and attacks of modesty during the official introduction of her *fiancé*, can think of nothing but the part she is playing, and this again is a certain means of stifling the imagination.

Modesty has far more to say against getting into bed with a man whom you have seen but twice, after three Latin words have been spoken in church, than against giving way despite yourself to the man whom for two years you have adored. But I am talking double Dutch.

The fruitful source of the vices and mishaps, which follow our marriages nowadays, is the Church of Rome. It makes liberty for girls impossible before marriage, and divorce impossible, when once they have made their mistake, or rather when they find out the mistake of the choice forced on them. Compare Germany, the land of happy marriages: a delightful princess (Madame la Duchesse de Sa——) has just married in all good faith for the fourth time, and has not failed to ask to the wedding her three first husbands, with whom she is on the best terms. That is going too far; but a single divorce, which punishes a husband for his tyranny, prevents a thousand cases of unhappy wedded life. What is amusing is that Rome is one of the places where you see most divorces.

Love goes out at first sight towards a face which reveals at once something to respect and something to pity.

Of Infatuation

46 THE most fastidious spirits are very given to curiosity and prepossession: this is to be seen, especially, in beings in which that sacred fire, the source of the passions, is extinct — in fact it is one of the most fatal symptoms. There is also the infatuation of schoolboys just admitted to society. At the two poles of life, with too much or too little sensibility, there is little chance of simple people getting the right effect from things, or feeling the genuine sensation which they ought to give. These beings, either too ardent or excessive in their ardor, amorous on credit, if one may use the expression, throw themselves at objects instead of awaiting them.

From afar off and without looking they enfold things in that imaginary charm, of which they find a perennial source within themselves, long before sensation, which is the consequence of the object's nature, has had time to reach them. Then, on coming to close quarters, they see these things not such as they are, but as they have made them; they think they are enjoying such and such an object, while, under cover of that object, they are enjoying themselves. But one fine day a man gets tired of keeping the whole thing going; he discovers that his idol is *not playing the game;* infatuation collapses and the resulting shock to his self-esteem makes him unfair to that which he appreciated too highly.

The Thunderbolt from the Blue

SO RIDICULOUS an expression ought to be changed, yet the thing exists. I have seen the amiable and noble Wilhelmina, the despair of the beaux of Berlin, making light of love and laughing at its folly. In the brilliance of youth, wit, beauty and all kinds of good luck — a boundless

fortune, giving her the opportunity of developing all her qualities, seemed to conspire with nature to give the world an example, rarely seen, of perfect happiness bestowed upon an object perfectly worthy. She was twenty-three years old and, already some time at Court, had won the homage of the bluest blood. Her virtue, unpretentious but invulnerable, was quoted as a pattern. Henceforth the most charming men, despairing of their powers of fascination, aspired only to make her their friend. One evening she goes to a ball at Prince Ferdinand's: she dances for ten minutes with a young Captain.

"From that moment," she writes subsequently to a friend,[1] "he was master of my heart and of me, and this to a degree that would have filled me with terror, if the happiness of seeing Herman had left me time to think of the rest of existence. My only thought was to observe whether he gave me a little notice.

"To-day the only consolation that I might find for my fault is to nurse the illusion within me, that it is through a superior power that I am lost to reason and to myself. I have no word to describe, in a way that comes at all near the reality, the degree of disorder and turmoil to which the mere sight of him could bring my whole being. I blush to think of the rapidity and the violence with which I was drawn towards him. If his first word, when at last he spoke to me, had been 'Do you adore me?' — truly I should not have had the power to have answered anything but 'yes.' I was far from thinking that the effect of a feeling could be at once so sudden and so unforeseen. In fact, for an instant, I believed that I had been poisoned.

"Unhappily you and the world, my dear friend, know how well I have loved Herman. Well, after a quarter of an hour he was so dear to me that he cannot have become dearer since. I saw then all his faults and I forgave them all, provided only he would love me.

"Soon after I had danced with him, the king left: Her-

[1] Translated *ad litteram* from the Memoirs of Bottmer.

man, who belonged to the suite, had to follow him. With him, everything in nature disappeared. It is no good to try to depict the excess of weariness with which I felt weighed down, as soon as he was out of my sight. It was equal only to the keenness of my desire to be alone with myself. At last I got away. No sooner the door of my room shut and bolted than I wanted to resist my passion. I thought I should succeed. Ah, dear friend, believe me I paid dear that evening and the following days for the pleasure of being able to credit myself with some virtue."

The preceding lines are the exact story of an event which was the topic of the day; for after a month or two poor Wilhelmina was unfortunate enough for people to take notice of her feelings. Such was the origin of that long series of troubles by which she perished so young and so tragically — poisoned by herself or her lover. All that we could see in this young Captain was that he was an excellent dancer; he had plenty of gaiety and still more assurance, a general air of good nature and spent his time with prostitutes; for the rest, scarcely a nobleman, quite poor and not seen at Court.

In these cases it is not enough to have no misgivings — one must be sick of misgivings — have, so to speak, the impatience of courage to face life's chances.

The soul of a woman, grown tired, without noticing it, of living without loving, convinced in spite of herself by the example of other women — all the fears of life surmounted and the sorry happiness of pride found wanting — ends in creating unconsciously a model, an ideal. One day she meets this model: crystallization recognizes its object by the commotion it inspires and consecrates for ever to the master of its fortunes the fruit of all its previous dreams.[1]

Women, whose hearts are open to this misfortune, have too much grandeur of soul to love otherwise than with passion. They would be saved if they could stoop to gallantry.

[1] Several phrases taken from Crébillon.

As "thunderbolts" come from a secret lassitude in what the catechism calls Virtue, and from boredom brought on by the uniformity of perfection, I should be inclined to think that it would generally be the privilege of what is known in the world as "a bad lot" to bring them down. I doubt very much whether rigidity *à la* Cato has ever been the occasion of a "thunderbolt."

What makes them so rare is that if the heart, thus disposed to love beforehand, has the slightest inkling of its situation, there is no thunderbolt.

The soul of a woman, whom troubles have made mistrustful, is not susceptible of this revolution.

Nothing facilitates a "thunderbolt" like praise, given in advance and by women, to the person who is to occasion it.

False "thunderbolts" form one of the most comic sources of love stories. A weary woman, but one without much feeling, thinks for a whole evening that she is in love for life. She is proud of having found at last one of those great commotions of the soul, which used to allure her imagination. The next day she no longer knows where to hide her face and, still more, how to avoid the wretched object she was adoring the night before.

Clever people know how to spot, that is to say, make capital out of these "thunderbolts."

Physical love also has its "thunderbolts." Yesterday in her carriage with the prettiest and most easy-going woman in Berlin, we saw her suddenly blush. She became deeply absorbed and preoccupied. Handsome Lieutenant Findorff had just passed. In the evening at the play, according to her own confession to me, she was out of her mind, she was beside herself, she could think of nothing but Findorff, to whom she had never spoken. If she had dared, she told me, she would have sent for him — that pretty face bore all the signs of the most violent passion. The next day it was still going on. After three days, Findorff having played the blockhead, she thought no more about it. A month later she loathed him.

I ADVISE the majority of people born in the North to skip the present chapter. It is an obscure dissertation upon certain phenomena relative to the orange-tree, a plant which does not grow or reach its full height except in Italy and Spain. In order to be intelligible elsewhere, I should have had to cut down the facts.

I should have had no hesitation about this, if for a single moment I had intended to write a book to be generally appreciated. But Heaven having refused me the writer's gift, I have thought solely of describing with all the ill-grace of science, but also with all its exactitude, certain facts, of which I became involuntarily the witness through a prolonged sojourn in the land of the orange-tree. Frederick the Great, or some such other distinguished man from the North, who never had the opportunity of seeing the orange-tree growing in the open, would doubtless have denied the facts which follow — and denied in good faith. I have an infinite respect for such good faith and can see its *wherefore*.

As this sincere declaration may seem presumption, I append the following reflection: —

We write haphazard, each one of us what we think true, and each gives the lie to his neighbor. I see in our books so many tickets in a lottery and in reality they have no more value. Posterity, forgetting some and reprinting others, declares the lucky numbers. And in so far, each one of us having written as best he can, what he thinks true, has no right to laugh at his neighbor — except where the satire is amusing. In that case he is always right, especially if he writes like M. Courrier to Del Furia.

After this preamble, I am going bravely to enter into the examination of facts which, I am convinced, have rarely been observed at Paris. But after all at Paris, superior as of course it is to all other towns, orange-trees are not seen growing out in the open, as at Sorrento, and it is there that

Lisio Visconti observed and noted the following facts — at Sorrento, the country of Tasso, on the Bay of Naples in a position half-way down to the sea, still more picturesque than that of Naples itself, but where no one reads the *Miroir*.

When we are to see in the evening the woman we love, the suspense, the expectation of so great a happiness makes every moment, which separates us from it, unbearable.

A devouring fever makes us take up and lay aside twenty different occupations. We look every moment at our watch — overjoyed when we see that we have managed to pass ten minutes without looking at the time. The hour so longed-for strikes at last, and when we are at her door ready to knock — we would be glad not to find her in. It is only on reflection that we would be sorry for it. In a word, the suspense before seeing her produces an unpleasant effect.

There you have one of the things which make good folk say that love drives men silly.

The reason is that the imagination, violently withdrawn from dreams of delight in which every step forward brings happiness, is brought back face to face with severe reality.

The gentle soul knows well that in the combat which is to begin the moment he sees her, the least inadvertency, the least lack of attention or of courage will be paid for by a defeat, poisoning, for a long time to come, the dreams of fancy and of passion, and humiliating to a man's pride, if he try to find consolation outside the sphere of passion. He says to himself: "I hadn't the wit, I hadn't the pluck"; but the only way to have pluck before the loved one is by loving her a little less.

It is a fragment of attention, torn by force with so much trouble from the dreams of crystallization, which allows the crowd of things to escape us during our first words with the woman we love — things which have no sense or which have a sense contrary to what we mean — or else, what is still more heart-rending, we exaggerate our feelings and they become ridiculous in our own eyes. We feel vaguely that we are not paying enough attention to our words and mechanically set about polishing and loading our oratory. And, also, it is impossible to hold one's tongue — silence would be embarrassing and make it still less possible to give one's thoughts to her. So we say in a feeling way a host of things that we do not feel, and would be quite embarrassed to repeat, obstinately keeping our distance from the woman before us, in order more really to be with her. In the early hours of my acquaintance with love, this oddity which I felt within me, made me believe that I did not love.

I understand cowardice and how recruits, to be delivered of their fear, throw themselves recklessly into the midst of the fire. The number of silly things I have said in the last two years, in order not to hold my tongue, makes me mad when I think of them.

And that is what should easily mark in a woman's eyes the difference between passion-love and gallantry, between the gentle soul and the prosaic.[1]

In these decisive moments the one gains as much as the other loses: the prosaic soul gets just the degree of warmth which he ordinarily wants, while excess of feeling drives mad the poor gentle heart, who, to crown his troubles, really means to hide his madness. Completely taken up with keeping his own transports in check, he is miles away from the self-possession necessary in order to seize opportunities, and leaves in a muddle after a visit, in which the prosaic soul would have made a great step forward. Directly it is a question of advancing his too violent passion, a gentle being with pride cannot be eloquent under the eye of the woman whom he loves: the pain of ill-success is too much for him. The vulgar being, on the contrary, calculates nicely the chances of success: he is stopped by no foretastes of the suffering of defeat, and, proud of that which makes him vulgar, laughs at the gentle soul, who, with all the cleverness he may have, is never quite enough at ease to say the simplest things and those most certain to

---

[1] The word was one of Léonore's.

succeed. The gentle soul, far from being able to grasp anything by force, must resign himself to obtaining nothing except through the *charity* of her whom he loves. If the woman one loves really has feelings, one always has reason to regret having wished to put pressure on oneself in order to make love to her. One looks shame-faced, looks chilly, would look deceitful, did not passion betray itself by other and surer signs. To express what we feel so keenly, and in such detail, at every moment of the day, is a task we take upon our shoulders because we have read novels; for if we were natural, we would never undertake anything so irksome. Instead of wanting to speak of what we felt a quarter of an hour ago, and of trying to make of it a general and interesting topic, we would express simply the passing fragment of our feelings at the moment. But no! we put the most violent pressure upon ourselves for a worthless success, and, as there is no evidence of actual sensation to back our words, and as our memory cannot be working freely, we approve at the time of things to say — and say them — comical to a degree that is more than humiliating.

When at last, after an hour's trouble, this extremely painful effort has resulted in getting away from the enchanted gardens of the imagination, in order to enjoy quite simply the presence of what you love, it often happens — that you've got to take your leave.

All this looks like extravagance, but I have seen better still. A woman, whom one of my friends loved to idolatry, pretending to take offence at some or other want of delicacy, which I was never allowed to learn, condemned him all of a sudden to see her only twice a month. These visits, so rare and so intensely desired, meant an attack of madness, and it wanted all Salviati's strength of character to keep it from being seen by outward signs.

From the very first, the idea of the visit's end is too insistent for one to be able to take pleasure in the visit. One speaks a great deal, deaf to one's own thoughts, saying often the contrary of what one thinks. One embarks upon discourses which have got suddenly to be cut short, because of their absurdity — if one manage to rouse oneself and listen to one's thoughts within. The effort we make is so violent that we seem chilly. Love hides itself in its excess.

Away from her, the imagination was lulled by the most charming dialogues: there were transports the most tender and the most touching. And thus for ten days or so you think you have the courage to speak; but two days before what should have been our day of happiness, the fever begins, and, as the terrible instant draws near, its force redoubles.

Just as you come into her *salon*, in order not to do or say some incredible piece of nonsense, you clutch in despair at the resolution of keeping your mouth shut and your eyes on her — in order at least to be able to remember her face. Scarcely before her, something like a kind of drunkenness comes over your eyes; you feel driven like a maniac to do strange actions; it is as if you had two souls — one to act and the other to blame your actions. You feel, in a confused way, that to turn your strained attention to folly would temporarily refresh the blood, and make you lose from sight the end of the visit and the misery of parting for a fortnight.

If some bore be there, who tells a pointless story, the poor lover, in his inexplicable madness, as if he were nervous of losing moments so rare, becomes all attention. That hour, of which he drew himself so sweet a picture, passes like a flash of lightning and yet he feels, with unspeakable bitterness, all the little circumstances which show how much a stranger he has become to her whom he loves. There he is in the midst of indifferent visitors and sees himself the only one who does not know her life of these past days, in all its details. At last he goes: and as he coldly says good-bye, he has the agonizing feelings of two whole weeks before another meeting. Without a doubt he would suffer less never to see the object of his love again. It is in the style, only far blacker, of the Duc de Policastro, who every six months travelled a hundred leagues to see for a quarter of an hour at Lecce a beloved mistress guarded by a jealous husband.

Here you can see clearly Will without influence upon Love. Out of all patience with one's mistress and oneself, how furious the desire to bury oneself in indifference! The only good of such visits is to replenish the treasure of crystallization.

Life for Salviati was divided into periods of two weeks, which took their color from the last evening he had been allowed to see Madame ——. For example, he was in the seventh heaven of delight the 21st of May, and the 2nd of June he kept away from home, for fear of yielding to the temptation of blowing out his brains.

I saw that evening how badly novelists have drawn the moment of suicide. Salviati simply said to me: "I'm thirsty, I must take this glass of water." I did not oppose his resolution, but said good-bye: then he broke down.

Seeing the obscurity which envelops the discourse of lovers, it would not be prudent to push too far conclusions drawn from an isolated detail of their conversation. They give a fair glimpse of their feelings only in sudden expressions — then it is the cry of the heart. Otherwise it is from the complexion of the bulk of what is said that inductions are to be drawn. And we must remember that quite often a man, who is very moved, has no time to notice the emotion of the person who is the cause of his own.

The Introduction

To SEE the subtlety and sureness of judgment with which women grasp certain details, I am lost in admiration: but a moment later, I see them praise a blockhead to the skies, let themselves be moved to tears by a piece of insipidity, or weigh gravely a fatuous affectation, as if it were a telling characteristic. I cannot conceive such simplicity. There must be some general law in all this, unknown to me.

Attentive to one merit in a man and absorbed by one detail, women feel it deeply and have no eyes for the rest. All the nervous fluid is used up in the enjoyment of this quality: there is none left to see the others.

I have seen the most remarkable men introduced to very clever women; it was always a particle of bias which decided the effect of the first inspection.

If I may be allowed a familiar detail, I shall tell the story how charming Colonel L. B—— was to be introduced to Madame de Struve of Koenigsberg — she a most distinguished woman. "*Farà colpo?*"[1] — we asked each other; and a wager was made as a result.

I go up to Madame de Struve, and tell her the Colonel wears his ties two days running — the second he turns them — she could notice on his tie the creases downwards. Nothing more palpably untrue!

As I finish, the dear fellow is announced. The silliest little Parisian would have made more effect. Observe that Madame de Struve was one who could love. She is also a respectable woman and there could have been no question of gallantry between them.

Never were two characters more made for each other. People blamed Madame de Struve for being romantic, and there was nothing could touch L. B. but virtue carried to the point of the romantic. Thanks to her, he had a bullet put through him quite young.

It has been given to women admirably to feel the fine shades of affection, the most imperceptible variations of the human heart, the lightest movements of susceptibility.

In this regard they have an organ which in us is missing: watch them nurse the wounded.

But, perhaps, they are equally unable to see what mind consists in — as a moral composition. I have seen the most distinguished women charmed with a clever man, who was not myself, and, at the same time and almost with the same word, admire the biggest fools. I felt caught like a connois-

[1] [Will he impress her?]

seur, who sees the loveliest diamonds taken for paste, and paste preferred for being more massive.

And so I concluded that with women you have to risk everything. Where General Lassale came to grief, a captain with moustaches and heavy oaths succeeded.[1] There is surely a whole side in men's merit which escapes them. For myself, I always come back to physical laws. The nervous fluid spends itself in men through the brain and in women through the heart: that is why they are more sensitive. Some great and obligatory work, within the profession we have followed all our life, is our consolation, but for them nothing can console but distraction.

Appiani, who only believes in virtue as a last resort, and with whom this evening I went routing out ideas (exposing meanwhile those of this chapter) answered: —

"The force of soul, which Eponina used with heroic devotion, to keep alive her husband in a cavern underground and to keep him from sinking into despair, would have helped her to hide from him a lover, if they had lived at Rome in peace. Strong souls must have their nourishment."

Of Modesty

IN Madagascar, a woman exposes without a thought what is here most carefully hidden, but would die of shame sooner than show her arm. Clearly three-quarters of modesty come from example. It is perhaps the one law, daughter of civilization, which produces only happiness.

People have noticed that birds of prey hide themselves to drink; the reason being that, obliged to plunge their heads in the water, they are at that moment defenseless. After a consideration of what happens at Tahiti,[2] I see no other natural basis for modesty.

[1] Posen, 1807.

[2] See the Travels of Bougainville, Cook, etc. In some animals, the female seems to retract at the moment she gives herself. We must expect from comparative anatomy some of the most important revelations about ourselves.

Love is the miracle of civilization. There is nothing but a physical love of the coarsest kind among savage or too barbarian peoples.

And modesty gives love the help of imagination — that is, gives it life.

Modesty is taught little girls very early by their mothers with such jealous care, that it almost looks like fellow-feeling; in this way women take measures in good time for the happiness of the lover to come.

There can be nothing worse for a timid, sensitive woman than the torture of having, in the presence of a man, allowed herself something for which she thinks she ought to blush; I am convinced that a woman with a little pride would sooner face a thousand deaths. A slight liberty, which touches a soft corner in the lover's heart, gives her a moment of lively pleasure.[1] If he seem to blame it, or simply not to enjoy it to the utmost, it must leave in the soul an agonizing doubt. And so a woman above the common sort has everything to gain by being very reserved in her manner. The game is not fair: against the chance of a little pleasure or the advantage of seeming a little more lovable, a woman runs the risk of a burning remorse and a sense of shame, which must make even the lover less dear. An evening gaily passed, in care-devil thoughtless fashion, is dearly paid for at the price. If a woman fears she has made this kind of mistake before her lover, he must become for days together hateful in her sight. Can one wonder at the force of a habit, when the lightest infractions of it are punished by such cruel shame?

As for the utility of modesty — she is the mother of love: impossible, therefore, to doubt her claims. And for the mechanism of the sentiment — it's simple enough. The soul is busy feeling shame instead of busy desiring. You deny yourelf desires and your desires lead to actions.

Evidently every woman of feeling and pride — and, these two things being cause and effect, one can hardly go with-

[1] Shows one's love in a new way.

out the other — must fall into ways of coldness, which the people whom they disconcert call prudery.

The accusation is all the more specious because of the extreme difficulty of steering a middle course: a woman has only to have little judgment and a lot of pride, and very soon she will come to believe that in modesty one cannot go too far. In this way, an Englishwoman takes it as an insult, if you pronounce before her the name of certain garments. An Englishwoman must be very careful, in the country, not to be seen in the evening leaving the drawing-room with her husband; and, what is still more serious, she thinks it an outrage to modesty, to show that she is enjoying herself a little in the presence of anyone *but* her husband.[1] It is perhaps due to such studied scrupulousness that the English, a people of judgment, betray signs of such boredom in their domestic bliss. Theirs the fault — why so much pride?[2]

To make up for this — and to pass straight from Plymouth to Cadiz and Seville — I found in Spain that the warmth of climate and passions caused people to overlook a little the necessary measure of restraint. The very tender caresses, which I noticed could be given in public, far from seeming touching, inspired me with feelings quite the reverse: nothing is more distressing.

We must expect to find incalculable the force of habits, which insinuate themselves into women under the pretext of modesty. A common woman, by carrying modesty to extremes, feels she is getting on a level with a woman of distinction.

Such is the empire of modesty, that a woman of feeling betrays her sentiments for her lover sooner by deed than by word.

The prettiest, richest and most easy-going woman of Bologna has just told me, how yesterday evening a fool of

[1] See the admirable picture of these tedious manners at the end of *Corinne;* and Madame de Staël has made a flattering portrait.

[2] The Bible and Aristocracy take a cruel revenge upon people who believe that duty is everything.

a Frenchman, who is here giving people a strange idea of his nation, thought good to hide under her bed. Apparently he did not want to waste the long string of absurd declarations, with which he has been pestering her for a month. But the great man should have had more presence of mind. He waited all right till Madame M—— sent away her maid and had got to bed, but he had not the patience to give the household time to go to sleep. She seized hold of the bell and had him thrown out ignominiously, in the midst of the jeers and cuffs of five or six lackeys. "And if he had waited two hours?" I asked her. "I should have been very badly off. 'Who is to doubt,' he would have said, 'that I am here by your orders?' "[1]

After leaving this pretty woman's house, I went to see a woman more worthy of being loved than any I know. Her extremely delicate nature is something greater, if possible, than her touching beauty. I found her alone, told the story of Madame M—— and we discussed it. "Listen," was what she said; "if the man, who will go as far as that, was lovable in the eyes of that woman beforehand, he'll have her pardon, and, all in good time, her love." I own I was dumbfounded by this unexpected light thrown on the recesses of the human heart. After a short silence I answered her — "But will a man, who loves, dare go to such violent extremities?"

There would be far less vagueness in this chapter had a woman written it. Everything relating to women's haughtiness or pride, to their habits of modesty and its excesses, to certain delicacies, for the most part dependent wholly on associations of feelings,[2] which cannot exist for men, and often delicacies not founded on Nature — all these things,

---

[1] I am advised to suppress this detail — "You take me for a very doubtful woman, to dare tell such stories in my presence."

[2] Modesty is one of the sources of taste in dress: by such and such an arrangement, a woman engages herself in a greater or less degree. This is what makes a dress lose its point in old age.
A provincial, who puts up to follow the fashion in Paris, engages herself in an awkward way, which makes people laugh. A woman coming to Paris from the provinces ought to begin by dressing as if she were thirty.

I say, can only find their way here so far as it is permissible to write from hearsay.

A woman once said to me, in a moment of philosophical frankness, something which amounts to this: —

"If ever I sacrificed my liberty, the man whom I should happen to favor would appreciate still more my affection, by seeing how sparing I had always been of favors — even of the slightest." It is out of preference for this lover, whom perhaps she will never meet, that a lovable woman will offer a cold reception to the man who is speaking to her at the moment. That is the first exaggeration of modesty; that one can respect. The second comes from women's pride. The third source of exaggeration is the pride of husbands.

To my idea, this possibility of love presents itself often to the fancy of even the most virtuous woman — and why not? Not to love, when given by Heaven a soul made for love, is to deprive yourself and others of a great blessing. It is like an orange-tree, which would not flower for fear of committing a sin. And beyond doubt a soul made for love can partake fervently of no other bliss. In the would-be pleasures of the world it finds, already at the second trial, an intolerable emptiness. Often it fancies that it loves Art and Nature in its grander aspects, but all they do for it is to hold out hopes of love and magnify it, if that is possible; until, very soon, it finds out that they speak of a happiness which it is resolved to forego.

The only thing I see to blame in modesty is that it leads to untruthfulness, and that is the only point of vantage, which light women have over women of feeling. A light woman says to you: "As soon, my friend, as you attract me, I'll tell you and I'll be more delighted than you; because I have a great respect for you."

The lively satisfaction of Constance's cry after her lover's victory! "How happy I am, not to have given myself to any-one, all these eight years that I've been on bad terms with my husband!" However comical I find the line of thought, this joy seems to me full of freshness.

Here I absolutely must talk about the sort of regrets, felt by a certain lady of Seville who had been deserted by her lover. I ought to remind the reader that, in love, everything is a sign, and, above all, crave the benefit of a little indulgence for my style.

.   .   .   .   .   .

As a man, I think my eye can distinguish nine points in modesty.

1. Much is staked against little; hence extreme reserve; hence often affectation. For example, one doesn't laugh at what amuses one the most. Hence it needs a great deal of judgment to have just the right amount of modesty.[1] That is why many women have not enough in intimate gatherings, or, to put it more exactly, do not insist on the stories told them being sufficiently disguised, and only drop their veils according to the degree of their intoxication or recklessness.[2]

Could it be an effect of modesty and of the deadly dullness it must impose on many women, that the majority of them respect nothing in a man so much as impudence? Or do they take impudence for character?

2. Second law: "My lover will think the more of me for it."

3. Force of habit has its way, even at the moments of greatest passion.

4. To the lover, modesty offers very flattering pleasures; it makes him feel what laws are broken for his sake.

5. And to women it offers more intoxicating pleasures, which, causing the fall of a strongly established habit, throw the soul into greater confusion. The Comte de Valmont finds himself in a pretty woman's bedroom at midnight. The thing happens every week to him; to her perhaps every

[1] See the tone of society at Geneva, above all in the "best" families — use of a Court to correct the tendency towards prudery by laughing at it — Duclos telling stories to Madame de Rochefort — "Really, you take us for too virtuous." Nothing in the world is so nauseous as modesty not sincere.

[2] "Ah, my dear Fronsac, there are twenty bottles of champagne between the story, that you're beginning to tell us, and our talk at this time of day."

other year. Thus continence and modesty must have pleasures infinitely more lively in store for women.[1]

6. The drawback of modesty is that it is always leading to falsehood.

7. Excess of modesty, and its severity, discourages gentle and timid hearts from loving[2] — just those made for giving and feeling the sweets of love.

8. In sensitive women, who have not had several lovers, modesty is a bar to ease of manner, and for this reason they are rather apt to let themselves be led by those friends, who need reproach themselves with no such failing.[3] They go into each particular case, instead of falling back blindly on habit. Delicacy and modesty give their actions a touch of restraint; by being natural they make themselves appear unnatural; but this awkwardness is akin to heavenly grace.

If familiarity in them sometimes resembles tenderness, it is because these angelic souls are coquettes without knowing it. They are disinclined to interrupt their dreams, and, to save themselves the trouble of speaking and finding something both pleasant and polite to say to a friend (which would end in being nothing but polite), they finish by leaning tenderly on his arm.[4]

---

[1] It is the story of the melancholy temperament and the sanguine. Consider a virtuous woman (even the mercenary virtue of certain of the faithful — virtue to be had for a hundredfold reward in Paradise) and a blasé debauchee of forty. Although the Valmont of the *Liaisons Dangereuses* is not as far gone as that, the Présidente de Tourvel is happier than he all the way through the book; and if the author, with all his wit, had had still more, that would have been the moral of his ingenious novel.

[2] Melancholy temperament, which may be called the temperament of love. I have seen women, the most distinguished and the most made for love, give the preference, for want of sense, to the prosaic, sanguine temperament. (Story of Alfred, Grande Chartreuse, 1810.)
I know no thought which incites me more to keep what is called bad company.
[Here poor Visconti loses himself in the clouds.
Fundamentally all women are the same so far as concerns the movements of the heart and passion: the forms the passions take are different. Consider the difference made by greater fortune, a more cultivated mind, the habit of higher thoughts, and, above all, (and more's the pity) a more irritable pride.
Such and such a word irritates a princess, but would not in the very least shock an Alpine shepherdess. Only, once their anger is up, the passion works in princess and shepherdess the same]. [The Editor's only note.]

[3] M.'s remark.

[4] Vol. *Guarna*.

9. Women only dare be frank by halves; which is the reason why they very rarely reach the highest, when they become authors, but which also gives a grace to their shortest note. For them to be frank means going out without a *fichu*. For a man nothing more frequent than to write absolutely at the dictate of his imagination, without knowing where he is going.

RÉSUMÉ

The usual fault is to treat woman as a kind of man, but more generous, more changeable and with whom, above all, no rivalry is possible. It is only too easy to forget that there are two new and peculiar laws, which tyrannize over these unstable beings, in conflict with all the ordinary impulses of human nature — I mean: —

Feminine pride and modesty, and those often inscrutable habits born of modesty.

The Glance

THIS is the great weapon of virtuous coquetry. With a glance, one may say everything, and yet one can always deny a glance; for it cannot be repeated textually.

This reminds me of Count G——, the Mirabeau of Rome. The delightful little government of that land has taught him an original way of telling stories by a broken string of words, which say everything — and nothing. He makes his whole meaning clear, but repeat who will his sayings word for word, it is impossible to compromise him. Cardinal Lante told him he had stolen this talent from women — yes, and respectable women, I add. This roguery is a cruel, but just, reprisal on man's tyranny.

Of Feminine Pride

ALL their lives women hear mention made by men of things claiming importance — large profits, success in war, people killed in duels, fiendish or admirable revenges, and so on. Those of them, whose heart is proud, feel that, being unable to reach these things, they are not in a position to display any pride remarkable for the importance of what it rests on. They feel a heart beat in their breast, superior by the force and pride of its movements to all which surrounds them, and yet they see the meanest of men esteem himself above them. They find out, that all their pride can only be for little things, or at least for things, which are without importance except for sentiment, and of which a third party cannot judge. Maddened by this desolating contrast between the meanness of their fortune and the conscious worth of their soul, they set about making their pride worthy of respect by the intensity of its fits or by the relentless tenacity with which they hold by its dictates. Before intimate intercourse women of this kind imagine, when they see their lover, that he has laid siege to them. Their imagination is absorbed in irritation at his endeavors, which, after all, cannot do otherwise than witness to his love — seeing that he does love. Instead of enjoying the feelings of the man of their preference, their vanity is up in arms against him; and it comes to this, that, with a soul of the tenderest, so long as its sensibility is not centred on a special object, they have only to love, in order, like a common flirt, to be reduced to the barest vanity.

A woman of generous character will sacrifice her life a thousand times for her lover, but will break with him for ever over a question of pride — for the opening or shutting of a door. Therein lies their point of honor. Well! Napoleon came to grief rather than yield a village.

I have seen a quarrel of this kind last longer than a year. It was a woman of the greatest distinction who sacrificed all her happiness, sooner than give her lover the chance of entertaining the slightest possible doubt of the magnanimity of her pride. The reconciliation was the work of chance, and, on my friend's side, due to a moment of weakness, which, on meeting her lover, she was unable to overcome. She imagined him forty miles away, and found him in a place, where certainly he did not expect to see her. She could not hide the first transports of delight; her lover was more overcome than she; they almost fell at each other's feet and never have I seen tears flow so abundantly — it was the unlooked-for appearance of happiness. Tears are the supreme smile.

The Duke of Argyll gave a fine example of presence of mind, in not drawing Feminine Pride into a combat, in the interview he had at Richmond with Queen Caroline.[1] The more nobility in a woman's character, the more terrible are these storms —

> As the blackest sky
> Foretells the heaviest tempest.
>
> (*Don Juan*)

Can it be that the more fervently, in the normal course of life, a woman delights in the rare qualities of her lover, the more she tries, in those cruel moments, when sympathy seems turned to the reverse, to wreak her vengeance on what usually she sees in him superior to other people? She is afraid of being confounded with them.

It is a precious long time since I read that boring *Clarissa;* but I think it is through feminine pride that she lets herself die, and does not accept the hand of Lovelace.

Lovelace's fault was great; but as she did love him a little, she could have found pardon in her heart for a crime, of which the cause was love.

Monime, on the contrary, seems to me a touching model of feminine delicacy. What cheek does not blush with pleasure to hear from the lips of an actress worthy of the part: —

[1] *The Heart of Midlothian.*

That fatal love which I had crushed and conquered,

.　　.　　.　　.　　.　　.　　.

Your wiles detected, and I cannot now
Disown what I confess'd; you cannot raze
Its memory; the shame of that avowal,
To which you forced me, will abide for ever
Present before my mind, and I should think
That you were always of my faith uncertain.
The grave itself to me were less abhorrent
Than marriage bed shared with a spouse, who took
Cruel advantage of my simple trust,
And, to destroy my peace for ever, fann'd
A flame that fired my cheek for other love
Than his.[1]

I can picture to myself future generations saying: "So that's what Monarchy[2] was good for — to produce that sort of character and its portrayal by great artists."

And yet I find an admirable example of this delicacy even in the republics of the Middle Ages; which seems to destroy my system of the influence of governments on the passions, but which I shall cite in good faith.

The reference is to those very touching verses of Dante:

Deh! quando tu sarai tornato al mondo

.　　.　　.　　.　　.　　.

Ricordati di me, che son la Pia;
Siena mi fè; disfecemi Maremma;
Salsi colui, che inanellata pria
Disposando, m'avea con la sua gemma.
Purgatorio, Cant. V.[3]

The woman, who speaks with so much restraint, had suffered in secret the fate of Desdemona, and, by a word, could make known her husband's crime to the friends, whom she had left on earth.

Nello della Pietra won the hand of Madonna Pia, sole heiress of the Tolomei, the richest and noblest family of

---

[1] Racine, *Mithridates*, Act. IV, Sc. 4.

[2] Monarchy without charter and without chambers.

[3] Ah! when you are returned to the world of the living, give me a passing thought. I am la Pia. Sienna gave me life, death took me in our fens. He who, wedding me, gave me his ring, knows my story.

Sienna. Her beauty, which was the admiration of Tuscany, sowed in her husband's heart the seed of jealousy, which, envenomed by false reports and suspicions ever and anon rekindled, led him to a heinous project. It is difficult, at this hour, to decide whether his wife was altogether innocent, but Dante represents her as such.

Her husband carried her off into the fens of Volterra, famous then, as now, for the effects of the *aria cattiva*. Never would he tell his unhappy wife the reason of her exile in so dangerous a place. His pride did not deign to utter complaint or accusation. He lived alone with her in a deserted tower, the ruins of which by the edge of the sea I have been myself to visit. There he never broke his scornful silence, never answered his young wife's questions, never listened to her prayers. Coldly he waited at her side for the pestilential air to have its effect. The exhalations of these morasses were not long in withering those features — the loveliest, it is said, which, in that century, the world had seen. In a few months she died. Some chroniclers of those remote times report that Nello used the dagger to hasten her end. She died in the fens in some horrible way; but the kind of death was a mystery even to her contemporaries. Nello della Pietra survived to pass the rest of his days in a silence which he never broke.

Nothing nobler and more delicate than the way in which young la Pia addresses Dante. She wishes to be recalled to the memory of the friends, whom she had left on earth so young; and yet, telling who she is and giving the name of her husband, she will not allow herself the slightest complaint against a piece of cruelty unheard of, but for the future irreparable; she only points out that he knows the story of her death.

This constancy in pride's revenge is not met, I think, except in the countries of the South.

In Piedmont I happened to be the involuntary witness of something very nearly parallel; though at the time I did not know the details. I was sent with twenty-five dragoons into the woods along the Sesia, to intercept contraband. Arriving in the evening at this wild and desolate spot, I caught sight, between the trees, of the ruins of an old castle. I went up to it and to my great surprise — it was inhabited. I found within a nobleman of the country, of sinister appearance, a man six foot high and forty years old. He gave me two rooms with a bad grace. I passed my time playing music with my quartermaster; after some days, we discovered that our friend kept a woman in the background, whom we used to call Camille, laughingly; but we were far from suspecting the fearful truth. Six weeks later she was dead. I had the morbid curiosity to see her in the coffin, paying a monk, who was watching, to introduce me into the chapel towards midnight, under pretext of going to sprinkle holy water. There I found one of those superb faces, which are beautiful even in the arms of death; she had a large aquiline nose — the nobility and delicacy of its outline I shall never forget. Then I left that deadly spot. Five years later, a detachment of my regiment accompanying the Emperor to his coronation as King of Italy, I had the whole story told me. I learned that the jealous husband, Count ——, had found one morning fastened to his wife's bed an English watch, belonging to a young man of the small town in which they lived. That very day he carried her off to the ruined castle in the midst of the woods of the Sesia. Like Nello della Pietra, he never uttered a single word. If she made him any request, he coldly and silently presented to her the English watch, which he carried always with him. Almost three years passed, spent thus alone with her. At last she died of despair, in the flower of life. Her husband tried to put a knife into the proprietor of the watch, missed him, passed on to Genoa, took ship and no one has heard of him since. His property has been divided.

As for these women with feminine pride, if you take their injuries with a good grace, which the habits of a military life make easy, you annoy these proud souls; they take you for a coward, and very soon become outrageous. Such lofty characters yield with pleasure to men whom they see overbearing with other men. That is, I fancy, the only way — you must often pick a quarrel with your neighbor in order to avoid one with your mistress.

One day Miss Cornel, the celebrated London actress, was surprised by the unexpected appearance of the rich colonel, whom she found useful. She happened to be with a little lover, whom she just liked — and nothing more. "Mr. So-and-so," says she in great confusion to the colonel, "has come to see the pony I want to sell." "I am here for something very different," put in proudly the little lover who was beginning to bore her, but whom, from the moment of that answer, she started to love again madly.[1] Women of that kind sympathize with their lover's haughtiness, instead of exercising at his expense their own disposition to pride.

The character of the Duc de Lauzun (that of 1660[2]), if they can forgive the first day its want of grace, is very fascinating for such women, and perhaps for all women of distinction. Grandeur on a higher plane escapes them; they take for coldness the calm gaze which nothing escapes, but which a detail never disturbs. Have I not heard women at the Court of Saint-Cloud maintain that Napoleon had a dry and prosaic character?[3] A great man is like an eagle: the

---

[1] I always come back from Miss Cornel's full of admiration and profound views on the passions laid bare. Her very imperious way of giving orders to her servants has nothing of despotism in it: she merely sees with precision and rapidity what has to be done.

Incensed against me at the beginning of the visit, she thinks no more about it at the end. She tells me in detail of the economy of her passion for Mortimer. "I prefer seeing him in company than alone with me." A woman of the greatest genius could do no better, for she has the courage to be perfectly natural and is unhampered by any theory. "I'm happier an actress than the wife of a peer." — A great soul whose friendship I must keep for my enlightenment.

[2] Loftiness and courage in small matters, but a passionate care for these small matters. — The vehemence of the choleric temperament. — His behavior towards Madame de Monaco (Saint-Simon, V. 383) and adventure under the bed of Madame de Montespan while the king was there. — Without the care for small matters, this character would remain invisible to the eye of women.

[3] When Minna Troil heard a tale of woe or of romance, it was then her blood rushed to her cheeks and showed plainly how warm it beat, notwithstanding the generally serious, composed and retiring disposition which her countenance and demeanor seemed to exhibit. (*The Pirate*, Chap. III.)

Souls like Minna Troil, in whose judgment ordinary circumstances are not worth emotion, by ordinary people are thought cold.

higher he rises the less he is visible, and he is punished for his greatness by the solitude of his soul.

From feminine pride arises what women call want of refinement. I fancy, it is not at all unlike what kings call *lèse majesté*, a crime all the more dangerous, because one slips into it without knowing. The tenderest lover may be accused of wanting refinement, if he is not very sharp, or, what is sadder, if he dares give himself up to the greatest charm of love — the delight of being perfectly natural with the loved one and of not listening to what he is told.

These are the sort of things, of which a well-born heart could have no inkling; one must have experience, in order to believe in them; for we are misled by the habit of dealing justly and frankly with our men friends.

It is necessary to keep in mind incessantly that we have to do with beings, who can, however wrongly, think themselves inferior in vigor of character, or, to put it better, can think that others believe they are inferior.

Should not a woman's true pride reside in the power of the feeling she inspires? A maid of honor to the queen and wife of Francis I was chaffed about the fickleness of her lover, who, it was said, did not really love her. A little time after, this lover had an illness and reappeared at Court — dumb. Two years later, people showing surprise one day that she still loved him, she turned to him, saying: "Speak." And he spoke.

Of Women's Courage

I tell thee, proud Templar, that not in thy fiercest battles hast thou displayed more of thy vaunted courage than has been shewn by women, when called upon to suffer by affection or duty — Ivanhoe

I REMEMBER meeting the following phrase in a book of history: "All the men lost their heads: that is the moment when women display an incontestable superiority."

Their courage has a reserve which that of their lover wants; he acts as a spur to their sense of worth. They find so much pleasure in being able, in the fire of danger, to dispute the first place for firmness with the man, who often wounds them by the proudness of his protection and his strength, that the vehemence of that enjoyment raises them above any kind of fear, which at the moment is the man's weak point. A man, too, if the same help were given him at the same moment, would show himself superior to everything; for fear never resides in the danger, but in ourselves.

Not that I mean to depreciate women's courage — I have seen them, on occasions, superior to the bravest men. Only they must have a man to love. Then they no longer feel except through him; and so the most obvious and personal danger becomes, as it were, a rose to gather in his presence.[1]

I have found also in women, who did not love, intrepidity, the coldest, the most surprising and the most exempt from nerves.

It is true, I have always imagined that they are so brave, only because they do not know the tiresomeness of wounds!

As for moral courage, so far superior to the other, the firmness of a woman who resists her love is simply the most admirable thing, which can exist on earth. All other possible marks of courage are as nothing compared to a thing so strongly opposed to nature and so arduous. Perhaps they find a source of strength in the habit of sacrifice, which is bred in them by modesty.

Hard on women it is that the proofs of this courage should always remain secret and be almost impossible to divulge. Still harder that it should always be employed against their own happiness: the Princesse de Clèves would have done better to say nothing to her husband and give herself to M. de Nemours.

Perhaps women are chiefly supported by their pride in making a fine defense, and imagine that their lover is staking his vanity on having them — a petty and miserable idea. A man of passion, who throws himself with a light heart into so many ridiculous situations, must have a lot of time

[1] Mary Stuart speaking of Leicester, after the interview with Elizabeth, where she had just met her doom. (Schiller)

to be thinking of vanity! It is like the monks who mean to catch the devil and find their reward in the pride of hair-shirts and macerations.

I should think that Madame de Clèves would have repented, had she come to old age, — to the period at which one judges life and when the joys of pride appear in all their meanness. She would have wished to have lived like Madame de la Fayette.[1]

I have just re-read a hundred pages of this essay: and a pretty poor idea I have given of true love, of love which occupies the entire soul, fills it with fancies, now the happiest, now heart-breaking — but always sublime — and makes it completely insensible to all the rest of creation. I am at a loss to express what I see so well; I have never felt more painfully the want of talent. How bring into relief the simplicity of action and of character, the high seriousness, the glance that reflects so truly and so ingenuously the passing shade of feeling, and above all, to return to it again, that inexpressible *What care I?* for all that is not the woman we love? A yes or a no spoken by a man in love has an *unction* which is not to be found elsewhere, and is not found in that very man at other times. This morning (August 3rd) I passed on horseback about nine o'clock in front of the lovely English garden of Marchese Zampieri, situated on the last crests of those tree-capped hills, on which Bologna rests, and from which so fine a view is enjoyed over Lombardy rich and green — the fairest country in the world. In a copse of laurels, belonging to the Giardino Zampieri, which dominates the path I was taking, leading to the cascade of the Reno at Casa Lecchio, I saw Count Delfante. He was absorbed in thought and scarcely returned my greeting, though we had passed the night together till two o'clock in the morning. I went to the cascade, I crossed the Reno; after which, passing again, at least three hours later,

[1] It is well known that that celebrated woman was the author, probably in company with M. de la Rochefoucauld, of the novel, *La Princesse de Clèves*, and that the two authors passed together in perfect friendship the last twenty years of their lives. That is exactly love *à l'Italienne*.

under the copse of the Giardino Zampieri, I saw him still there. He was precisely in the same position, leaning against a great pine, which rises above the copse of laurels — but this detail I am afraid will be found too simple and pointless. He came up to me with tears in his eyes, asking me not to go telling people of his trance. I was touched, and suggested retracing my steps and going with him to spend the day in the country. At the end of two hours he had told me everything. His is a fine soul, but oh! the coldness of these pages, compared to his story.

Furthermore, he thinks his love is not returned — which is not my opinion. In the fair marble face of the Contessa Ghigi, with whom we spent the evening, one can read nothing. Only now and then a light and sudden blush, which she cannot check, just betrays the emotions of that soul, which the most exalted feminine pride disputes with deeper emotions. You see the color spread over her neck of alabaster and as much as one catches of those lovely shoulders, worthy of Canova. She somehow finds a way of diverting her black and sombre eyes from the observation of those, whose penetration alarms her woman's delicacy; but last night, at something which Delfante was saying and of which she disapproved, I saw a sudden blush spread all over her. Her lofty soul found him less worthy of her.

But when all is said, even if I were mistaken in my conjectures on the happiness of Delfante, vanity apart, I think him happier than I, in my indifference, although I am in a thoroughly happy position, in appearance and in reality.

Bologna, *August 3rd, 1818.*

A Mournful Spectacle

WOMEN with their feminine pride visit the iniquities of the fools upon the men of sense, and those of the prosaic, prosperous and brutal upon the noble-minded. A very pretty result — you'll agree!

The petty considerations of pride and worldly proprieties are the cause of many women's unhappiness, for, through pride, their parents have placed them in their abominable position. Destiny has reserved for them, as a consolation far superior to all their misfortunes, the happiness of loving and being loved with passion, when suddenly one fine day they borrow from the enemy this same mad pride, of which they were the first victims — all to kill the one happiness which is left them, to work their own misfortune and the misfortune of those who love them. A friend, who has had ten famous intrigues (and by no means all one after another), gravely persuades them that if they fall in love, they will be dishonored in the eyes of the public, and yet this worthy public, which never rises above low ideas, gives them generously a lover a year; because that, it says, "is the thing." Thus the soul is saddened by this odd spectacle: a woman of feeling, supremely refined and an angel of purity, on the advice of a low t——, runs away from the boundless, the only happiness which is left to her, in order to appear in a dress of dazzling white, before a great fat brute of a judge, whom everyone knows has been blind a hundred years, and who bawls out at the top of his voice: "She is dressed in black!"

Extract from the Diary of Salviati

Ingenium nobis ipsa puella facit — Propertius, II, 1

BOLOGNA, *April 29th, 1818*

DRIVEN to despair by the misfortune to which love has reduced me, I curse existence. I have no heart for anything. The weather is dull; it is raining, and a late spell of cold has come again to sadden Nature, who after a long winter was hurrying to meet the spring.

Schiassetti, a half-pay colonel, my cold and reasonable friend, came to spend a couple of hours with me.

"You should renounce your love."

"How? Give me back my passion for war."

"It is a great misfortune for you to have known her."

I agree very nearly — so low-spirited and craven do I feel — so much has melancholy taken possession of me to-day. We discuss what interest can have led her friend to libel me, but find nothing but that old Neapolitan proverb: "Woman, whom love and youth desert, a nothing piques." What is certain is that that cruel woman is *enraged* with me — it is the expression of one of her friends. I could revenge myself in a fearful way, but, against her hatred, I am without the smallest means of defense. Schiassetti leaves me. I go out into the rain, not knowing what to do with myself. My rooms, this drawing-room, which I lived in during the first days of our acquaintance, and when I saw her every evening, have become insupportable to me. Each engraving, each piece of furniture, brings up again the happiness I dreamed of in their presence — which now I have lost for ever.

I tramped the streets through a cold rain: chance, if I can call it chance, made me pass under her windows. Night was falling and I went along, my eyes full of tears fixed on the window of her room. Suddenly the curtains were just drawn aside, as if to give a glimpse into the square, then instantly closed again. I felt within me a physical movement about the heart. I was unable to support myself and took refuge under the gateway of the next house. A thousand feelings crowd upon my soul. Chance may have produced this movement of the curtains; but oh! if it was her hand that had drawn them aside.

There are two misfortunes in the world: passion frustrated and the "dead blank."

In love — I feel that two steps away from me exists a boundless happiness, something beyond all my prayers, which depends upon nothing but a word, nothing but a smile.

Passionless like Schiassetti, on gloomy days I see happiness nowhere, I come to doubt if it exists for me, I fall into depression. One ought to be without strong passions and have only a little curiosity or vanity.

It is two o'clock in the morning; I have seen that little movement of the curtain; at six o'clock I paid some calls and went to the play, but everywhere, silent and dreaming, I passed the evening examining this question:

"After so much anger with so little foundation (for after all did I wish to offend her and is there a thing on earth which the intention does not excuse?) — has she felt a moment of love?"

Poor Salviati, who wrote the preceding lines on his Petrarch, died a short time after. He was the intimate friend of Schiassetti and myself; we knew all his thoughts, and it is from him that I have all the tearful part of this essay. He was imprudence incarnate; moreover, the woman, for whom he went to such wild lengths, is the most interesting creature that I have met.

Schiassetti said to me: "But do you think that that unfortunate passion was without advantages for Salviati? To begin with, the most worrying of money troubles that can be imagined came upon him. These troubles, which reduced him to a very middling fortune after his dazzling youth, and would have driven him mad with anger in any other circumstances, crossed his mind not once in two weeks.

"And then — a matter of importance of a quite different kind for a mind of his range — that passion is the first true course of logic, which he ever had. That may seem peculiar in a man who has been at Court; but the fact is explained by his extreme courage. For example, he passed without winking the day of ——, the day of his undoing; he was surprised then, as in Russia, not to feel anything extraordinary. It is an actual fact, that his fear of anything had never gone so far as to make him think about it for two days together. Instead of this callousness, the last two years he was trying every minute to be brave. Before he had never seen danger.

"When as a result of his imprudence and his faith in the

generosity of critics,[1] he had managed to get condemned to not seeing the woman he was in love with, except twice a month, we would see him pass those evenings, talking to her as if intoxicated with joy, because he has been received with that noble frankness which he worshipped. He held that Madame —— and he were two souls without their like, who should understand each other with a glance. It was beyond him to grasp that she should pay the least attention to petty bourgeois comments, which tried to make a criminal of him. The result of this fine confidence in a woman, surrounded by his enemies, was to find her door closed to him. 'With M——,' I used to say to him, 'you forget your maxim — that you mustn't believe in greatness of soul, except in the last extremity.'

" 'Do you think,' he answered, 'that the world contains another heart which is more suited to hers? True, I pay for this passionate way of being, which Léonore, in anger, made me see on the horizon in the line of the rocks of Poligny, with the ruin of all the practical enterprises of my life — a disaster which comes from my lack of patient industry and imprudence due to the force of momentary impressions.' "

One can see the touch of madness!

For Salviati life was divided into periods of a fortnight, which took their hue from the last interview which he had been granted. But I noticed often, that the happiness he owed to a welcome, which he thought less cold, was far inferior in intensity to the unhappiness with which a hard reception overwhelmed him.[2] At times Madame —— failed to be quite honest with him; and these are the only two criticisms I ever dared offer him. Beyond the more intimate side of his sorrow, of which he had the delicacy never to speak even to the friends dearest to him and most devoid

---

[1] Sotto l'usbergo del sentirsi pura. [Under the shield of conscious purity.] (Dante, *Inferno*, XXVIII, 117)

[2] That is a thing which I have often seemed to notice in love — that propensity to reap more unhappiness from what is unhappy than happiness from what is happy.

of envy, he saw in a hard reception from Léonore the triumph of prosaic and scheming beings over the open-hearted and the generous. At those times he lost faith in virtue and, above all, in glory. It was his way to talk to his friends only of sad notions, to which it is true his passion led up, but notions capable besides of having some interest in the eyes of philosophy. I was curious to observe that uncommon soul. Ordinarily passion-love is found in people, a little simple in the German way.[1] Salviati, on the contrary, was among the firmest and sharpest men I have known.

I seemed to notice that, after these cruel visits, he had no peace until he had found a justification for Léonore's severities. So long as he felt that she might have been wrong in ill-using him, he was unhappy. Love, so devoid of vanity, I should never have thought possible.

He was incessantly singing us the praises of love.

"If a supernatural power said to me: Break the glass of that watch and Léonore will be for you, what she was three years ago, an indifferent friend — really I believe I would never as long as I live have the courage to break it." I saw in these discourses such signs of madness, that I never had the courage to offer my former objections.

He would add: "Just as Luther's Reformation at the end of the Middle Ages, shaking society to its base, renewed and reconstructed the world on reasonable foundations, so is a generous character renewed and retempered by love.

"It is only then, that he casts off all the baubles of life; without this revolution he would always have had in him a pompous and theatrical *something*. It is only since I began to love that I have learned to put greatness into my character — such is the absurdity of education at our military academy.

"Although I behaved well, I was a child at the Court of Napoleon and at Moscow. I did my duty, but I knew nothing of that heroic simplicity, the fruit of entire and wholehearted sacrifice. For example, it is only this last year, that

[1] Don Carlos, Saint-Preux, Racine's *Hippolyte* and *Bajazet*.

my heart takes in the simplicity of the Romans in Livy. Once upon a time, I thought them cold compared to our brilliant colonels. What they did for their Rome, I find in my heart for Léonore. If I had the luck to be able to do anything for her, my first desire would be to hide it. The conduct of a Regulus or a Decius was something confirmed beforehand, which had no claim to surprise them. Before I loved, I was small, precisely because I was tempted sometimes to think myself great; I felt a certain effort, for which I applauded myself.

"And, on the side of affection, what do we not owe to love?

After the hazards of early youth, the heart is closed to sympathy. Death and absence remove our early companions, and we are reduced to passing our life with lukewarm partners, measure in hand, for ever calculating ideas of interest and vanity. Little by little all the sensitive and generous region of the soul becomes waste, for want of cultivation, and at less than thirty a man finds his heart steeled to all sweet and gentle sensations. In the midst of this arid desert, love causes a well of feelings to spring up, fresher and more abundant even than that of earliest youth. In those days it was a vague hope, irresponsible and incessantly distracted[1] — no devotion to one thing, no deep and constant desire; the soul, at all times light, was athirst for novelty and forgot to-day its adoration of the day before. But nothing is more concentrated, more mysterious, more eternally single in its object, than the crystallization of love. In those days only agreeable things claimed to please and to please for an instant: now we are deeply touched by everything which is connected with the loved one — even by objects the most indifferent. Arriving at a great town, a hundred miles from that which Léonore lives in, I was in a state of fear and trembling; at each street corner I shuddered to meet Alviza, the intimate friend of Madame ——, although I did not know her. For me everything took a mysterious

[1] Mordaunt Mertoun, *Pirate*, Vol. I.

and sacred tint. My heart beat fast, while talking to an old scholar; for I could not hear without blushing the name of the city gate, near which the friend of Léonore lives.

"Even the severities of the woman we love have an infinite grace, which the most flattering moments in the company of other women cannot offer. It is like the great shadows in Correggio's pictures, which far from being, as in other painters, passages less pleasant, but necessary in order to give effect to the lights and relief to the figures, have graces of their own which charm and throw us into a gentle reverie.[1]

"Yes, half and the fairest half of life is hidden from the man, who has not loved with passion."

Salviati had need of the whole force of his dialectic powers, to hold his own against the wise Schiassetti, who was always saying to him: "You want to be happy, then be content with a life exempt from pains and with a small quantity of happiness every day. Keep yourself from the lottery of great passions."

"Then give me your curiosity," was Salviati's answer.

I imagine there were not a few days, when he would have liked to be able to follow the advice of our sensible colonel; he made a little struggle and thought he was succeeding; but this line of action was absolutely beyond his strength. And yet what strength was in that soul!

A white satin hat, a little like that of Madame ——, seen in the distance in the street, made his heart stop beating, and forced him to rest against the wall. Even in his blackest moments, the happiness of meeting her gave him always some hours of intoxication, beyond the reach of all misfortune and all reasoning.[2] For the rest, at the time of his death[3] his character had certainly contracted more than one

---

[1] As I have mentioned Correggio, I will add that in the sketch of an angel's head in the gallery of the museum at Florence, is to be seen the glance of happy love, and at Parma in the Madonna crowned by Jesus the downcast eyes of love.

[2] Come what sorrow can
It cannot countervail the exchange of joy
That one short moment gives me in her sight. — (*Romeo and Juliet*)

[3] Some days before the last he made a little ode, which has the merit of expressing just the sentiments, which formed the subject of our conversations: —

noble habit, after two years of this generous and boundless passion; and, in so far at least, he judged himself correctly. Had he lived, and circumstances helped him a little, he would have made a name for himself. Maybe also, just through his simplicity, his merit would have passed on this earth unseen.

L'ULTIMO DI. ANACREONTICA. A ELVIRA

Vedi tu dove il rio
　　Lambendo un mirto va,
　　Là del riposo mio
　　La pietra surgerà.

Il passero amoroso,
　　E il nobile usignuol
　　Entro quel mirto ombroso
　　Raccoglieranno il vol.

Vieni, diletta Elvira,
　　A quella tombia vien,
　　E sulla muta lira,
　　Appoggia il bianco sen.

Su quella bruna pietra,
　　Le tortore verran,
　　E intorno alla mia cetra,
　　Il nido intrecieran.

E ogni anno, il di che offendere
　　M'osasti tu infedel,
　　Faro la su discendere
　　La folgore del ciel.

Odi d'un uom che muore
　　Odi i'estremo suon
　　Questo appassito fiore
　　Ti lascio, Elvira, in don

Quanto prezioso ei sia
　　Saper tu il devi appien
　　Il di che fosti mia,
　　Te l'involai dal sen.

Simbolo allor d'affetto
　　Or pegno di dolor
　　Torno a posarti in petto
　　Quest' appassito fior.

E avrai nel cuor-scolpito
　　Se crudo il cor non è,
　　Come ti fu rapito,
　　Come fu reso a te. — (S. Radael)*

* [Lo! where the passing stream laps round the myrtle-tree, raise there the stone of my resting-place. The amorous sparrow and the noble nightingale within the shade of that myrtle will rest from flight. Come, beloved Elvira, come to that tomb and press my mute lyre to your white bosom. Turtles shall perch on that dark stone and will twine their nest about my harp. And every year on the day when you did dare cruelly betray me, on this spot will I make the lightning of heaven descend. Listen, listen to the last utterances of a dying man. This faded flower, Elvira, is the gift I leave you. How precious it is you must know full well: from your bosom I stole it the day you became mine. Then it was a symbol of love; now as a pledge of suffering I will put it back in your bosom — this faded flower. And you shall have engraved on your heart, if a woman's heart you have, how it was snatched from you, how it was returned.]

O lasso
Quanti dolci pensier, quanto desio
Menò costui al doloroso passo!
Biondo era, e bello, e di gentile aspetto;
Ma l'un de' cigli un colpo avea diviso.

(Dante)[1]

Of Intimate Intercourse

THE greatest happiness that love can give — 'tis first join-
ing your hand to the hand of a woman you love.

The happiness of gallantry is quite otherwise — far more
real, and far more subject to ridicule.

In passion-love intimate intercourse is not so much perfect delight itself, as the last step towards it.

But how depict a delight, which leaves no memories
behind?

Mortimer returned from a long voyage in fear and trembling; he adored Jenny, but Jenny had not answered his
letters. On his arrival in London, he mounts his horse and
goes off to find her at her country home. When he gets
there, she is walking in the park; he runs up to her, with
beating heart, meets her and she offers him her hand and
greets him with emotion; he sees that she loves him. Roam-
ing together along the glades of the park, Jenny's dress became entangled in an acacia bush. Later on Mortimer won
her; but Jenny was faithless. I maintain to him that Jenny
never loved him and he quotes, as proof of her love, the
way in which she received him at his return from the Con-
tinent; but he could never give me the slightest details of
it. Only he shudders visibly directly he sees an acacia bush:
really, it is the only distinct remembrance he succeeded in
preserving of the happiest moment of his life.[2]

---

[1] "Poor wretch, how many sweet thoughts, what constancy brought him to
his last hour. He was fair and beautiful and gentle of countenance, only a noble
scar cut through one of his eyebrows."

[2] *Life of Haydn.*

A sensitive and open man, a former *chevalier*, confided to me this evening (in the depth of our craft buffeted by a high sea on the Lago di Garda[1]) the history of his loves, which I in my turn shall not confide to the public. But I feel myself in a position to conclude from them that the day of intimate intercourse is like those fine days in May, a critical period for the fairest flowers, a moment which can be fatal and wither in an instant the fairest hopes.

.   .   .   .   .   .[2]

Naturalness cannot be praised too highly. It is the only coquetry permissible in a thing so serious as love *à la* Werther; in which a man has no idea where he is going, and in which at the same time by a lucky chance for virtue, that is his best policy. A man, really moved, says charming things unconsciously; he speaks a language which he does not know himself.

Woe to the man the least bit affected! Given he were in love, allow him all the wit in the world, and he loses three-quarters of his advantages. Let him relapse for an instant into affectation — a minute later comes a moment of frost.

The whole art of love, as it seems to me, reduces itself to saying exactly as much as the degree of intoxication at the moment allows of, that is to say in other terms, to listen to one's heart. It must not be thought, that this is so easy; a man, who truly loves, has no longer strength to speak, when his mistress says anything to make him happy.

Thus he loses the deeds which his words[3] would have given birth to. It is better to be silent than say things too tender at the wrong time, and what was in point ten seconds

[1] 20 September, 1811.

[2] At the first quarrel Madame Ivernetta gave poor Bariac his *congé*. Bariac was truly in love and this *congé* threw him into despair; but his friend Guillaume Balaon, whose life we are writing, was of great help to him and managed, finally, to appease the severe Ivernetta. Peace was restored, and the reconciliation was accompanied by circumstances so delicious, that Bariac swore to Balaon that the hour of the first favors he had received from his mistress had not been as sweet as that of this voluptuous peacemaking. These words turned Balaon's head; he wanted to know this pleasure, of which his friend had just given him a description, etc. etc. (*Vie de quelques Troubadours*, by Nivernois, Vol. I, p. 32.)

[3] It is this kind of timidity which is decisive, and which is proof of passion-love in a clever man.

ago, is now no longer — in fact at this moment it makes a mess of things. Every time that I used to infringe this rule[1] and say something, which had come into my head three minutes earlier and which I thought pretty, Léonore never failed to punish me. And later I would say to myself, as I went away — "She is right." This is the sort of thing to upset women of delicacy extremely; it is indecency of sentiment. Like tasteless rhetoricians, they are readier to admit a certain degree of weakness and coldness. There being nothing in the world to alarm them but the falsity of their lover, the least little insincerity of detail, be it the most innocent in the world, robs them instantly of all delight and puts mistrust into their hearts.

Respectable women have a repugnance to what is vehement and unlooked for — those being none the less characteristics of passion — and, furthermore, that vehemence alarms their modesty; they are on the defensive against it.

When a touch of jealousy or displeasure has occasioned some chilliness, it is generally possible to begin subjects, fit to give birth to the excitement favorable to love, and, after the first two or three phrases of introduction, as long as a man does not miss the opportunity of saying exactly what his heart suggests, the pleasure he will give to his loved one will be keen. The fault of most men is that they want to succeed in saying something, which they think either pretty or witty or touching — instead of releasing their soul from the false gravity of the world, until a degree of intimacy and *naturalness* brings out in simple language what they are feeling at the moment. The man, who is brave enough for this, will have instantly his reward in a kind of peace-making. It is this reward, as swift as it is involuntary, of the pleasure one gives to the object of one's love, which puts this passion so far above the others.

If there is perfect *naturalness* between them, the happi-

---

[1] Remember that, if the author uses sometimes the expression "I," it is an attempt to give the form of this essay a little variety. He does not in the least pretend to fill the readers' ears with the story of his own feelings. His aim is to impart, with as little monotony as possible, what he has observed in others.

ness of two individuals comes to be fused together.[1] This is simply the greatest happiness which can exist, by reason of sympathy and several other laws of human nature.

It is quite easy to determine the meaning of this word *naturalness* — essential condition of happiness in love.

We call *natural* that which does not diverge from an habitual way of acting. It goes without saying that one must not merely never lie to one's love, but not even embellish the least bit or tamper with the simple outline of truth. For if a man is embellishing, his attention is occupied in doing so and no longer answers simply and truly, as the keys of a piano, to the feelings mirrored in his eye. The woman finds it out at once by a certain chilliness within her, and she, in her turn, falls back on coquetry. Might not here be found hidden the cause why it is impossible to love a woman with a mind too far below one's own — the reason being that, in her case, one can make pretense with impunity, and, as that course is more convenient, one abandons oneself to unnaturalness by force of habit? From that moment love is no longer love; it sinks to the level of an ordinary transaction — the only difference being that, instead of money, you get pleasure or flattery or a mixture of both. It is hard not to feel a shade of contempt for a woman, before whom one can with impunity act a part, and consequently, in order to throw her over, one only needs to come across something better in her line. Habit or vow may hold, but I am speaking of the heart's desire, whose nature it is to fly to the greatest pleasure.

To return to this word *natural* — natural and habitual are two different things. If one takes these words in the same sense, it is evident that the more sensibility in a man, the harder it is for him to be natural, since the influence of *habit* on his way of being and acting is less powerful, and he himself is more powerful at each new event. In the life-story of a cold heart every page is the same: take him to-day or take him to-morrow, it is always the same dummy.

[1] Resides in exactly the same actions.

A man of sensibility, so soon as his heart is touched, loses all traces of habit to guide his action; and how can he follow a path, which he has forgotten all about?

He feels the enormous weight attaching to every word which he says to the object of his love — it seems to him as if a word is to decide his fate. How is he not to look about for the right word? At any rate, how is he not to have the feeling that he is trying to say "the right thing?" And then, there is an end of candor. And so we must give up our claim to candor, that quality of our being, which never reflects upon itself. We are the best we can be, but we feel what we are.

I fancy this brings us to the last degree of *naturalness*, to which the most delicate heart can pretend in love.

A man of passion can but cling might and main, as his only refuge in the storm, to the vow never to change a jot or tittle of the truth and to read the message of his heart correctly. If the conversation is lively and fragmentary, he may hope for some fine moments of *naturalness:* otherwise he will only be perfectly natural in hours when he will be a little less madly in love.

In the presence of the loved one, we hardly retain *naturalness* even in our movements, however deeply such habits are rooted in the muscles. When I gave my arm to Léonore, I always felt on the point of stumbling, and I wondered if I was walking properly. The most one can do is never to be affected willingly: it is enough to be convinced that want of *naturalness* is the greatest possible disadvantage, and can easily be the source of the greatest misfortunes. For the heart of the woman, whom you love, no longer understands your own; you lose that nervous involuntary movement of sincerity, which answers the call of sincerity. It means the loss of every way of touching, I almost said of winning, her. Not that I pretend to deny, that a woman worthy of love may see her fate in that pretty image of the ivy, which "dies if it does not cling" — that is a law of Nature; but to make your lover's happiness is none the less a step that will decide your own. To me it seems that a reasonable woman ought not to give in completely to her lover, until she can hold out no longer, and the slightest doubt thrown on the sincerity of your heart gives her there and then a little strength — enough at least to delay her defeat still another day.[1]

Is it necessary to add that to make all this the last word in absurdity you have only to apply it to gallant-love?

The Role of Doubt

ALWAYS a little doubt to allay — that is what whets our appetite every moment, that is what makes the life of happy love. As it is never separated from fear, so its pleasures can never tire. The characteristic of this happiness is its high seriousness.

Of Confidences

THERE is no form of insolence so swiftly punished as that which leads you, in passion-love, to take an intimate friend into your confidence. He knows that, if what you say is true, you have pleasures a thousand times greater than he, and that your own make you despise his.

It is far worse between women — their lot in life being to inspire a passion, and the *confidante* having commonly also displayed her charms for the advantage of the lover.

On the other hand, for anyone a prey to his fever, there is no moral need more imperative than that of a friend, before whom to dilate on the fearful doubts which at every instant beset his soul; for in this terrible passion, always a thing imagined is a thing existent.

---

[1] Haec autem ad acerbam rei memoriam, amara quadam dulcedine, scribere visum est — ut cogitem nihil esse debere quod amplius mihi placeat in hac vita. (*Petrarch*, Ed. Marsand.) [These things, to be a painful reminder, yet not without a certain bitter charm, I have seen good to write — to remind me that nothing any longer can give me pleasure in this life.]
15 January, 1819.

"A great fault in Salviati's character," he writes in 1817, "— in this point how opposed to Napoleon's! — is that when, in the discussion of interests in which passion is concerned, something is at last morally proved, he cannot resolve to take that as a fact once and for all established and as a point to start from. In spite of himself and greatly to his hurt, he brings it again and again under discussion." The reason is that, in the field of ambition, it is easy to be brave. Crystallization, not being subjected to the desire of the thing to be won, helps to fortify our courage; in love it is wholly in the service of the object against which our courage is wanted.

A woman may find an unfaithful friend, she also may find one with nothing to do.

A princess of thirty-five,[1] with nothing to do and dogged by the need of action, of intrigue, etc. etc., discontented with a lukewarm lover and yet unable to hope to sow the seeds of another love, with no use to make of the energy which is consuming her, with no other distraction than fits of black humor, can very well find an occupation, that is to say a pleasure, and a life's work, in accomplishing the misfortune of a true passion — passion which someone has the insolence to feel for another than herself, while her own lover falls to sleep at her side.

It is the only case in which hate produces happiness; the reason being that it procures occupation and work.

Just at first, the pleasure of doing something, and, as soon as the design is suspected by society, the prick of doubtful success, add a charm to this occupation. Jealousy of the friend takes the mask of hatred for the lover; otherwise how would it be possible to hate so madly a man one has never set eyes on?

You cannot recognize the existence of envy, or, first, you would have to recognize the existence of merit; and there are flatterers about you who only hold their place at Court by poking fun at your good friend.

[1] Venice, 1819.

The faithless *confidante*, all the while she is indulging in villainies of the deepest dye, may quite well think herself solely animated by the desire not to lose a precious friendship. A woman with nothing to do tells herself that even friendship languishes in a heart devoured by love and its mortal anxieties. Friendship can only hold its own, by the side of love, by the exchange of confidences; but then what is more odious to envy than such confidences?

The only kind of confidences well received between women are those accompanied by, in all its frankness, a statement of the case such as this: — "My dear friend, in this war, as absurd as it is relentless, which the prejudices, brought into vogue by our tyrants, wage upon us, you help me to-day — to-morrow it will be my turn."[1]

Beyond this exception there is another — that of true friendship born in childhood and not marred since by any jealousy . . .

.   .   .   .   .   .

The confidences of passion-love are well received only between schoolboys in love with love, and girls eaten up with unemployed curiosity and tenderness or led on perhaps by the instinct,[2] which whispers to them that there lies the great business of their life, and that they cannot look after it too early.

Apart from the danger, there is the difficulty of confidences. In passion-love, things one cannot express (because the tongue is too gross for such subtleties) exist none the less; only, as these are things of extreme delicacy, we are more liable in observing them to make mistakes.

90

[1] Memoirs of Madame d'Epinay, Geliotte.
Prague, Klagenfurth, all Moravia, etc. etc. Their women are great wits and their men are great hunters. Friendship is very common between the women. The country enjoys its fine season in the winter; among the nobles of the province a succession of hunting parties takes place, each lasting from fifteen to twenty days. One of the cleverest of these nobles said to me one day that Charles V had reigned legitimately over all Italy, and that, consequently, it was all in vain for the Italians to want to revolt. The wife of this good man read the Letters of Mlle. de Lespinasse. (Znaym, 1816)

[2] Important point. It seems to me that independent of their education, which begins at eight or ten months, there is a certain amount of instinct.

Also, an observer in a state of emotion is a bad observer; he won't allow for chance.

Perhaps the only safe way is to make yourself your own confidant. Write down this evening, under borrowed names, but with all the characteristic details, the dialogue you had just now with the woman you care for, and the difficulty which troubles you. In a week, if it is passion-love, you will be a different man, and then, rereading your consultation, you will be able to give a piece of good advice to yourself.

In male society, as soon as there are more than two together, and envy might make its appearance, politeness allows none but physical love to be spoken of — think of the end of dinners among men. It is Baffo's sonnets[1] that are quoted and which give such infinite pleasure; because each one takes literally the praises and excitement of his neighbor, who, quite often, merely wants to appear lively or polite. The sweetly tender words of Petrarch or French madrigals would be out of place.

Of Jealousy

WHEN you are in love, as each new object strikes your eye or your memory, whether crushed in a gallery and patiently listening to a parliamentary debate, or galloping to the relief of an outpost under the enemy's fire, you never fail to add a new perfection to the idea you have of your mistress, or discover a new means (which at first seems excellent) of winning her love still more.

Each step the imagination takes is repaid by a moment of sweet delight. No wonder that existence, such as this, takes hold of one.

---

[1] The Venetian dialect boasts descriptions of physical love which for vivacity leave Horace, Propertius, La Fontaine and all the poets a hundred miles behind. M. Buratti of Venice is at the moment the first satirical poet of our unhappy Europe. He excels above all in the description of the physical grotesqueness of his heroes; and he finds himself frequently in prison. (See *l'Elefanteide*, *l'Uomo*, *la Strefeide*)

Directly jealousy comes into existence, this turn of feelings continues in itself the same, though the effect it is to produce is contrary. Each perfection that you add to the crown of your beloved, who now perhaps loves someone else, far from promising you a heavenly contentment, thrusts a dagger into your heart.

A voice cries out: "This enchanting pleasure is for my rival to enjoy."[1]

Even the objects which strike you, without producing this effect, instead of showing you, as before, a new way of winning her love, cause you to see a new advantage for your rival.

You meet a pretty woman galloping in the park;[2] your rival is famous for his fine horses which can do ten miles in fifty minutes.

In this state, rage is easily fanned into life; you no longer remember that in love possession is nothing, enjoyment everything. You exaggerate the happiness of your rival, exaggerate the insolence happiness produces in him, and you come at last to the limit of tortures, that is to say to the extremest unhappiness, poisoned still further by a lingering hope.

The only remedy is, perhaps, to observe your rival's happiness at close quarters. Often you will see him fall peacefully asleep in the same *salon* as the woman for whom your heart stops beating at the mere sight of a hat like hers some way off in the street.

To wake him up you have only to show your jealousy. You may have, perhaps, the pleasure of teaching him the price of the woman who prefers him to you, and he will owe to you the love he will learn to have for her.

Face to face with a rival there is no mean — you must either banter with him in the most off-hand way you can, or frighten him.

[1] Here you see one of love's follies; for this perfection, seen by your eyes, is not one for him.

[2] Montaguola, 13th April, 1819.

Jealousy being the greatest of all evils, endangering one's life will be found an agreeable diversion. For then not all our fancies are embittered and blackened (by the mechanism explained above) — sometimes it is possible to imagine that one kills this rival.

According to this principle, that it is never right to add to the enemy's forces, you must hide your love from your rival, and, under some pretext of vanity as far as possible removed from love, say to him very quietly, with all possible politeness, and in the calmest, simplest tone: "Sir, I cannot think why the public sees good to make little So-and-so mine; people are even good enough to believe that I am in love with her. As for you, if you want her, I would hand her over with all my heart, if unhappily there were not the risk of placing myself into a ridiculous position. In six months, take her as much as ever you like, but at the present moment, honor, such as people attach (why, I don't know) to these things, forces me to tell you, to my great regret, that, if by chance you have not the justice to wait till your turn comes round, one of us must die."

Your rival is very likely a man without much passion, and perhaps a man of much prudence, who once convinced of your resolution, will make haste to yield you the woman in question, provided he can find any decent pretext. For that reason you must give a gay tone to your challenge, and keep the whole move hidden with the greatest secrecy.

What makes the pain of jealousy so sharp is that vanity cannot help you to bear it. But, according to the plan I have spoken of, your vanity has something to feed on; you can respect yourself for bravery, even if you are reduced to despising your powers of pleasing.

If you would rather not carry things to such tragic lengths, you must pack up and go miles away, and keep a chorus-girl, whose charms people will think have arrested you in your flight.

Your rival has only to be an ordinary person and he will think you are consoled.

Very often the best way is to wait without flinching, while he wears himself out in the eyes of the loved one through his own stupidity. For, except in a serious passion formed little by little and in early youth, a clever woman does not love an undistinguished man for long.[1] In the case of jealousy after intimate intercourse, there must follow also apparent indifference or real inconstancy. Plenty of women, offended with a lover whom they still love, form an attachment with the man, of whom he has shown himself jealous, and the play becomes a reality.[2]

I have gone into some detail, because in these moments of jealousy one often loses one's head. Counsels, made in writing a long time ago, are useful, and, the essential thing being to feign calmness, it is not out of place in a philosophical piece of writing, to adopt that tone.

As your adversaries' power over you consists in taking away from you or making you hope for things, whose whole worth consists in your passion for them, once manage to make them think you are indifferent, and suddenly they are without a weapon.

If you have no active course to take, but can distract yourself in looking for consolation, you will find some pleasure in reading *Othello;* it will make you doubt the most conclusive appearances. You will feast your eyes on these words: —

> Trifles light as air
> Seem to the jealous confirmations strong
> As proofs from Holy Writ.

It is my experience that the sight of a fine sea is consoling.

The morning which had arisen calm and bright gave a pleasant effect to the waste mountain view, which was seen from the castle on looking to the landward, and the glorious ocean crisped with a thousand rippling waves of silver extended on the other side in

---

[1] *La Princesse de Tarente.* Story by Scarron.

[2] As in the *Curieux-impertinent,* story by Cervantes.

awful, yet complacent majesty to the verge of the horizon. With such scenes of calm sublimity the human heart sympathizes even in its most disturbed moods, and deeds of honor and virtue are inspired by their majestic influence. (*The Bride of Lammermoor,* Chap. VII)

I find this written by Salviati: —

July 20th, 1818. — I often — and I think unreasonably — apply to life as a whole the feelings of a man of ambition or a good citizen, if he finds himself set in battle to guard the baggage or in any other post without danger or action. I should have felt regret at forty to have passed the age of loving without deep passion. I should have had that bitter and humiliating displeasure, to have found out too late that I had been fool enough to let life pass, without living.

Yesterday I spent three hours with the woman I love and a rival, whom she wants to make me think she favors. Certainly, there were moments of bitterness, in watching her lovely eyes fixed on him, and, on my departure, there were wild transports from utter misery to hope. But what changes, what sudden lights, what swift thoughts, and, in spite of the apparent happiness of my rival, with what pride and what delight my love felt itself superior to his! I went away saying to myself: The most vile fear would bleach those cheeks at the least of the sacrifices, which my love would make for the fun of it, nay, with delight — for example, to put this hand into a hat and draw one of these two lots: "Be loved by her," the other — "Die on the spot." And this feeling in me is so much second nature, that it did not prevent me being amiable and talkative.

If someone had told me all that two years ago, I should have laughed.

I find in the *Travels to the Source of the Missouri River ... in 1804-6* of Captains Lewis and Clarke (p. 215): —

The Ricaras are poor and generous; we stayed some time in three of their villages. Their women are more beautiful than those of the other tribes we came across; they are also not in the least inclined to let their lover languish. We found a new example of the truth that you only have to travel to find out that there is variety everywhere. Among the Ricaras, for a woman to grant her favors without the consent of her husband or her brother, gives great offence. But then the brothers and the husband are only too delighted to have the opportunity of showing this courtesy to their friends.

There was a negro in our crew; he created a great sensation among a people who had never seen a man of his color before. He was soon a favorite with the fair sex, and we noticed that the husbands, instead of being jealous, were overjoyed to see him come to visit them. The funny part was that the interior of the huts was so narrow that everything was visible.[1]

More of Jealousy

Now for the woman suspected of inconstancy!

She leaves you, because you have discouraged crystallization, but it is possible that in her heart you have habit to plead for you.

She leaves you, because she is too sure of you. You have killed fear, and there is nothing left to give birth to the little doubts of happy love. Just make her uneasy, and, above all, beware of the absurdity of protestations!

During all the time you have lived in touch with her, you will doubtless have discovered what woman, in society or outside it, she is most jealous or most afraid of. Pay court to that woman, but so far from blazoning it about, do your best to keep it secret, and do your best sincerely; trust to the eyes of anger to see everything and feel everything. The strong aversion you will have felt for several months to all women ought to make this easy.[2] Remember that in the

[1] There ought to be instituted at Philadelphia an academy, whose sole occupation would be the collection of materials for the study of man in the savage state, instead of waiting till these curious peoples have been exterminated.

I know quite well that such academies exist — but apparently regulated in a way worthy of our academies in Europe. (Memoir and Discussion on the Zodiac of Denderah at the Académie des Sciences of Paris, 1821.) I notice that the academy of, I fancy, Massachusetts, wisely charges a member of the clergy (Mr. Jarvis) to make a report on the religion of the savage. The priest, of course, refutes energetically an impious Frenchman, called Volney. According to the priest, the savage has the most exact and noble ideas of the Divinity, etc. If he lived in England, such a report would bring the worthy academician a preferment of three or four hundred pounds and the protection of all the noble lords in the county. But in America! For the rest, the absurdity of this academy reminds me of the free Americans, who set the greatest store on seeing fine coats-of-arms painted on the panels of their carriages; what upsets them is that, through their carriage-painter's want of instruction, the blazoning is often wrong.

[2] You compare the branch adorned with diamonds to the branch left bare, and contrast adds sting to your memories.

position you are in, everything is spoiled by a show of passion: avoid seeing much of the woman you love, and drink champagne with the wits.

In order to judge of your mistress' love, remember: —

1. The more physical pleasure counts for in the basis of her love and in what formerly determined her to yield, the more prone it is to inconstancy, and, still more, to infidelity. This applies especially in which crystallization has been favored by the fire of sweet seventeen.

2. Two people in love are hardly ever equally in love:[1] passion-love has its phases, during which now one, now the other is more impassioned. Often, too, it is merely gallantry or vain love which responds to passion-love, and it is generally the woman who is carried away by passion. But whatever the love may be that either of them feels, directly one of them is jealous, he insists on the other fulfilling all the conditions of passion-love; vanity pretends to all the claims of a heart that feels.

Furthermore, nothing wearies gallant-love like passion-love from the other side.

Often a clever man, paying court to a woman, just sets her thinking of love in a sentimental frame of mind. She receives this clever man kindly for giving her this pleasure — he conceives hopes.

But one fine day that woman meets the man, who makes her feel what the other has described.

I do not know what are the effects of a man's jealousy on the heart of the woman he loves. Displayed by an admirer who wearies her, jealousy must inspire a supreme disgust, and it may even turn to hatred, if the man he is jealous of is nicer than the jealous one; for we want jealousy, said Madame de Coulanges, only from those of whom we could be jealous.

[1] e.g. the love of Alfieri for that great English lady (Lady Ligonier) who also philandered with her footman and prettily signed herself Penelope. (*Vita*, Epoca III, Chaps. X and XI)

If the jealous one is liked, but has no real claims, his jealousy may offend that feminine pride so hard to keep in humor or even to recognize. Jealousy may please women of pride, as a new way of showing them their power.

Jealousy can please as a new way of giving proof of love. It can also offend the modesty of a woman who is over-refined.

It can please as a sign of the lover's hot blood — *ferrum est quod amant*. But note that it *is* hot blood they love, and not courage *à la* Turenne, which is quite compatible with a cold heart.

One of the consequences of crystallization is that a woman can never say "yes" to the lover, to whom she has been unfaithful, if she ever means to make anything of him.

Such is the pleasure of continuing to enjoy the perfect image we have formed of the object of our attachment, that until that fatal "yes" —

> L'on va chercher bien loin, plutôt que de mourir,
> Quelque prétexte ami pour vivre et pour souffrir.
>
> (*André Chénier*)[1]

Everyone in France knows the anecdote of Mademoiselle de Sommery, who, caught in *flagrante delicto* by her lover, flatly denied the fact. On his protesting, she replied: "Very well, I see you don't love me any more: you believe what you see before what I tell you."

To make it up with an idol of a mistress, who has been unfaithful, is to set yourself to undo with the point of a dagger a crystallization incessantly forming afresh. Love has got to die, and your heart will feel the cruel pang of every stage in its agony.

It is one of the saddest dispositions of this passion and of life. You must be strong enough to make it up only as friends.

---

[1] ["Sooner than die, we will go very far in search of some friendly pretext to live and suffer."]

Roxana

As for women's jealousy — they are suspicious, they have infinitely more at stake than we, they have made a greater sacrifice to love, have far fewer means of distraction and, above all, far fewer means of keeping a check on their lover's actions. A woman feels herself degraded by jealousy; she thinks her lover is laughing at her, or, still worse, making fun of her tenderest transports. Cruelty must tempt her — and yet, legally, she cannot kill her rival!

For women, jealousy must be a still more abominable evil than it is for men. It is the last degree of impotent rage and self-contempt[1] which a heart can bear without breaking.

I know no other remedy for so cruel an evil, than the death of the one who is the cause of it or of the one who suffers. An example of French jealousy is the story of Madame de la Pommeraie in *Jacques le Fataliste*.

La Rochefoucauld says: "We are ashamed of owning we are jealous, but pride ourselves on having been and of being capable of jealousy."[2] Poor woman dares not own even to having suffered this torture, so much ridicule does it bring upon her. So painful a wound can never quite heal up.

If cold reason could be unfolded before the fire of imagination with the merest shade of success, I would say to those wretched women, who are unhappy from jealousy: "There is a great difference between infidelity in man and in you. In you, the importance of the act is partly direct, partly symbolic. But, as an effect of the education of our military schools, it is in man the symbol of nothing at all. On the contrary, in women, through the effect of modesty, it is the most decisive of all the symbols of devotion. Bad habit makes it almost a necessity to men. During all our early years, the example set by the so-called 'bloods' makes us set

[1] This contempt is one of the great causes of suicide: people kill themselves to give their sense of honor satisfaction.

[2] *Pensée* 495. The reader will have recognized, without my marking it each time, several other thoughts of celebrated writers. It is history which I am attempting to write, and such thoughts are the facts.

all our pride on the number of successes of this kind — as the one and only proof of our worth. For you, your education acts in exactly the opposite direction."

As for the value of an action as symbol — in a moment of anger I upset a table on to the foot of my neighbor; that gives him the devil of a pain, but can quite easily be fixed up — or again, I make as if to give him a slap in the face. . . .

The difference between infidelity in the two sexes is so real, that a woman of passion may pardon it, while for a man that is impossible.

Here we have a decisive ordeal to show the difference between passion-love and love from pique: infidelity in women all but kills the former and doubles the force of the latter.

Haughty women disguise their jealousy from pride. They will spend long and dreary evenings in silence with the man whom they adore, and whom they tremble to lose, making themselves consciously disagreeable in his eyes. This must be one of the greatest possible tortures, and is certainly one of the most fruitful sources of unhappiness in love. In order to cure these women, who merit so well all our respect, it needs on the man's side a strong and out-of-the-way line of action — but, mind, he must not seem to notice what is going on — for example, a long journey with them undertaken at a twenty-four hours' notice.

Of Self-Esteem Piqued [1]

PIQUE is a manifestation of vanity; I do not want my antagonist to go higher than myself and *I take that antagonist himself as judge of my worth*. I want to produce an effect on his heart. It is this that carries us so far beyond all reasonable limits.

Sometimes, to justify our own extravagance, we go so far as to tell ourselves that this rival has a mind to dupe us.

[1] In Italian *puntiglio*.

Pique, being an infirmity of honor, is far more common in monarchies; it must, surely, be exceedingly rare in counties, where the habit is rampant of valuing things according to their utility — for example, in the United States.

Every man, and a Frenchman sooner than any other, loathes being taken for a dupe; and yet the lightness of the French character under the old monarchy[1] prevented pique from working great havoc beyond the domains of gallantry and gallant-love. Pique has produced serious tragedies only in monarchies, where, through the climate, the shade of character is darker (Portugal, Piedmont).

The provincial in France forms a ludicrous idea of what is considered a gentleman in good society — and then he takes cover behind his model, and waits there all his life to see that no one trespasses. And so good-bye naturalness! He is always in a state of pique, a mania which gives a laughable character even to his love affairs. This enviousness is what makes it most unbearable to live in small towns, and one should remind oneself of this, when one admires the picturesque situation of any of them. The most generous and noble emotions are there paralyzed by contact with all that is most low in the products of civilization. In order to put the finishing touch to their awfulness, these bourgeois talk of nothing but the corruption of great cities.[2]

Pique cannot exist in passion-love; it is feminine pride. "If I let my lover treat me badly, he will despise me and no longer be able to love me." It may also be jealousy in all its fury.

Jealousy desires the death of the object it fears. The man in a state of pique is miles away from that — he wants his enemy to live, and, above all, be witness of his triumph.

He would be sorry to see his rival renounce the struggle, for the fellow may have the insolence to say in the depth

[1] Three-quarters of the great French noblemen about 1778 would have been on the high road to prison in a country where the laws were executed without respect of persons.

[2] As the one keeps strict watch on the other in all that touches love, there is less love and more immorality in provincial towns. Italy is luckier.

of his heart: "If I had persevered in my original object, I should have outdone him."

With pique, there is no interest in the apparent purpose — the point of everything is victory. This is well brought out in the love affairs of chorus-girls; take away the rival, and the boasted passion, which threatened suicide from the fifth-floor window, instantly subsides.

Love from pique, contrary to passion-love, passes in a moment; it is enough for the antagonist by an irrevocable step to own that he renounces the struggle. I hesitate, however, to advance this maxim, having only one example, and that leaves doubts in my mind. Here are the facts — the reader will judge.

Dona Diana is a young person of twenty-three, daughter of one of the richest and proudest citizens of Seville. She is beautiful, without any doubt, but of a peculiar type of beauty, and is credited with ever so much wit and still more pride. She was passionately in love, to all appearances at least, with a young officer, with whom her family would have nothing to do. The officer left for America with Morillo, and they corresponded continuously. One day in the midst of a lot of people, assembled round the mother of Dona Diana, a fool announced the death of the charming officer. All eyes are turned upon Dona Diana; Dona Diana says nothing but these words: "What a pity — so young."

Just that day we had been reading a play of old Massinger, which ends tragically, but in which the heroine takes the death of her lover with this apparent tranquillity. I saw the mother shudder in spite of her pride and dislike; the father went out of the room to hide his joy. In the midst of this scene and the dismay of all present, who were making eyes at the fool who had told the story, Dona Diana, the only one at ease, proceeded with the conversation, as if nothing had happened. Her mother, in apprehension, set her maid to watch her, but nothing seemed to be altered in her behavior.

Two years later, a very fine young man paid his attentions to her. This time again, and, still for the same reason, Dona Diana's parents violently opposed the marriage, because the aspirant was not of noble birth. She herself declared it should take place. A state of pique ensues between the daughter's sense of honor and the father's. The young man is forbidden the house. Dona Diana is no longer taken to the country and hardly ever to church. With scrupulous care, every means of meeting her lover is taken from her. He disguises himself and sees her secretly at long intervals. She becomes more and more resolute, and refuses the most brilliant matches, even a title and a great establishment at the Court of Ferdinand VII. The whole town is talking of the misfortunes of the two lovers and of their heroic constancy. At last the majority of Dona Diana draws near. She gives her father to understand that she means to make use of her right of disposing of her own hand. The family, driven back on its last resources, opens negotions for the marriage. When it is half concluded, at an official meeting of the two families, the young man, after six years' constancy, refuses Dona Diana.[1]

A quarter of an hour later no trace of anything — she was consoled. Did she love from pique? Or are we face to face with a great soul, that disclaims to parade its sorrow before the eyes of the world?

In passion-love satisfaction, if I can call it such, is often only to be won by piquing the loved one's self-esteem. Then, in appearance, the lover realizes all that can be desired; complaints would be ridiculous and seem senseless. He cannot speak of his misfortune, and yet how constantly he knows and feels its prick! Its traces are inwoven, so to speak, with circumstances, the most flattering and the most fit to awaken illusions of enchantment. This misfortune rears its monstrous head at the tenderest moments, as if to taunt the

[1] Every year there is more than one example of women abandoned just as vilely, and so I can pardon suspiciousness in respectable women. Mirabeau, *Lettres à Sophie*. Opinion is powerless in despotic countries: there is nothing solid but the friendship of the pasha.

lover and make him feel, at one and the same instant, all the delight of being loved by the charming and unfeeling creature in his arms, and the impossibility of this delight being his. Perhaps after jealousy, this is the cruellest unhappiness.

The story is still fresh in a certain large town[1] of a man of soft and gentle nature, who was carried away by a rage of this kind to spill the blood of his mistress, who only loved him from pique against her sister. He arranged with her, one evening, to come for a row on the sea by themselves, in a pretty little boat he had devised himself. Once well out to sea, he touches a spring, the boat divides and disappears for ever.

I have seen a man of sixty set out to keep an actress, the most capricious, irresponsible, delightful and wonderful on the London stage — Miss Cornel. "And you expect that she'll be faithful?" people asked him.

"Not in the least. But she'll be in love with me — perhaps madly in love."

And for a whole year she did love him — often to distraction. For three whole months together she never even gave him subject for complaint. He had put a state of pique, disgraceful in many ways, between his mistress and his daughter.

Pique wins the day in gallant-love, being its very life and blood. It is the ordeal best fitted to differentiate between gallant-love and passion-love. There is an old maxim of war, given to young fellows new to their regiment, that if you are billeted on a house, where there are two sisters, and you want to have one, you must pay your attentions to the other. To win the majority of Spanish women, who are still young and ready for love affairs, it is enough to give out, seriously and modestly, that you have no feelings whatever for the lady of the house. I have this useful maxim from dear General Lassale. This is the most dangerous way of attacking passion-love.

[1] Leghorn, 1819.

Piqued self-esteem is the bond which ties the happiest marriages, after those formed by love. Many husbands make sure of their wives' love for many years, by taking up with some little woman a couple of months after their marriage.[1] In this way the habit is engendered of thinking only of one man, and family ties succeed in making the habit invincible.

If in the past century at the Court of Louis XV a great lady (Madame de Choiseul) was seen to worship her husband,[2] the reason is that he seemed to take a keen interest in her sister, the Duchesse de Grammont.

The most neglected mistress, once she makes us see that she prefers another man, robs us of our peace and afflicts our heart with all the semblance of passion.

The courage of an Italian is an access of rage; the courage of a German a moment of intoxication; that of a Spaniard an outburst of pride. If there were a nation, in which courage were generally a matter of piqued self-esteem between the soldiers of each company and the regiments of each division, in the case of a rout there would be no support, and consequently there would be no means of rallying the armies of such a nation. To foresee the danger and try to remedy it, would be the greatest of all absurdities with such conceited runaways.

"It is enough to have opened any single description of a voyage among the savages of North America," says one of the most delightful philosophers of France,[3] "to know that the ordinary fate of prisoners of war is not only to be burnt alive and eaten, but first to be bound to a stake near a flaming bonfire and to be tortured there for several hours, by all the most ferocious and refined devices that fury can imagine. Read what travellers, who have witnessed these fearful scenes, tell of the cannibal joy of the assistants, above all, of the fury of the women and children, and of their gruesome delight in this competition of cruelty. See also what they add about the heroic firmness and immutable self-possession of the prisoner, who not only gives no sign of pain, but taunts and defies his torturers, by all that pride can make most haughty, irony most bitter, and

[1] See *The Confessions of an Odd-tempered Man.* Story by Mrs. Opie.
[2] Letters of Madame du Deffant, Memoirs of Lauzun.
[3] Volney, *Tableau des Etats-Unis d'Amérique*, pp. 491-96.

sarcasm most insulting — singing his own glorious deeds, going through the number of the relations and friends of the onlookers whom he has killed, detailing the sufferings he has inflicted on them, and accusing all that stand around him of cowardice, timidity and ignorance of the methods of torture; until falling limb from limb, devoured alive under his own eyes by enemies drunk with fury, he gasps out his last whisper and his last insult together with his life's breath.[1] All this would be beyond belief in civilized nations, will look like fable to the most fearless captains of our grenadiers, and will one day be brought into doubt by posterity."

This physiological phenomenon is closely connected with a particular moral state in the prisoner, which constitutes, between him on the one side and all his torturers on the other, a combat of self-esteem — of vanity against vanity, as to who can hold out longer.

Our brave military doctors have often observed that wounded soldiers, who, in a calm state of mind and senses, would have shrieked out, during certain operations, display, on the contrary, only calmness and heroism, if they are prepared for it in a certain manner. It is a matter of piquing their sense of honor; you have to pretend, first in a roundabout way, and then with irritating persistence, that it is beyond their present power to bear the operation without shrieking.

Of Quarrelsome Love

IT is of two kinds:
1. In which the originator of the quarrel loves.
2. In which he does not love.

If one of the lovers is too superior in advantages which both value, the love of the other must die; for sooner or later comes the fear of contempt, to cut short crystallization.

[1] Anyone accustomed to a spectacle like this, who feels the risk of being the hero of such another, may possibly be interested only in its heroic aspect, and, in that case, the spectacle must be the foremost and most intimate of the nonactive pleasures.

Nothing is so odious to the mediocre as mental superiority. There lies the source of hatred in the world of to-day, and if we do not have to thank this principle for desperate enmities, it is solely due to the fact that the people it comes between are not forced to live together. What then of love? For here, everything being natural, especially on the part of the superior being, superiority is not masked by any social precaution.

For the passion to be able to survive, the inferior must ill-treat the other party; otherwise the latter could not shut a window, without the other taking offense.

As for the superior party, he deludes himself: the love he feels is beyond the reach of danger, and, besides, almost all the weaknesses in that which we love, make it only the dearer to us.

In point of duration, directly after passion-love reciprocated between people on the same level, one must put quarrelsome love, in which the quarreller does not love. Examples of this are to be found in the anecdotes, relative to the Duchesse de Berri (Memoirs of Duclos).

Partaking, as it does, of the nature of set habits, which are rooted in the prosaic and egoistic side of life and follow man inseparably to the grave, this love can last longer than passion-love itself. But it is no longer love, it is a habit engendered by love, which has nothing of that passion but memories and physical pleasure. This habit necessarily presupposes a less noble kind of being. Each day a little scene is got ready — "Will he make a fuss?" — which occupies the imagination, just as, in passion-love, every day a new proof of affection had to be found. See the anecdotes about Madame d'Houdetot and Saint-Lambert.[1]

It is possible that pride refuses to get used to this kind of occupation; in which case, after some stormy months, pride kills love. But we see the nobler passion make a long resistance before giving in. The little quarrels of happy love foster a long time the illusion of a heart that still loves

[1] Memoirs of Madame d'Epinay, I think, or of Marmontel.

and sees itself badly treated. Some tender reconciliations may make the transition more bearable. A woman excuses the man she has deeply loved, on the score of a secret sorrow or a blow to his prospects. At last she grows used to being scolded. Where, really, outside passion-love, outside gambling or the possession of power,[1] can you find any other unfailing entertainment to be compared with it for liveliness? If the scolder happens to die, the victim who survives proves inconsolable. This is the principle which forms the bond of many middle-class marriages; the scolder can listen to his own voice all day long talking of his favorite subject.

There is a false kind of quarrelsome love. I took from the letters of a woman of extraordinary brilliance this in Chapter XXXIII: —

"Always a little doubt to allay — that is what whets our appetite in passion-love every moment. . . . As it is never separated from fear, so its pleasures can never tire."

With rough and ill-mannered people, or those with a very violent nature, this little doubt to calm, this faint misgiving shows itself in the form of a quarrel.

If the loved one has not the extreme susceptibility, which comes of a careful education, she may find that love of this kind has more life in it, and consequently is more enjoyable. Even with all the refinement in the world, it is hard not to love "your savage" all the more, if you see him the first to suffer for his transports. What Lord Mortimer thinks back on, perhaps, with most regret for his lost mistress, are the candlesticks she threw at his head. And, really, if pride forgives and permits such sensations, it must also be allowed that they do wage implacable warfare upon boredom — that arch-enemy of the happy!

Saint-Simon, the one historian France has had, says: —

After several passing fancies, the Duchesse de Berri had fallen in love, in real earnest, with Riom, cadet of the house of d'Aydie, son

---

[1] Whatever certain hypocritical ministers may say, power is the foremost of pleasures. I believe love alone can beat it, and love is a lucky illness, which cannot be got like a ministry.

of a sister of Madame de Biron. He had neither looks nor sense: a stout, short youth, with a puffy white face, who with all his spots looked like one big abscess — though, true, he had fine teeth. He had no idea of having inspired a passion, which in less than no time went beyond all limits and lasted ever after, without, indeed, preventing passing fancies and cross-attachments. He had little property, and many brothers and sisters who had no more. M. and Madame de Pons, lady-in-waiting to the Duchesse de Berri were related to them and of the same province, and they sent for the young man, who was a lieutenant in the dragoons, to see what could be made of him. He had scarcely arrived before the Duchess's weakness for him became public and Riom was master of the Luxembourg.

M. de Lauzun, whose grand-nephew he was, laughed in his sleeve; he was delighted to see in Riom a reincarnation at the Luxembourg of himself from the time of Mademoiselle. He gave Riom instructions which were listened to by him, as befitted a mild and naturally polite and respectful young fellow, well behaved and straightforward. But before long Riom began to feel the power of his own charms, which could only captivate the incomprehensible humor of this princess. Without abusing his power with others, he made himself liked by everyone, but he treated his duchess as M. de Lauzun had treated Mademoiselle. He was soon dressed in the richest laces, the richest suits, furnished with money, buckles, jewels. He made himself an object of admiration and took a delight in making the princess jealous or pretending to be jealous himself — bringing her often to tears. Little by little he reduced her to the state of doing nothing without his permission, not even in matters of indifference. At one time, ready to go out to the Opera, he made her stay at home; at another he made her go against her will. He forced her to do favors to ladies she disliked, or of whom she was jealous, and to injure people she liked, or of whom he pretended to be jealous. Even as far as dress, she was not allowed the smallest liberty. He used to amuse himself by making her have her hair done all over again, or have her dress changed when she was completely ready — and this happened so often and so publicly, that he had accustomed her to take in the evening his orders for dress and occupation for the next day. The next day he would change it all and make the princess cry still more. At last she came to sending him messages by trusted valets — for he lived in the Luxembourg almost from the day of his arrival — and the messages had often to be repeated during her toilet for her to know what ribbons to wear and about her frock and other details of dress; and nearly always he made her wear what she disliked. If sometimes she gave herself some liberty in the smallest matter without leave, he treated her like a servant, and often her tears lasted several days.

This haughty princess, who was so fond of display and indulging her boundless pride, could bring herself so low as to partake of obscene parties with him and unmentionable people — she with whom no one could dine unless he were prince of the blood. The Jesuit Riglet, whom she as a child had known, and who had brought her up, was admitted to these private meals, without feeling ashamed himself or the Duchess being embarrassed. Madame de Mouchy was admitted into the secret of all these strange events; she and Riom summoned the company and chose the days. This lady was the peacemaker between the two lovers, and the whole of this existence was a matter of general knowledge at the Luxembourg. Riom was there looked to, as the centre of everything, while on his side he was careful to live on good terms with all, honoring them with a show of respect, which he refused in public only to his princess. Before everybody he would give her curt answers, which would make the whole company lower their eyes and bring blushes to the cheeks of the Duchess, who put no constraint upon her idolatry of him.

Riom was a sovereign remedy, for the Duchess, against the monotony of life.

A famous woman said once off-hand to General Bonaparte, then a young hero covered with glory and with no crimes against liberty on his conscience: "General, a woman could only be a wife or a sister to you." The hero did not understand the compliment, which the world has made up for with some pretty slanders.

The women, of whom we are speaking, like to be despised by their lover, whom they only love in his cruelty.

Remedies Against Love

THE leap of Leucas was a fine image of antiquity. It is true, the remedy of love is almost impossible. A danger is needed to call man's attention back sharply to look to his own preservation.[1] But that is not all. What is harder to realize — a pressing danger must continue, and one that

[1] Danger of Henry Morton in the Clyde. (*Old Mortality*, Vol. IV, Chap. X)

can only be averted with care, in order that the habit of thinking of his own preservation may have time to take root. I can see nothing that will do but a storm of sixteen days, like that in *Don Juan*[1] or the shipwreck of M. Coche-let among the Moors. Otherwise, one gets soon used to the peril, and even drops back into thoughts of the loved one with still more charm — when reconnoitering at twenty yards' range from the enemy.

We have repeated over and over again that the love of a man, who loves well, delights in and vibrates to every movement of his imagination, and that there is nothing in nature which does not speak to him of the object of his love. Well, this delight and this vibration form a most interesting occupation, next to which all others pale.

A friend who wants to work the cure of the patient, must, first of all, be always on the side of the woman the patient is in love with — and all friends, with more zeal than sense, are sure to do exactly the opposite.

It is attacking with forces too absurdly inferior that combination of sweet illusions, which earlier we called crystallization.[2]

The *friend in need* should not forget this fact, that, if there is an absurdity to be believed, as the lover has either to swallow it or renounce everything which holds him to life, he will swallow it. With all the cleverness in the world, he will deny in his mistress the most palpable vices and the most villainous infidelities. This is how, in passion-love, everything is forgiven after a little.

In the case of reasonable and cold characters, for the lover to swallow the vices of a mistress, he must only find them out after several months of passion.[3]

Far from trying bluntly and openly to distract the lover, the *friend in need* ought to tire him with talking of his love

---

[1] Of the over-extolled Lord Byron.

[2] Merely in order to abbreviate, and with apologies for the new word.

[3] Madame Dornal and Serigny, *Confessions of le Comte* —— of Duclos. See the note to p. 50: death of General Abdallah at Bologna.

and his mistress, and at the same time manage that a host of little events force themselves upon his notice. Even if travel isolates,[1] it is still no remedy, and in fact nothing recalls so tenderly the object of our love as change of scene. It was in the midst of the brilliant Paris *salons*, next to women with the greatest reputation for charm, that I was most in love with my poor mistress, solitary and sad in her little room in the depth of the Romagna.[2]

I looked at the superb clock in the brilliant *salon*, where I was exiled, for the hour she goes out on foot, even in the rain, to call on her friend. Trying to forget her, I have found that change of scene is the source of memories of one's love, less vivid but far more heavenly than those one goes in search for in places where once upon a time one met her.

In order that absence may prove useful, the *friend in need* must be always at hand, and suggest to the lover's mind all possible reflections on the history of his love, trying to make these reflections tiresome through their length and importunity. In this way he gives them the appearance of commonplaces. For example, tender sentimental talk after a dinner enlivened with good wine.

It is hard to forget a woman, with whom one has been happy; for, remember, that there are certain moments the imagination can never be tired of evoking and beautifying.

I leave out all mention of pride, cruel but sovereign remedy, which, however, is not to be applied to sensitive souls.

The first scenes of Shakespeare's *Romeo* form an admirable picture; there is so vast a gap between the man who says sorrowfully to himself: "She hath forsworn to love," and he who cries out in the height of happiness: "Come what sorrow can!"

---

[1] I cried almost every day. (Precious words of the 10th of June.)
[2] Salviati.

Further Remedies against Love

Her passion will die like a lamp for want of what the flame should feed upon — Bride of Lammermoor, II, Chap. VI.

113

THE *friend in need* must beware of faulty reasoning — for example, of talking about ingratitude. You are giving new life to crystallization, by procuring it a victory and a new enjoyment.

In love there is no such things as ingratitude; the actual pleasure always repays, and more than repays, sacrifices that seem the greatest. In love no other crime but want of honesty seems to me possible: one should be scrupulous as to the state of one's heart.

The *friend in need* has only to attack fair and square, for the lover to answer: —

"To be in love, even while enraged with the loved one, is nothing less, to bring myself down to your dollars and cents style, than having a ticket in a lottery, in which the prize is a thousand miles above all that you can offer me, in your world of indifference and selfish interests. One must have plenty of vanity — and precious petty vanity — to be happy, because people receive you well. I do not blame men for going on like this, in their world, but in the love of Léonore I found a world where everything was heavenly, tender and generous. The most lofty and almost incredible virtue of your world counted, between her and me, only as any ordinary and everyday virtue. Let me at all events dream of the happiness of passing my life close to such a creature. Although I understand that slander has ruined me, and that I have nothing to hope for, at least I shall make her the sacrifice of my vengeance."

It is quite impossible to put a stop to love except in its first stages. Besides a prompt departure, and the forced distractions of society (as in the case of the Comtesse Kalember), there are several other little ruses, which the *friend in need* can bring into play. For example, he can bring to your notice, as if by chance, the fact that the woman you love, quite outside the disputed area, does not even observe towards you the same amount of politeness and respect, with which she honors your rival. The smallest details are enough; for in love everything is a sign: for example, she does not take your arm to go up to her box. This sort of nonsense, taken tragically by a passionate heart, couples a pang of humiliation to every judgment formed by crystallization, poisons the source of love and may destroy it.

One way against the woman, who is behaving badly to our friend, is to bring her under suspicion of some absurd physical defect, impossible to verify. If it were possible for the lover to verify the calumny, and even if he found it substantiated, it would be disqualified by his imagination, and soon have no place with him at all. It is only imagination itself which can resist imagination: Henry III knew that very well when he scoffed at the famous Duchesse de Montpensier.

Hence it is the imagination you must look to — above all, in a girl whom you want to keep safe from love. And the less her spirit has of the common stuff, the more noble and generous her soul, in a word the worthier she is of our respect, just so much greater the danger through which she must pass.

It is always perilous, for a girl, to suffer her memories to group themselves too repeatedly and too agreeably around the same individual. Add gratitude, admiration or curiosity to strengthen the bonds of memory, and she is almost certainly on the edge of the precipice. The greater the monotony of her everyday life, the more active are those poisons called gratitude, admiration and curiosity. The only thing, then, is a swift, prompt and vigorous distraction.

Just so, a little roughness and "slap-dash" in the first encounter, is an almost infallible means of winning the respect of a clever woman, if only the drug be administered in a natural and simple manner.

BOOK THE SECOND

The Varieties of Love

EVERY kind of love and every kind of imagination, takes its color from one of these six temperaments:

The sanguine, or French, — M. de Francueil (Memoirs of Madame d'Epinay);

The choleric, or Spanish, — Lauzun (the Peguilhen of Saint-Simon's Memoirs);

The melancholy, or German, — Schiller's Don Carlos;

The phlegmatic, or Dutch;

The nervous —Voltaire;

The athletic — Milo of Croton[1]

If the influence of temperament makes itself felt in ambition, avarice, friendship, etc. etc., what must it be in the case of love, in which the physical also is perforce an ingre-

[1] See Cabanis, influence of the physical, etc.

dient? Let us suppose that all kinds of love can be referred to the four varieties, which we have noted: —

Passion-love — Julie d'Etanges;

Gallant-love or gallantry;

Physical love;

Vanity-love — "a duchess is never more than thirty for a bourgeois."

We must submit these four kinds of love to the six different characters, with which habits, dependent upon the six kinds of temperament, stamp the imagination. Tiberius did not have the wild imagination of Henry VIII.

Then let us submit all these combinations, thus obtained, to the differences of habit which depend upon government or national character: —

1. Asiatic despotism, such as may be seen at Constantinople;

2. Absolute monarchy *à la* Louis XIV;

3. Aristocracy masked by a charter, or government of a nation for the profit of the rich, as in England — all according to the rules of a self-styled biblical morality;

4. A federal republic, or government for the profit of all, as in the United States of America;

5. Constitutional monarchy, or —

6. A state in revolution, as Spain, Portugal, France. This state of things in a country gives lively passions to everyone, makes manners more natural, destroys puerilities, the conventional virtues and senseless proprieties[1] — gives seriousness to youth and causes it to despise vanity-love and neglect gallantry.

This state can last a long time and form the habits of a generation. In France it began in 1788, was interrupted in 1802, and began again in 1818 — to end God knows when!

After all these general ways of considering love, we have the differences of age, and come finally to individual peculiarities.

[1] The laces missing from Minister Roland's shoes: "Ah, Monsieur, all is lost," answers Dumouriez. At the royal sitting, the President of the Assembly crosses his legs.

For example, we might say: —

I found at Dresden, in Count Wolstein, vanity-love, a melancholy temperament, monarchical habits, thirty years, and ... his individual peculiarities.

For anyone who is to form a judgment on love, this way of viewing things is conveniently short and cooling to the head — an essential, but difficult operation.

Now, as in physiology man has learnt scarcely anything about himself, except by means of comparative anatomy, so in the case of passions, through vanity and many other causes of illusion, we can only get enlightenment on what goes on in ourselves from the foibles we have observed in others. If by chance this essay has any useful effect, it will be by bringing the mind to make comparisons of this sort. To lead the way, I am going to attempt a sketch of some general traits in the character of love in different nations.

I beg for pardon if I often come back to Italy; in the present state of manners in Europe, it is the only country where the plant, which I describe, grows in all freedom. In France, vanity; in Germany, a pretentious and highly comical philosophy; in England, pride, timid, painful and rancorous, torture and stifle it, or force it into a crooked channel.[1]

Of Different Nations: France

I MEAN to put aside my natural affections and be only a cold philosopher. French women, fashioned by their amiable men, themselves creatures only of vanity and physical desires, are less active, less energetic, less feared, and,

[1] The reader will have perceived only too easily that this treatise is made up of Lisio Visconti's fragmentary account of events, written in the order that they were presented to him on his travels. All these events may be found related at length in the journal of his life; perhaps I ought to have inserted them — but they might have been found scarcely suitable. The oldest notes bear the date, Berlin 1807, and the last are some days before his death, June 1819. Some dates have been altered expressly to avoid indiscretion; but the changes, which I have made, go no further than that. I have not thought myself authorized to recast the style. This book was written in a hundred different places — so may it be read!

what's more, less loved and less powerful, than Spanish and Italian women.

A woman is powerful only according to the degree of unhappiness which she can inflict as punishment on her lover. Where men have nothing but vanity, every woman is useful, but none is indispensable. It is success in winning a woman's love, not in keeping it, which flatters a man. When men have only physical desires, they go to prostitutes, and that is why the prostitutes of France are charming and those of Spain the very reverse. In France, to a great many men prostitutes can give as much happiness as virtuous women — happiness, that is to say, without love. There is always one thing for which a Frenchman has much more respect than for his mistress — his vanity.

In Paris a young man sees in his mistress a kind of slave, whose destiny it is, before everything, to please his vanity. If she resist the orders of this dominating passion, he leaves her — and is only the better pleased with himself, when he can tell his friends in what a piquant way, with how smart a gesture, he waved her off.

A Frenchman, who knew his own country well (Meilhan), said: "In France, great passions are as rare as great men." No language has words to express how impossible it is for a Frenchman to play the rôle of a deserted and desperate lover, in full view of a whole town — yet no sight is commoner at Venice or Bologna.

To find love at Paris, we must descend to those classes, in which the absence of education and of vanity, and the struggle against real want, have left more energy.

To let oneself be seen with a great and unsatisfied desire, is to let oneself be seen in a position of inferiority — and that is impossible in France, except for people of no position at all. It means exposing oneself to all kinds of sneers — hence come the exaggerated praises bestowed on prostitutes by young men who mistrust their own hearts. A vulgar susceptibility and dread of appearing in a position of inferiority forms the principle of conversation among provincial people. Think of the man who only lately, when told of the assassination of H.R.H. the Duke of Berri, answered: "I knew it."[1]

In the Middle Ages hearts were tempered by the presence of danger, and therein, unless I am mistaken, lies another cause of the astonishing superiority of the men of the sixteenth century. Originality, which among us is rare, comical, dangerous and often affected, was then of everyday and unadorned. Countries where even to-day danger often shows its iron hand, such as Corsica,[2] Spain or Italy, can still produce great men. In those climates, where men's gall cooks for three months under the burning heat, it is activity's direction that is to seek; at Paris, I fear, it is activity itself.[3]

Many young men, fine enough to be sure at Montmirail or the Bois de Boulogne, are afraid of love; and when you see them, at the age of twenty, fly the sight of a young girl who has struck them as pretty, you may know that cowardice is the real cause. When they remember what they have read in novels is expected of a lover, their blood runs cold. These chilly spirits cannot conceive how the storm of passion, which lashes the sea to waves, also fills the sails of the ship and gives her the power of riding over them.

[1] This is historical. Many people, though very curious, are annoyed at being told news; they are frightened of appearing inferior to him who tells them the news.

[2] Memoirs of M. Realier-Dumas. Corsica, which, as regards its population of one hundred and eighty thousand souls, would not form a half of most French Departments, has produced in modern times Salliceti, Pozzo di Borgo, General Sebastiani, Cervioni, Abbatucci, Lucien and Napoleon Bonaparte and Aréna. The Département du Nord, with its nine hundred thousand inhabitants, is far from being able to show a similar list. The reason is that in Corsica anyone, on leaving his house, may be greeted by a bullet; and the Corsican, instead of submitting like a good Christian, tries to defend himself and still more to be revenged. That is the way spirits like Napoleon are forged. It's a long cry from such surroundings to a palace with its lords-in-waiting and chamberlains, and a Fénelon obliged to find reasons for his respect to His Royal Highness, when speaking to H.R.H. himself, aged twelve years. See the works of that great writer.

[3] At Paris, to get on, you must pay attention to a million little details. None the less there is this very powerful objection. Statistics show many more women who commit suicide from love at Paris than in all the towns of Italy together. This fact gives me great difficulty; I do not know what to say to it for the moment, but it doesn't change my opinion. It may be that our ultra-civilized life is so wearisome, that death seems a small matter to the Frenchman of to-day — or more likely, overwhelmed by the wreck of his vanity, he blows out his brains.

Love is a delicious flower, but one must have the courage to go and pick it on the edge of a frightful precipice. Besides ridicule, love has always staring it in the face the desperate plight of being deserted by the loved one, and in her place only a *dead blank* for all the rest of one's life.

Civilization would be perfect, if it could continue the delicate pleasures of the nineteenth century with a more frequent presence of danger.[1]

It ought to be possible to augment a thousandfold the pleasures of private life by exposing it frequently to danger. I do not speak only of military danger. I would have this danger present at every instant, in every shape, and threatening all the interests of existence, such as formed the essence of life in the Middle Ages. Such danger as our civilization has trained and refined, goes hand in hand quite naturally with the most insipid feebleness of character.

I hear the words of a great man in *A Voice from St. Helena* by Mr. O'Meara: —

Order Murat to attack and destroy four or five thousand men in such a direction, it was done in a moment; but leave him to himself, he was an imbecile without judgment. I cannot conceive how so brave a man could be so "lâche." He was nowhere brave unless before the enemy. There he was probably the bravest man in the world. . . . He was a paladin, in fact a Don Quixote in the field; but take him into the Cabinet, he was a poltroon without judgment or decision. Murat and Ney were the bravest men I ever witnessed.

More on France

I BEG leave to speak ill of France a little longer. The reader need have no fear of seeing my satire remain unpunished; if this essay finds readers, I shall pay for my insults with interest. Our national honor is wide awake.

[1] I admire the manners of the time of Louis XIV: many a man might pass in three days from the *salons* of Marly to the battlefield of Senet or Ramillies. Wives, mothers, sweethearts, were all in a continual state of apprehension. See the *Letters* of Madame de Sévigné. The presence of danger had kept in the language an energy and a freshness that we would not dare to hazard nowadays; and yet M. de Lameth killed his wife's lover. If a Walter Scott were to write a novel of the times of Louis XIV, we should be a good deal surprised.

France fills an important place in the plan of this book, because Paris, thanks to the superiority of its conversation and its literature, is, and will always be, the *salon* of Europe.

Three-quarters of the *billets* in Vienna, as in London, are written in French or are full of French allusions and quotations — Lord knows what French![1]

As regards great passions, France, in my opinion, is void of originality from two causes: —

1. True honor — the desire to resemble Bayard — in order to be honored in the world and there, every day, to see your vanity satisfied.

2. The fool's honor, or the desire to resemble the upper classes, the fashionable world of Paris. The art of entering a drawing-room, of showing aversion to a rival, of breaking with your mistress, etc.

The fool's honor is much more useful than true honor in ministering to the pleasures of our vanity, both in itself, as being intelligible to fools, and also as being applicable to the actions of every day and every hour. We see people, with only this fool's honor and without true honor, very well received in society; but the contrary is impossible.

This is the way of the fashionable world: —

1. To treat all great interests ironically. 'Tis natural enough. Formerly people, really in society, could not be profoundly affected by anything; they hadn't the time. Residence in the country has altered all this. Besides, it is contrary to a Frenchman's nature to let himself be seen in a posture of admiration,[2] that is to say, in a position of inferiority, not only in relation to the object of his admiration — that goes without saying — but also in relation to his neighbor, if his neighbor choose to mock at what he admires.

---

[1] In England, the gravest writers think they give themselves a smart tone by quoting French words, which, for the most part, have never been French, except in English grammars. See the writers for the *Edinburgh Review;* see the *Memoirs* of the Comtesse de Lichtnau, mistress of the last King of Prussia but one.

[2] The fashionable admiration of Hume in 1775, for example, or of Franklin in 1784, is no objection to what I say.

In Germany, Italy and Spain, on the contrary, admiration is genuine and happy; there the admirer is proud of his transports and pities the man who turns up his nose. I don't say the mocker, for that's an impossible rôle in countries, where it is not in failing in the imitation of a particular line of conduct, but in failing to strike the road to happiness, that the only ridicule exists. In the South, mistrust and horror at being troubled in the midst of pleasures vividly felt, plants in men an inborn admiration of luxury and pomp. See the Courts of Madrid and Naples; see a *funzione* at Cadiz — things are carried to a point of delirium.[1]

2. A Frenchman thinks himself the most miserable of men, and almost the most ridiculous, if he is obliged to spend his time alone. But what is love without solitude?

3. A passionate man thinks only of himself; a man who wants consideration thinks only of others. Nay more: before 1789, individual security was only found in France by becoming one of a body, the Robe, for example,[2] and by

---

[1] *Voyage en Espagne,* by M. Semple; he gives a true picture, and the reader will find a description of the Battle of Trafalgar heard in the distance which sticks in the memory.

[2] *Correspondance* of Grimm, January, 1783. "Comte de N———, Captain commanding the guards of the Duke of Orleans, being piqued at finding no place left in the balcony, the day of the opening of the new hall, was so ill-advised as to dispute his place with an honest Procureur; the latter, one Maitre Pernot, was by no means willing to give it up. — 'You've taken my place.' — 'I'm in my own.' — 'Who are you?' — 'I'm Mr. Six Francs' . . . (that is to say, the price of these places.) Then, angrier words, insults, jostling. Comte de N——— pushed his indiscretion so far as to treat the poor joker as a thief, and finally took it upon himself to order the sergeant on duty to arrest the person of the Procureur, and to conduct him to the guard-room. Maitre Pernot surrendered with great dignity, and went out, only to go and depose his complaint before a Commissary. The redoubtable body, of which he had the honor to be a member, had no intention of letting the matter drop. The affair came up before the Parlement. M. de N——— was condemned to pay all the expenses, to make reparation to the Procureur, to pay him two thousand crowns damages and interest, which were to be applied, with the Procureur's consent, to the poor prisoners of the Conciergerie; further, the said Count was very expressly enjoined never again, under pretext of the king's orders, to interfere with a performance, etc. This adventure made a lot of noise, and great interests were mixed up in it: the whole Robe has considered itself insulted by an outrage done to a man who wears its livery, etc. M. de N———, that his affair may be forgotten, has gone to seek his laurels at the Camp of St. Roch. He couldn't do better, people say, for no one can doubt of his talent for carrying places by sheer force. Now suppose an obscure philosopher in the place of Maitre Pernot. Use of the Duel. (Grimm, Part III, Vol. II, p. 102)

See further on, p. 496, a most sensible letter of Beaumarchais refusing a closed box (*loge grillée*) for Figaro, which one of his friends had asked of him. So long as people thought that his answer was addressed to a Duke, there was great excitement, and they talked about severe punishment. But it turned to

being protected by the members of that body. The thoughts of your neighbor were then an integral and necessary part of your happiness. This was still truer at the Court than in Paris. It is easy to see how far such manners, which, to say the truth, are every day losing their force, but which Frenchmen will retain for another century, are favorable to great passions.

Try to imagine a man throwing himself from a window, and at the same time trying to reach the pavement in a graceful position. In France, the passionate man, merely as such, is the object of general ridicule. Altogether he offends his fellow-men, and that gives wings to ridicule.

Italy

ITALY's good fortune is that it has been left to the inspiration of the moment, a good fortune which it shares, up to a certain point, with Germany and England.

Furthermore, Italy is a country where Utility, which was the guiding principle of the mediæval republic,[1] has not been dethroned by Honor or Virtue, disposed to the advantages of monarchy.[2] True honor leads the way to the

laughter when Beaumarchais declared that his letter was addressed to Monsieur le Président du Paty. It is a far cry from 1785 to 1822! We no longer understand these feelings. And yet people pretend that the same tragedies that touched those generations are still good for us!

[1] G. Pecchio, in his very lively *Letters* to a beautiful young English woman, says on the subject of free Spain, where the Middle Ages are not a revival, but have never ceased to exist (p. 60): "The aim of the Spaniards was not glory, but independence. If the Spaniards had only fought for honor, the war had ended with the battle of Tudela. Honor is a thing of an odd nature — once soiled, it loses all its power of action. . . . The Spanish army of the line, having become imbued in its turn with prejudices in favor of honor (that means having become modern-European) disbanded, once beaten, with the thought that, with honor, all was lost, etc."

[2] In 1620 a man was honored by saying unceasingly and as servilely as he could: "The King my Master" (See the Memoirs of Noailles, Torcy and all Louis XIV's ambassadors). Quite simple — by this turn of phrase, he proclaims the rank he occupies among subjects. This rank, dependent on the King, takes the place, in the eyes and esteem of these subjects, of the rank which in ancient Rome depended on the good opinion of his fellow-citizens, who had seen him fighting at Trasimene and speaking in the Forum. You can batter down absolute monarchy by destroying vanity and its advance works, which it calls *conventions*. The dispute between Shakespeare and Racine is only one form of the dispute between Louis XIV and constitutional government.

fool's honor. It accustoms men to ask themselves: What will my neighbor think of my happiness? But how can happiness of the heart be an object of vanity, since no one can see it?[1] In proof of all this, France is the country, where there are fewer marriages from inclination than anywhere else in the world.[2]

And Italy has other advantages. The Italian has undisturbed leisure and an admirable climate, which makes men sensible to beauty under every form. He is extremely, yet reasonably, mistrustful, which increases the aloofness of intimate love and doubles its charms. He reads no novels, indeed hardly any books, and this leaves still more to the inspiration of the moment. He has a passion for music, which excites in the soul a movement very similar to that of love.

In France, towards 1770, there was no mistrust; on the contrary, it was good form to live and die before the public. As the Duchess of Luxemburg was intimate with a hundred friends, there was no intimacy and no friendship, properly so-called.

In Italy, passion, since it is not a very rare distinction, is not a subject of ridicule,[3] and you may hear people in the *salons* openly quoting general maxims of love. The public knows the symptoms and periods of this illness, and is very much concerned with it. They say to a man who has been deserted: "You'll be in despair for six months, but you'll get over it in the end, like So-and-so, etc."

In Italy, public opinion is the very humble attendant on passion. Real pleasure there exercises the power, which elsewhere is in the hands of society. 'Tis quite simple — for society can give scarcely any pleasure to a people who have no time to be vain, and can have but little authority over those, who are only trying to escape the notice of their

[1] It can only be estimated in unpremeditated actions.

[2] Miss O'Neill, Mrs. Couts, and most of the great English actresses, leave the stage in order to marry rich husbands.

[3] One can allow women gallantry, but love makes them laughed at, wrote the judicious Abbé Girard in Paris in 1740.

"pacha." The *blasés* censure the passionate — but who cares for them? South of the Alps, society is a despot without a prison.

As in Paris honor challenges, sword in hand, or, if possible, *bon mot* in the mouth, every approach to every recognized great interest, it is much more convenient to take refuge in irony. Many young men have taken up a different attitude, and become disciples of J. J. Rousseau and Madame de Staël. As irony had become vulgar, one had to fall back on feelings. A. de Pezai in our days writes like M. Darlincourt. Besides, since 1789, everything tends to favor utility or individual sensibility, as opposed to honor or the empire of opinion. The sight of the two Chambers teaches people to discuss everything, even mere nonsense. The nation is becoming serious, and gallantry is losing ground.

As a Frenchman, I ought to say that it is not a small number of colossal fortunes, but the multiplicity of middling ones, that makes up the riches of a country. In every country passion is rare, and gallantry is more graceful and refined: in France, as a consequence, it has better fortune. This great nation, the first in the world,[1] has the same kind of aptitude for love as for intellectual achievements. In 1822 we have, to be sure, no Moore, no Walter Scott, no Crabbe, no Byron, no Monti, no Pellico; but we have among us more men of intellect, clear-sighted, agreeable and up to the level of the lights of this century, than England has, or Italy. It is for this reason that the debates in our Chamber of Deputies in 1822, are so superior to those in the English Parliament, and that when a Liberal from England comes to France, we are quite surprised to find in him several opinions which are distinctly feudal.

A Roman artist wrote from Paris: —

I am exceedingly uncomfortable here; I suppose it's because I have no leisure for falling in love at my ease. Here, sensibility is spent drop by drop, just as it forms, in such a way, at least so I find

[1] I want no other proof than the world's envy. See the *Edinburgh Review* for 1821. See the German and Italian literary journals, and the *Scimiatigre* of Alfieri.

it, as to be a drain on the source. At Rome, owing to the little interest created by the events of every day and the somnolence of the outside world, sensibility accumulates to the profit of passion.

Rome

ONLY at Rome[1] can a respectable woman, seated in her carriage, say effusively to another woman, a mere acquaintance, what I heard this morning: "Ah, my dear, beware of love with Fabio Vitteleschi; better for you to fall in love with a highwayman! For all his soft and measured air, he is capable of stabbing you to the heart with a knife, and of saying with the sweetest smile, while he plunged the knife into your breast: 'Poor child, does it hurt?' " And this conversation took place in the presence of a pretty young lady of fifteen, daughter of the woman who received the advice, and a very wide-awake young lady.

If a man from the North has the misfortune not to be shocked at first by the candor of this southern capacity for love, which is nothing but the simple product of a magnificent nature, favored by the twofold absence of *good form* and of all interesting novelty, after a stay of one year the women of all other countries will become intolerable to him.

He will find Frenchwomen, perfectly charming, with their little graces,[2] seductive for the first three days, but boring the fourth — fatal day, when one discovers that all these graces, studied beforehand, and learned by rote, are eternally the same, every day and for every lover.

He will see German women, on the contrary, so very natural, and giving themselves up with so much ardor to their imagination, but often with nothing to show in the end, for all their naturalness, but barrenness, insipidity, and blue-stocking tenderness. The phrase of Count Alma-

[1] September 30th, 1819.

[2] Not only had the author the misfortune not to be born at Paris, but he had also lived there very little. (Editor's note)

viva seems made for Germany: "And one is quite astonished, one fine evening, to find satiety, where one went to
look for happiness."

At Rome, the foreigner must not forget that, if nothing
is tedious in countries where everything is natural, the bad
is there still more bad than elsewhere. To speak only of the
men,[1] we can see appearing here in society a kind of monster, who elsewhere lies low — a man passionate, clear-
sighted and base, all in an equal degree. Suppose evil chance
has set him near a woman in some capacity or other: madly
in love with her, suppose, he will drink to the very dregs
the misery of seeing her prefer a rival. There he is to oppose her happier lover. Nothing escapes him, and everyone
sees that nothing escapes him; but he continues none the
less, in despite of every honorable sentiment, to trouble
the woman, her lover and himself. No one blames him —
"That's his way of getting pleasure." — "He is doing what
gives him pleasure." One evening, the lover, at the end of
his patience, gives him a kick. The next day the wretch is
full of excuses, and begins again to torment, constantly and
imperturbably, the woman, the lover and himself. One
shudders, when one thinks of the amount of unhappiness
that these base spirits have every day to swallow — and
doubtless there is but one grain less of cowardice between
them and a poisoner.

It is also only in Italy that you can see young and elegant
millionaires entertaining with magnificence, in full view
of a whole town, ballet girls from a big theatre, at a cost of
thirty halfpence a day.[2]

Two brothers X——, fine young fellows, always hunting
and on horseback, are jealous of a foreigner. Instead of going
and laying their complaint before him, they are sullen, and
spread abroad unfavorable reports of this poor foreigner.

[1] Heu! male nunc artes miseras haec secula tractant;
Jam tener assuevit munera velle puer. (Tibullus, I, iv)

[2] See in the manners of the age of Louis XV how Honor and Aristocracy load
with profusion such ladies as Duthé, La Guerre and others. Eighty or a hundred
thousand francs a year was nothing extraordinary; with less, a man of fashion
would have lowered himself.

In France, public opinion would force such men to prove their words or give satisfaction to the foreigner. Here public opinion and contempt mean nothing. Riches are always certain of being well received everywhere. A millionaire, dishonored and excluded from every house in Paris, can go quite securely to Rome; there he will be estimated just according to the value of his dollars.

England

I HAVE lived a good deal of late with the ballet-girls of the Teatro Del Sol, at Valencia. People assure me that many of them are very chaste; the reason being that their profession is too fatiguing. Vigano makes them rehearse his ballet, the *Jewess of Toledo*, every day, from ten in the morning to four, and from midnight to three in the morning. Besides this, they have to dance every evening in both ballets.

This reminds me that Rousseau prescribes a great deal of walking for Emile. This evening I was strolling at midnight with these little ballet girls out along the seashore, and I was thinking especially how unknown to us, in our sad lands of mist, is this superhuman delight in the freshness of a sea breeze under this Valencian sky, under the eyes of these resplendent stars that seem close above us. This alone repays the journey of four hundred leagues; this it is that banishes thought, for feeling is too strong. I thought that the chastity of my little ballet girls gives the explanation of the course adopted by English pride, in order, little by little, to bring back the morals of the harem into the midst of a civilized nation. One sees how it is that some of these young English girls, otherwise so beautiful and with so touching an expression, leave something to be desired as regards ideas. In spite of liberty, which has only just been banished from their island, and the admirable originality of their national character, they lack interesting ideas and originality. Often there is nothing remarkable in them but the extravagance of their refinements. It's simple enough — in England the modesty of the women is the pride of their husbands. But, however submissive a slave may be, her society becomes sooner or later a burden. Hence, for the men, the necessity of getting drunk solemnly every evening,[1] instead of as in Italy, passing the evening with their mistresses. In England, rich people, bored with their homes and under the pretext of necessary exercise, walk four or five leagues a day, as if man were created and put into the world to trot up and down it. They use up their nervous fluid by means of their legs, not their hearts; after which, they may well talk of female refinement and look down on Spain and Italy.

No life, on the other hand, could be less busy than that of young Italians; to them all action is importunate, if it take away their sensibility. From time to time they take a walk of half a league for health's sake, as an unpleasant medicine. As for the women, a Roman woman in a whole year does not walk as far as a young Miss in a week.

It seems to me that the pride of an English husband exalts very adroitly the vanity of his wretched wife. He persuades her, first of all, that one must not be vulgar, and the mothers, who are getting their daughters ready to find husbands, are quick enough to seize upon this idea. Hence fashion is far more absurd and despotic in reasonable England than in the midst of light-hearted France: in Bond Street was invented the idea of the "carefully careless." In England fashion is a duty, at Paris it is a pleasure. In London fashion raises a wall of bronze between New Bond Street and Fenchurch Street far different from that between the Chaussée d'Antin and the rue Saint-Martin at Paris. Husbands are quite willing to allow their wives this aristocratic nonsense, to make up for the enormous amount of unhappiness, which they impose on them. I recognize a perfect picture of women's society in England, such as the taciturn pride

---

[1] This custom begins to give way a little in very good society, which is becoming French, as everywhere; but I'm speaking of the vast generality.

of its men produces, in the once celebrated novels of Miss Burney. Since it is vulgar to ask for a glass of water, when one is thirsty, Miss Burney's heroines do not fail to let themselves die of thirst. While flying from vulgarity, they fall into the most abominable affectation.

Compare the prudence of a young Englishman of twenty-two with the profound mistrust of a young Italian of the same age. The Italian must be mistrustful to be safe, but this mistrust he puts aside, or at least forgets, as soon as he becomes intimate, while it is apparently just in his most tender relationships that you see the young Englishman redouble his prudence and aloofness. I once heard this: —

"In the last seven months I haven't spoken to her of the trip to Brighton." This was a question of a necessary economy of twenty-four pounds, and a lover of twenty-two years speaking of a mistress, a married woman, whom he adored. In the transports of his passion prudence had not left him: far less had he let himself go enough to say to his mistress: "I shan't go to Brighton, because I should feel the pinch."

Note that the fate of Gianone de Pellico, and of a hundred others, forces the Italian to be mistrustful, while the young English *beau* is only forced to be prudent by the excessive and morbid sensibility of his vanity. A Frenchman, charming enough with his inspiration of the minute, tells everything to her he loves. It is habit. Without it he would lack ease, and he knows that without ease there is no grace.

It is with difficulty and with tears in my eyes that I have plucked up courage to write all this; but, since I would not, I'm sure, flatter a king, why should I say of a country anything but what seems to me the truth? Of course it may be all very absurd, for the simple reason that this country gave birth to the most lovable woman that I have known.

It would be another form of cringing before a monarch. I will content myself with adding that in the midst of all this variety of manners, among so many Englishwomen, who are the spiritual victims of Englishmen's pride, a perfect form of originality does exist, and that a family, brought up aloof from these distressing restrictions (invented to reproduce the morals of the harem) may be responsible for charming characters. And how insufficient, in spite of its etymology, — and how common — is this word "charming" to render what I would express. The gentle Imogen, the tender Ophelia might find plenty of living models in England; but these models are far from enjoying the high veneration that is unanimously accorded to the true accomplished Englishwoman, whose destiny is to show complete obedience to every convention and to afford a husband full enjoyment of the most morbid aristocratic pride and a happiness that makes him die of boredom.[1]

In the great suites of fifteen or twenty rooms, so fresh and so dark, in which Italian women pass their lives softly propped on low divans, they hear people speak of love and of music for six hours in the day. At night, at the theatre, hidden in their boxes for four hours, they hear people speak of music and love.

Then, besides the climate, the whole way of living is in Spain or Italy as favorable to music and love, as it is the contrary in England.

I neither blame nor approve; I observe.

More on England

I LOVE England too much and I have seen of her too little to be able to speak on the subject. I shall make use of the observations of a friend.

In the actual state of Ireland (1822) is realized, for the twentieth time in two centuries,[2] that curious state of society which is so fruitful of courageous resolutions, and so opposed to a monotonous existence, and in which people,

[1] See Richardson: the manners of the Harlowe family, translated into modern manners, are frequent in England. Their servants are worth more than they.

[2] The young child of Spenser was burnt alive in Ireland.

who breakfast gaily together, may meet in two hours' time on the field of battle. Nothing makes a more energetic and direct appeal to that disposition of the spirit, which is most favorable to the tender passions — to naturalness. Nothing is further removed from the two great English vices — cant and bashfulness, — moral hypocrisy and haughty, painful timidity. (See the Travels of Mr. Eustace in Italy.) If this traveller gives a poor picture of the country, in return he gives a very exact idea of his own character, and this character, as that of Mr. Beattie, the poet (see his *Life* written by an intimate friend), is unhappily but too common in England. For the priest, honest in spite of his cloth, refer to the letters of the Bishop of Landaff.[1]

One would have thought Ireland already unfortunate enough, bled as it has been for two centuries by the cowardly and cruel tyranny of England; but now there enters into the moral state of Ireland a terrible personage: the PRIEST. . . .

For two centuries Ireland has been almost as badly governed as Sicily. A thorough comparison between these two islands, in a volume of five hundred pages, would offend many people and overwhelm many established theories with ridicule. What is evident is that the happier of these two countries — both of them governed by fools, only for the profit of a minority — is Sicily. Its governors have at least left it its love of pleasure; they would willingly have robbed it of this as of the rest, but, thanks to its climate, Sicily knows little of that moral evil called Law and Government.[2]

It is old men and priests who make the laws and have them executed, and this seems quite in keeping with the comic jealousy, with which pleasure is hunted down in the British Isles. The people there might say to its governors as Diogenes said to Alexander: "Be content with your sine-

---

[1] To refute otherwise than by insults the portraiture of a certain class of Englishmen presented in these three works seems to me an impossible task. Satanic school.

[2] I call moral evil, in 1822, every government which has not got two chambers; the only exception can be when the head of the government is great by reason of his probity, a miracle to be seen in Saxony and at Naples.

cures, but please don't step between me and my daylight."[1]

By means of laws, rules, counter-rules and punishments, the Government in Ireland has created the potato, and the population of Ireland exceeds by far that of Sicily. This is to say, they have produced several millions of degenerate and half-witted peasants, broken down by work and misery, dragging out a wretched life of some forty or fifty years among the marshes of old Erin — and, you may be sure, paying their taxes! A real miracle! With the pagan religion these poor wretches would at least have enjoyed some happiness — but not a bit of it, they must adore St. Patrick.

Everywhere in Ireland one sees none but peasants more miserable than savages. Only, instead of there being a hundred thousand, as there would be in a state of nature, there are eight millions,[2] who allow five hundred "absentees" to live in prosperity at London or Paris.

Society is infinitely more advanced in Scotland,[3] where, in very many respects, government is good (the rarity of crime, the diffusion of reading, the non-existence of bishops, etc.). There the tender passions can develop much more freely, and it is possible to leave these sombre thoughts and approach the humorous.

One cannot fail to notice a foundation of melancholy in Scottish women. This melancholy is particularly seductive at dances, where it gives a singular piquancy to the extreme ardor and energy with which they perform their national dances. Edinburgh has another advantage, that of being withdrawn from the vile empire of money. In this, as well as in the singular and savage beauty of its site, this city forms

[1] See in the trial of the late Queen of England, a curious list of the peers with the sums which they and their families receive from the State. For example, Lord Lauderdale and his family, £36,000. The half-pint of beer that is necessary to the miserable existence of the poorest Englishman, is taxed a halfpenny for the profit of the noble peer. And, what is very much to the point, both of them know it. As a result, neither the lord nor the peasant have leisure enough to think of love; they are sharpening their arms, the one publicly and haughtily, the other secretly and enraged. (Yeomanry and Whiteboys)

[2] Plunkett Craig, *Life of Curran.*

[3] Degree of civilization to be seen in the peasant Robert Burns and his family; a peasants' club with a penny subscription each meeting; the questions discussed there. (See the *Letters* of Burns)

a complete contrast with London. Like Rome, fair Edinburgh seems rather the sojourn of the contemplative life. At London you have the ceaseless whirlwind and restless interests of active life, with all its advantages and inconveniences. Edinburgh seems to me to pay its tribute to the devil by a slight disposition to pedantry. Those days when Mary Stuart lived at old Holyrood, and Riccio was assassinated in her arms, were worth more to Love (and here all women will agree with me) than to-day, when one discusses at such length, and even in their presence, the preference to be accorded to the neptunian system over the vulcanian system of . . . I prefer a discussion on the new uniform given by the king to the Guards, or on the peerage which Sir B. Bloomfield failed to get — the topic of London in my day — to a learned discussion as to who has best explored the nature of rocks, de Werner or de . . .

I say nothing about the terrible Scottish Sunday, after which a Sunday in London looks like a beanfeast. That day, set aside for the honor of Heaven, is the best image of Hell that I have ever seen on earth. "Don't let's walk so fast," said a Scotchman returning from church to a Frenchman, his friend; "people might think we were going for a walk."[1]

Of the three countries, Ireland is the one in which there is the least hypocrisy. See the *New Monthly Magazine* thundering against Mozart and the *Nozze di Figaro*.

In every country it is the aristocrats, who try to judge a literary magazine and literature; and for the last four years in England these have been hand in glove with the bishops. As I say, that of the three countries where, it seems to me, there is the least hypocrisy, is Ireland: on the contrary, you find there a reckless, a most fascinating vivacity. In Scotland there is the strict observance of Sunday, but on Monday they dance with a joy and an abandon unknown to London. There is plenty of love among the peasant class in Scotland. The omnipotence of imagination gallicized the country in the sixteenth century.

[1] The same in America. In Scotland, display of titles.

The terrible fault of English society, that which in a single day creates a greater amount of sadness than the national debt and its consequences, and even than the war to the death waged by the rich against the poor, is this sentence which I heard last autumn at Croydon, before the beautiful statue of the bishop: "In society no one wants to put himself forward, for fear of being deceived in his expectations."

Judge what laws, under the name of modesty, such men must impose on their wives and mistresses.

Spain

ANDALUSIA is one of the most charming sojourns that Pleasure has chosen for itself on earth. I had three or four anecdotes to show how my ideas about the three or four different acts of madness, which together constitute Love, hold good for Spain: I have been advised to sacrifice them to French refinement. In vain I protested that I wrote in French, but emphatically not French literature. God preserve me from having anything in common with the French writers esteemed to-day!

The Moors, when they abandoned Andalusia, left it their architecture and much of their manners. Since it is impossible for me to speak of the latter in the language of Madame de Sevigné, I'll at least say this of Moorish architecture: — its principal trait consists in providing every house with a little garden surrounded by an elegant and graceful portico. There, during the unbearable heat of summer, when for whole weeks together the Réaumur thermometer never falls below a constant level of thirty degrees, a delicious obscurity pervades these porticoes. In the middle of the little garden there is always a fountain, monotonous and voluptuous, whose sound is all that stirs this charming retreat. The marble basin is surrounded by a dozen orange-trees and laurels. A thick canvas, like a tent, covers in the whole of the little garden, and, while it protects it from the rays of the sun and from the light, lets in the gentle breezes which, at midday, come down from the mountains.

There live and receive their guests the fair ladies of Andalusia: a simple black silk robe, ornamented with fringes of the same color, and giving glimpses of a charming ankle; a pale complexion and eyes that mirror all the most fugitive shades of the most tender and ardent passion — such are the celestial beings, whom I am forbidden to bring upon the scene.

I look upon the Spanish people as the living representatives of the Middle Age.

It is ignorant of a mass of little truths (the puerile vanity of its neighbors); but it has a profound knowledge of great truths and enough character and wit to follow their consequences down to their most remote effects. The Spanish character offers a fine contrast to French intellect — hard, brusque, inelegant, full of savage pride, and unconcerned with others. It is just the contrast of the fifteenth with the eighteenth century.

Spain provides me with a good contrast; the only people, that was able to withstand Napoleon, seems to me to be absolutely lacking in the fool's honor and in all that is foolish in honor. Instead of making fine military ordinances, of changing uniforms every six months and of wearing large spurs, Spain has general *No importa.*[1]

German Love

IF the Italian, always agitated between love and hate, is a creature of passion, and the Frenchman of vanity, the good and simple descendants of the ancient Germans are assuredly creatures of imagination. Scarcely raised above social interests, the most directly necessary to their sub-

[1] See the charming *Letters* of M. Pecchio. Italy is full of people of this wonderful type; but, instead of letting themselves be seen, they try to keep quiet — *paese della virtù scunosciuta* — "Land of mute, inglorious virtue."

sistence, one is amazed to see them soar into what they call their philosophy, which is a sort of gentle, lovable, quite harmless folly. I am going to cite, not altogether from memory, but from hurriedly taken notes, a work whose author, though writing in a tone of opposition, illustrates clearly, even in his admirations, the military spirit in all its excesses — I speak of the *Travels in Austria* of M. Cadet-Gassicourt, in 1809. What would the noble and generous Desaix have said, if he had seen the pure heroism of '95 lead on to this execrable egoism?

Two friends find themselves side by side with a battery at the battle of Talavera, one as Captain in command, the other as lieutenant. A passing bullet lays the Captain low. "Good," says the lieutenant, quite beside himself with joy, "that's done for Francis — now I shall be Captain." "Not so quick," cries Francis, as he gets up. He had only been stunned by the bullet. The lieutenant, as well as the Captain, were the best fellows in the world, not a bit ill-natured, and only a little stupid; the excitement of the chase and the furious egoism which the Emperor had succeeded in awakening, by decorating it with the name of glory, made these enthusiastic worshippers of him forget their humanity.

After the harsh spectacle offered by men like this, who dispute on parade at Schoenbrunn for a look from their master and a barony — see how the Emperor's apothecary describes German love, page 188:

"Nothing can be more sweet, more gentle, than an Austrian woman. With her, love is a cult, and when she is attached to a Frenchman, she adores him — in the full force of the word.

"There are light, capricious women everywhere, but in general the Viennese are faithful and in no way coquettes; when I say that they are faithful, I mean to the lover of their own choice, for husbands are the same at Vienna as everywhere else" (June 7, 1809).

The most beautiful woman of Vienna accepts the homage of one of my friends, M. M——, a captain attached to the Emperor's headquarters. He's a young man, gentle and witty, but certainly neither his figure nor face are in any way remarkable.

For some days past his young mistress has made a very great sensation among our brilliant staff officers, who pass their life ferreting about in every corner of Vienna. It has become a contest of daring. Every possible manœuvre has been employed. The fair one's house has been put in a state of siege by all the best-looking and richest. Pages, brilliant colonels, generals of the guard, even princes, have gone to waste their time under her windows, and their money on the fair lady's servants. All have been turned away. These princes were little accustomed to find a deaf ear at Paris or Milan. When I laughed at their discomfiture before this charming creature: "But good Heavens," she said, "don't they know that I'm in love with M. M....?"

A singular remark and certainly a most improper one!

Page 290: "While we were at Schoenbrunn I noticed that two young men, who were attached to the Emperor, never received anyone in their lodgings at Vienna. We used to chaff them a lot on their discretion. One of them said to me one day: 'I'll keep no secrets from you: a young woman of the place has given herself to me, on condition that she need never leave my apartment, and that I never receive anyone at all without her leave.' I was curious," says the traveller, "to know this voluntary recluse, and my position as doctor giving me, as in the East, an honorable pretext, I accepted a breakfast offered me by my friend. The woman I found was very much in love, took the greatest care of the household, never wanted to go out, though it was just a pleasant time of the year for walking — and for the rest, was quite certain that her lover would take her back with him to France.

"The other young man, who was also never to be found in his rooms, soon after made me a similar confession. I also saw his mistress. Like the first, she was fair, very pretty, and an excellent figure.

"The one, eighteen years of age, was the daughter of a well-to-do upholsterer; the other, who was about twenty-four, was the wife of an Austrian officer, on service with the army of the Archduke John. This latter pushed her love to the verge of what we, in our land of vanity, would call heroism. Not only was her lover faithless to her, he also found himself under the necessity of making a confession of a most unpleasant nature. She nursed him with complete devotion; the seriousness of his illness attached her to her lover; and perhaps she only cherished him the more for it, when soon after his life was in danger.

"It will be understood that I, a stranger and a conqueror, have had no chance of observing love in the highest circles, seeing that the whole of the aristocracy of Vienna had retired at our approach to their estates in Hungary. But I have seen enough of it to be convinced that it is not the same love as at Paris.

"The feeling of love is considered by the Germans as a virtue, as an emanation of the Divinity, as something mystical. It is not quick, impetuous, jealous, tyrannical, as it is in the heart of an Italian woman: it is profound and something like illuminism; in this Germany is a thousand miles away from England.

"Some years ago a Leipsic tailor, in a fit of jealousy, waited for his rival in the public garden and stabbed him. He was condemned to lose his head. The moralists of the town, faithful to the German traditions of kindness and unhampered emotion (which makes for feebleness of character) discussed the sentence, decided that it was severe and, making a comparison between the tailor and Orosmanes, were moved to pity for his fate. Nevertheless they were unable to have his sentence mitigated. But the day of the execution, all the young girls of Leipsic, dressed in white, met together and accompanied the tailor to the scaffold, throwing flowers in his path.

"No one thought this ceremony odd; yet, in a country which considers itself logical, it might be said that it was honoring a species of murder. But it was a ceremony — and everything which is a ceremony, is always safe from ridicule in Germany. See the ceremonies at the Courts of the small princes, which would make us Frenchmen die with laughter, but appear quite imposing at Meiningen or Koethen. In the six gamekeepers who file past their little prince, adorned with his star, they see the soldiers of Arminius marching out to meet the legions of Varus.

"A point of difference between the Germans and all other peoples: they are exalted, instead of calming themselves, by meditation. A second subtle point: they are all eaten up with the desire to have character.

"Life at Court, ordinarily so favorable to love, in Germany deadens it. You have no idea of the mass of incomprehensible *minutiæ* and the pettinesses that constitute what is called a German Court,[1] — even the Court of the best princes. (Munich, 1820).

"When we used to arrive with the staff in a German town, at the end of the first fortnight the ladies of the district had made their choice. But that choice was constant; and I have heard it said that the French were a shoal, on which foundered many a virtue till then irreproachable."

.   .   .   .   .   .

The young Germans whom I have met at Gottingen, Dresden, Koenigsberg, etc., are brought up among pseudo-systems of philosophy, which are merely obscure and badly written poetry, but, as regards their ethics, of the highest and holiest sublimity. They seem to me to have inherited from their Middle Age, not like the Italians, republicanism, mistrust and the dagger, but a strong disposition to enthusiasm and good faith. Thus it is that every ten years they have a new great man who's going to efface all the others. (Kant, Steding, Fichte, etc. etc.[2])

Formerly Luther made a powerful appeal to the moral

---

[1] See the Memoirs of the Margrave de Bayreuth and *Vingt ans de séjour à Berlin*, by M. Thiébaut.

[2] See in 1821 their enthusiasm for the tragedy, the *Triumph of the Cross*, which has caused *Wilhelm Tell* to be forgotten.

sense, and the Germans fought thirty years on end, in order to obey their conscience. It's a fine word and one quite worthy of respect, however absurd the belief; I say worthy of respect even from an artist. See the struggle in the soul of S—— between the third [sixth] commandment of God — "Thou shalt not kill" — and what he believed to be the interest of his country.

Already in Tacitus we find a mystical enthusiasm for women and love, at least if that writer was not merely aiming his satire at Rome.[1]

One has not been five hundred miles in Germany, before one can distinguish in this people, disunited and scattered, a foundation of enthusiasm, soft and tender, rather than ardent and impetuous.

If this disposition were not so apparent, it would be enough to reread three or four of the novels of Auguste La Fontaine, whom the pretty Louise, Queen of Prussia, made Canon of Magdeburg, as a reward for having so well painted the Peaceful Life.[2]

I see a new proof of this disposition, which is common to all the Germans, in the Austrian code, which demands the confession of the guilty for the punishment of almost all crimes. This code is calculated to fit a people, among whom crime is a rare phenomenon, and sooner an excess of madness in a feeble being than the effect of interests, daring, reasoned and for ever in conflict with society. It is precisely the contrary of what is wanted in Italy, where they are trying to introduce it — a mistake of well-meaning people.

I have seen German judges in Italy in despair over sentences of death or, what's the equivalent, the irons, if they were obliged to pronounce it without the confession of the guilty.

[1] I have had the good fortune to meet a man of the liveliest wit, and at the same time as learned as ten German professors, and one who discloses his discoveries in terms clear and precise. If ever M. F. publishes, we shall see the Middle Age revealed to our eyes in a full light, and we shall love it.

[2] The title of one of the novels of Auguste la Fontaine. The peaceful life, another great trait of German manners — it is the "farniente" of the Italian, and also the physiological commentary on a Russian *droski* and on the English "horseback."

FLORENCE, *February 12, 1819*

THIS evening, in a box at the theatre, I met a man who had some favor to ask of a magistrate, aged fifty. His first question was: "Who is his mistress? *Chi avvicina adesso?*" Here everyone's affairs are absolutely public; they have their own laws; there is an approved manner of acting, which is based on justice without any conventionality — if you act otherwise, you are a *porco*.

"What's the news?" one of my friends asked yesterday, on his arrival from Volterra. After a word of vehement lamentation about Napoleon and the English, someone adds, in a tone of the liveliest interest: "La Vitteleschi has changed her lover: poor Gherardesca is in despair." — "Whom has she taken?" — "Montegalli, the good-looking officer with a moustache, who had Princess Colonna; there he is down in the stalls, nailed to her box; he's there the whole evening, because her husband won't have him in the house, and there near the door you can see poor Gherardesca, walking about so sadly and counting afar the glances, which his faithless mistress throws his successor. He's very changed and in the depths of despair; it's quite useless for his friends to try to send him to Paris or London. He is ready to die, he says, at the very idea of leaving Florence."

Every year there are twenty such cases of despair in high circles; some of them I have seen last three or four years. These poor devils are without any shame and take the whole world into their confidence. For the rest, there's little society here, and besides, when one's in love, one hardly mixes with it. It must not be thought that great passions and great hearts are at all common, even in Italy; only, in Italy, hearts which are more inflamed and less stunted by the thousand little cares of our vanity, find delicious pleasures even in the subaltern species of love. In Italy I have seen love from caprice, for example, cause transports and

moments of madness, such as the most violent passion has never brought with it under the meridian of Paris.[1]

I noticed this evening that there are proper names in Italian for a million particular circumstances in love, which, in French, would need endless paraphrases; for example, the action of turning sharply away, when from the floor of the house you are quizzing a woman you are in love with, and the husband or a servant come towards the front of her box.

The following are the principal traits in the character of this people: —

1. The attention, habitually at the service of deep passions, cannot move rapidly. This is the most marked difference between a Frenchman and an Italian. You have only to see an Italian get into a diligence or make a payment, to understand "la furia francese." It's for this reason that the most vulgar Frenchman, provided that he is not a witty fool, like Démasure, always seems a superior being to an Italian woman. (The lover of Princess D—— at Rome.)

2. Everyone is in love, and not under cover, as in France; the husband is the best friend of the lover.

3. No one reads.

4. There is no society. A man does not reckon, in order to fill up and occupy his life, on the happiness which he derives from two hours' conversation and the play of vanity in this or that house. The word *causerie* cannot be translated into Italian. People speak when they have something to say, to forward a passion, but they rarely talk just in order to talk on any given subject.

5. Ridicule does not exist in Italy.

In France, both of us are trying to imitate the same model, and I am a competent judge of the way in which you copy it.[2] In Italy I cannot say whether the peculiar

---

[1] Of that Paris which has given the world Voltaire, Molière and so many men of distinguished wit — but one can't have everything, and it would show little wit to be annoyed at it.

[2] This French habit, growing weaker every day, will increase the distance between us and Molière's heroes.

action, which I see this man perform, does not give pleasure to the performer and might not, perhaps, give pleasure to me.

What is affectation of language or manner at Rome, is good form or unintelligible at Florence, which is only fifty leagues away. The same French is spoken at Lyons as at Nantes. Venetian, Neapolitan, Genoese, Piedmontese are almost entirely different languages, and only spoken by people who are agreed never to print except in a common language, namely that spoken at Rome. Nothing is so absurd as a comedy, with the scene laid at Milan and the characters speaking Roman. It is only by music that the Italian language, which is far more fit to be sung than spoken, will hold its own against the clearness of French, which threatens it.

In Italy, fear of the "pacha" and his spies causes the useful to be held in esteem; the fool's honor simply doesn't exist.[1] Its place is taken by a kind of petty hatred of society, called "petegolismo." Finally, to make fun of a person is to make a mortal enemy, a very dangerous thing in a country where the power and activity of governments is limited to exacting taxes and punishing everything above the common level.

6. The patriotism of the antechamber.

That pride which leads a man to seek the esteem of his fellow-citizens and to make himself one of them, but which in Italy was cut off, about the year 1550, from any noble enterprise by the jealous despotism of the small Italian princes, has given birth to a barbarous product, to a sort of Caliban, to a monster full of fury and sottishness, the patriotism of the antechamber, as M. Turgot called it, *à propos* of the siege of Calais (the *Soldat laboureur* of those times.) I have seen this monster blunt the sharpest spirits. For example, a stranger will make himself unpopular, even with pretty women, if he thinks fit to find anything wrong

[1] Every infraction of this honor is a subject of ridicule in bourgeois circles in France. (See M. Picard's *Petite Ville*.)

with the painter or poet of the town; he will be soon told, and that very seriously, that he ought not to come among people to laugh at them, and they will quote to him on this topic a saying of Louis XIV about Versailles.

At Florence people say: "our Benvenuti," as at Brescia — "our Arrici": they put on the word "our" a certain emphasis, restrained yet very comical, not unlike the *Miroir* talking with unction about national music and of M. Monsigny, the musician of Europe.

In order not to laugh in the face of these fine patriots one must remember that, owing to the dissensions of the Middle Age, envenomed by the vile policy of the Popes,[1] each city has a mortal hatred for its neighbor, and the name of the inhabitants in the one always stands in the other as a synonym for some gross fault. The Popes have succeeded in making this beautiful land into the kingdom of hate.

This patriotism of the antechamber is the greatest moral sore in Italy, a corrupting germ that will still show its disastrous effects long after Italy has thrown off the yoke of its ridiculous little priests.[2] The form of this patriotism is an inexorable hatred for everything foreign. Thus they look on the Germans as fools, and get angry when someone says: "What has Italy in the eighteenth century produced the equal of Catherine II or Frederick the Great? Where have you an English garden comparable to the smallest German garden, you who, with your climate, have a real need of shade?"

7. Unlike the English or French, the Italians have no political prejudices; they all know by heart the line of La Fontaine: —

Notre ennemi c'est notre M.[3]

Aristocracy, supported by the priest and a biblical state of society, is a worn-out illusion which only makes them

[1] See the excellent and curious *Histoire de l'Eglise*, by M. de Potter.

[2] 1822.

[3] [Our enemy is our Master. — *Fables*, VI. 8.]

smile. In return, an Italian needs a stay of three months in France to realize that a draper may be a conservative.

8. As a last trait of character I would mention intolerance in discussion, and anger as soon as they do not find an argument ready to hand, to throw out against that of their adversary. At that point they visibly turn pale. It is one form of their extreme sensibility, but it is not one of its most amiable forms: consequently it is one of those that I am most willing to admit as proof of the existence of sensibility.

I wanted to see love without end, and, after considerable difficulty, I succeeded in being introduced this evening to Chevalier C—— and his mistress, with whom he has lived for fifty-four years. I left the box of these charming old people, my heart melted; there I saw the art of being happy, an art ignored by so many young people.

Two months ago I saw Monsignor R——, by whom I was well received, because I brought him some copies of the *Minerve.* He was at his country house with Madame D——, whom he is still pleased, after thirty-four years, *"avvicinare,"* [to come near] as they say. She is still beautiful, but there is a touch of melancholy in this household. People attribute it to the loss of a son, who was poisoned long ago by her husband.

Here, to be in love does not mean, as at Paris, to see one's mistress for a quarter of an hour every week, and for the rest of the time to obtain a look or a shake of the hand: the lover, the happy lover, passes four or five hours every day with the woman he loves. He talks to her about his actions at law, his English garden, his hunting parties, his prospects, etc. There is the completest, the most tender intimacy. He speaks to her with the familiar *"tu,"* even in the presence of her husband and everywhere.

A young man of this country, one very ambitious as he believed, was called to a high position at Vienna (nothing less than ambassador). But he could not get used to his stay abroad. At the end of six months he said good-bye to his job, and returned to be happy in his mistress's box at the opera.

Such continual intercourse would be inconvenient in France, where one must display a certain degree of affectation, and where your mistress can quite well say to you: "Monsieur So-and-so, you're glum this evening; you don't say a word." In Italy it is only a matter of telling the woman you love everything that passes through your head — you must actually think aloud. There is a certain nervous state which results from intimacy; freedom provokes freedom, and is only to be got in this way. But there is one great inconvenience; you find that love in this way paralyzes all your tastes and renders all the other occupations of your life insipid. Such love is the best substitute for passion.

Our friends at Paris, who are still at the stage of trying to conceive that it's possible to be a Persian, not knowing what to say, will cry out that such manners are indecent. To begin with, I am only an historian; and secondly, I reserve to myself the right to show one day, by dint of solid reasoning, that as regards manners, and fundamentally, Paris is not superior to Bologna. Quite unconsciously these poor people are still repeating their twopence-halfpenny catechism.

12 July, 1821. There is nothing odious in the society of Bologna. At Paris the rôle of a deceived husband is execrable; here (at Bologna) it is nothing — there are no deceived husbands. Manners are the same, it is only hate that is missing; the recognized lover is always the husband's friend, and this friendship, which has been cemented by reciprocal services, quite often survives other interests. Most love-affairs last five or six years, many for ever. People part at last, when they no longer find it sweet to tell each other everything, and when the first month of the rupture is over, there is no bitterness.

January, 1822. The ancient mode of the *cavaliere servente*, imported into Italy by Philip II, along with Spanish pride and manners, has entirely fallen into disuse in the large towns. I know of only one exception, and that's Calabria, where the eldest brother always takes orders, marries his younger brother, sets up in the service of his sister-in-law and becomes at the same time her lover.

Napoleon banished libertinism from upper Italy, and even from here (Naples).

The morals of the present generation of pretty women shame their mothers; they are more favorable to passion-love, but physical love has lost a great deal.[1]

Love in the United States

A FREE government is a government which does no harm to its citizens, but which, on the contrary, gives them security and tranquillity. But 'tis a long cry from this to happiness. That a man must find for himself; for he must be a gross creature who thinks himself perfectly happy, because he enjoys security and tranquillity. We mix these things up in Europe, especially in Italy. Accustomed as we are to governments, which do us harm, it seems to us that to be delivered from them would be supreme happiness; in this we are like invalids, worn out with the pain of our sufferings. The example of America shows us just the contrary. There government discharges its office quite well, and does harm to no one. But we have been far removed, for very many centuries, thanks to the unhappy state of Europe, from any actual experience of the kind, and now destiny, as if to disconcert and give the lie to all our philosophy, or rather to accuse it of not knowing all the elements of human nature, shows us, that just when the unhappiness of bad government is wanting to America, the Americans are wanting to themselves.

One is inclined to say that the source of sensibility is dried up in this people. They are just, they are reasonable, but they are essentially not happy.

[1] Towards 1780 the maxim ran:
Molti averne, un goderne, e cambiar spesso.
Travels of Shylock [Sherlock?]

Is the Bible, that is to say, the ridiculous consequences and rules of conduct which certain fantastic wits deduce from that collection of poems and songs, sufficient to cause all this unhappiness? To me it seems a very considerable effect for such a cause.

M. de Volney related that, being at table in the country at the house of an honest American, a man in easy circumstances, and surrounded by children already grown up, there entered into the dining-room a young man. "Good day, William," said the father of the family; "sit down." The traveller inquired who this young man was. "He's my second son." "Where does he come from?" — "From Canton."

The arrival of one of his sons from the end of the world caused no more sensation than that.

All their attention seems employed on finding a reasonable arrangement of life, and on avoiding all inconveniences. When finally they arrived at the moment of reaping the fruit of so much care and of the spirit of order so long maintained, there is no life left for enjoyment.

One might say that the descendants of Penn never read that line, which looks like their history: —

> Et propter vitam vivendi perdere causas.

The young people of both sexes, when winter comes, which in this country, as in Russia, is the gay season, go sleighing together day and night over the snow, often going quite gaily distances of fifteen or twenty miles, and without anyone to look after them. No inconvenience ever results from it.

They have the physical gaiety of youth, which soon passes away with the warmth of their blood, and is over at twenty-five. But I find no passions which give pleasure. In America there is such a reasonable habit of mind that crystallization has been rendered impossible.

I admire such happiness, but I do not envy it; it is like the happiness of human beings of a different and lower species. I augur much better things from Florida and Southern America.[1]

What strengthens my conjecture about the North is the absolute lack of artists and writers. The United States have not yet sent us over one scene of a tragedy, one picture, or one life of Washington.

Love in Provence

UP TO THE CONQUEST OF TOULOUSE,
IN 1328, BY THE BARBARIANS
FROM THE NORTH

LOVE took a singular form in Provence, from the year 1100 up to 1328. It had an established legislation for the relations of the two sexes in love, as severe and as exactly followed as the laws of Honor could be to-day. The laws of Love began by putting completely aside the sacred rights of husbands. They presuppose no hypocrisy. These laws, taking human nature such as it is, were of the kind to produce a great deal of happiness.

There was an official manner of declaring oneself a woman's lover, and another of being accepted by her as lover. After so many months of making one's court in a certain fashion, one obtained her leave to kiss her hand. Society, still young, took pleasure in formalities and ceremonies, which were then a sign of civilization, but which to-day would bore us to death. The same trait is to be found in the language of Provence, in the difficulty and interlacing of its rhymes, in its masculine and feminine words to express the same object, and indeed in the infinite number of its poets. Everything formal in society, which is so insipid to-day, then had all the freshness and savor of novelty.

After having kissed a woman's hand, one was promoted

[1] See the manners of the Azores: there, love of God and the other sort of love occupy every moment. The Christian religion, as interpreted by the Jesuits, is much less of an enemy to man, in this sense, than English protestantism; it permits him at least to dance on Sunday; and one day of pleasure in the seven is a great thing for the agricultural laborer, who works hard for the other six.

from grade to grade by force of merit, and without extra-ordinary promotion.

It should be remarked, however, that if the husbands were always left out of the question, on the other hand the official promotion of the lover stopped at what we should call the sweetness of a most tender friendship between persons of a different sex.[1] But after several months or several years of probation, in which a woman might become perfectly sure of the character and discretion of a man, and he enjoy at her hand all the prerogatives and outward signs which the tenderest friendship can give, her virtue must surely have had to thank his friendship for many a violent alarm.

I have spoken of extraordinary promotion, because a woman could have more than one lover, but one only in the higher grades. It seems that the rest could not be promoted much beyond that degree of friendship which consisted in kissing her hand and seeing her every day. All that is left to us of this singular civilization is in verse, and in a verse that is rhymed in a very fantastic and difficult way; and it need not surprise us if the notions, which we draw from the ballads of the troubadours, are vague and not at all precise. Even a marriage contract in verse has been found. After the conquest in 1328, as a result of its heresy, the Pope, on several occasions, ordered everything written in the vulgar tongue to be burnt. Italian cunning proclaimed Latin the only language worthy of such clever people. 'Twere a most advantageous measure could we renew it in 1822.

Such publicity and such official ordering of love seem at first sight to ill-accord with real passion. But if a lady said to her lover: "Go for your love of me and visit the tomb of our Lord Jesus Christ at Jerusalem; there you will pass three years and then return" — the lover was gone immediately: to hesitate a moment would have covered him with

---

[1] Memoirs of the life of Chabanon, written by himself. The rapping of a cane on the ceiling.

the same ignominy as would nowadays a sign of wavering on a point of honor. The language of this people has an extreme fineness in expressing the most fugitive shades of feeling. Another sign that their manners were well advanced on the road of real civilization is that, scarcely out of the horrors of the Middle Ages and of Feudalism, when force was everything, we see the feebler sex less tyrannized over than it is to-day with the approval of the law; we see the poor and feeble creatures, who have the most to lose in love and whose charms disappear the quickest, mistresses over the destiny of the men who approach them. An exile of three years in Palestine, the passage from a civilization full of gaiety to the fanaticism and boredom of the Crusaders' camp, must have been a painful duty for any other than an inspired Christian. What can a woman do to her lover who has basely deserted her at Paris?

I can only see one answer to be made here: at Paris no self-respecting woman has a lover. Certainly prudence has much more right to counsel the woman of to-day not to abandon herself to passion-love. But does not another prudence, which, of course, I am far from approving, counsel her to make up for it with physical love? Our hypocrisy and asceticism[1] imply no homage to virtue; for you can never oppose nature with impunity: there is only less happiness on earth and infinitely less generous inspiration.

A lover who, after ten years of intimate intercourse, deserted his poor mistress, because he began to notice her two-and-thirty years, was lost to honor in this lovable Provence; he had no resource left but to bury himself in the solitude of a cloister. In those days it was to the interest of a man, not only of generosity but even of prudence, to make display of no more passion than he really had. We conjecture all this; for very few remains are left to give us any exact notions. . . .

We must judge manners as a whole, by certain particular facts. You know the anecdote of the poet who had offended

[1] The ascetic principle of Jeremy Bentham.

his lady: after two years of despair she deigned at last to answer his many messages and let him know that if he had one of his nails torn off and had this nail presented to her by fifty loving and faithful knights, she might perhaps pardon him. The poet made all haste to submit to the painful operation. Fifty knights, who stood in their ladies' good graces, went to present this nail with all imaginable pomp to the offended beauty. It was as imposing a ceremony as the entry of a prince of the blood into one of the royal towns. The lover, dressed in the garb of a penitent, followed his nail from afar. The lady, after having watched the ceremony, which was of great length, right through, deigned to pardon him; he was restored to all the sweets of his former happiness. History tells that they spent long and happy years together. Sure it is that two such years of unhappiness prove a real passion and would have given birth to it, had it not existed before in that high degree.

I could cite twenty anecdotes which show us everywhere gallantry, pleasing, polished and conducted between the two sexes on principles of justice. I say gallantry, because in all ages passion-love is an exception, rather curious than frequent, a something we cannot reduce to rules. In Provence every calculation, everything within the domain of reason, was founded on justice and the equality of rights between the two sexes; and I admire it for this reason especially, that it eliminates unhappiness as far as possible. The absolute monarchy under Louis XV, on the contrary, had come to make baseness and perfidy the fashion in these relations.[1]

Although this charming Provençal language, so full of delicacy and so labored in its rhymes,[2] was probably not the language of the people, the manners of the upper classes had permeated the lower classes, which in Provence were at that time far from coarse, for they enjoyed a great deal

---

[1] The reader should have heard charming General Laclos talk at Naples in 1802. If he has not had the luck he can open the *Vie privée du maréchal de Richelieu*, nine volumes very pleasantly put together.

[2] It originated at Narbonne — a mixture of Latin and Arabic.

of comfort. They were in the first enjoyment of a very prosperous and very valuable trade. The inhabitants of the shores of the Mediterranean had just realized (in the ninth century) that to engage in commerce, by risking a few ships on this sea, was less troublesome and almost as amusing as following some little feudal lord and robbing the passers-by on the neighboring high-road. Soon after the Provençals of the tenth century learned from the Arabs that there are sweeter pleasures than pillage, violence and war.

One must think of the Mediterranean as the home of European civilization. The happy shores of this lovely sea, so favored in its climate, were still more favored in the prosperous state of their inhabitants and in the absence of all religion or miserable legislation. The eminently gay genius of the Provençals had by then passed through the Christian religion, without being altered by it.

We see a lively image of a like effect from a like cause in the cities of Italy, whose history has come down to us more distinctly and which have had the good fortune besides of bequeathing to us Dante, Petrarch and the art of painting.

The Provençals have not left us a great poem like the *Divine Comedy*, in which are reflected all the peculiarities of the manners of the time. They had, it seems to me, less passion and much more gaiety than the Italians. They learned this pleasant way of taking life from their neighbors, the Moors of Spain. Love reigned with joy, festivity and pleasure in the castles of happy Provence.

Have you seen at the opera the finale of one of Rossini's beautiful operettas? On the stage all is gaiety, beauty, ideal magnificence. We are miles away from all the mean side of human nature. The opera is over, the curtain falls, the spectators go out, the great chandelier is drawn up, the lights are extinguished. The house is filled with the smell of lamps hastily put out; the curtain is pulled up half-way, and you see dirty, ill-dressed roughs tumble on to the stage; they bustle about it in a hideous way, occupying the place of the young women who filled it with their graces only a moment ago.

Such for the kingdom of Provence was the effect of the conquest of Toulouse by the army of Crusaders. Instead of love, of grace, of gaiety, we have the Barbarians from the North and Saint Dominic. I shall not darken these pages with a blood-curdling account of the horrors of the Inquisition in all the zeal of its early days. As for the Barbarians, they were our fathers; they killed and plundered everywhere; they destroyed, for the pleasure of destroying, whatever they could not carry off; a savage madness animated them against everything that showed the least trace of civilization; above all, they understood not a word of that beautiful southern language; and that redoubled their fury. Highly superstitious and guided by the terrible S. Dominic, they thought to gain Heaven by killing the Provençals. For the latter all was over; no more love, no more gaiety, no more poetry. Less than twenty years after the conquest (1335), they were almost as barbarous and as coarse as the French, as our fathers.[1]

Whence had lighted on this corner of the world that charming form of civilization, which for two centuries was the happiness of the upper classes of society? Apparently from the Moors of Spain.

Provence in the Twelfth Century

I AM going to translate an anecdote from the Provençal manuscripts. The facts, of which you are going to read, happened about the year 1180 and the history was written about 1250.[2] The anecdote, to be sure, is very well known: the style especially gives the color of the society which produced it.

[1] See *The State of the Military Power of Russia*, a truthful work by General Sir Robert Wilson.

[2] The manuscript is in the Laurentian Library. M. Raynouard gives it in Vol. V of his *Troubadours*, p. 187. There are a good many faults in his text; he has praised the Troubadours too much and understood them too little.

I beg that I be allowed to translate it word for word, and without seeking in any way after the elegance of the language of to-day:

"My Lord Raymond of Roussillon was a valiant baron, as you know, and he took to wife my Lady Marguerite, the most beautiful woman of all her time and one of the most endowed with all good qualities, with all worth and with all courtesy. Now it happened that William of Cabstaing came to the Court of my Lord Raymond of Roussillon, presented himself to him and begged, if it so pleased him, that he might be a page in his Court. My Lord Raymond, who saw that he was fair and of good grace, told him that he was welcome and that he might dwell at his Court. Thus William dwelt with him, and succeeded in bearing himself so gently that great and small loved him; and he succeeded in placing himself in so good a light that my Lord Raymond wished him to be page to my Lady Marguerite, his wife; and so it was. Then William set himself to merit yet more both in word and deed. But now, as is wont to happen in love, it happened that Love wished to take hold of my Lady Marguerite and to inflame her thoughts. So much did the person of William please her, both his word and his air, that one day she could not restrain herself from saying to him: 'Now listen, William, if a woman showed you likelihood of love, tell me would you dare love her well?' 'Yes, that I would, madam, provided only that the likelihood were the truth' — 'By S. John,' said the lady, 'you have answered well, like a man of valor; but at present I wish to try you, whether you can understand and distinguish in matter of likelihood the difference between what is true and what is not.'

"When William heard these words he answered: 'My lady, it is as it shall please you.'

"He began to be pensive, and at once Love sought war with him; and the thoughts that love mingled with his entered into the depth of his heart, and straightway he was of the servants of Love and began to 'find'[1] little couplets, gracious and gay, and tunes for the dance and tunes with sweet words,[2] by which he was well received, and the more so by reason of her for whom he sang. Now Love, that grants to his servants their reward, when he pleases, wished to grant William the price of his; and behold, he began to take hold of the lady with such keen thoughts and meditations on love that neither night nor day could she rest, thinking of the valor and prowess that had been so beautifully disposed and set in William.

"One day it happened that the lady took William and said to him: 'William, come now, tell me, have you up to this hour taken note of our likelihood, whether it truly is or lies?' William answered: 'My lady, so help me God, from that moment onward that I have been your servant, no thought has been able to enter my heart but that you were the best woman that was ever born, and the truest in the world and the most likely. So I think, and shall think, all my life.' And the lady answered: 'William, I tell you that, if God help me, you shall never be deceived by me, and that what you think shall not prove vain or nothing.' And she opened her arms and kissed him softly in the room where they two sat together, and they began their *druerie*;[3] and straightway there wanted not those, whom God holds in wrath, who set themselves to talk and gossip of their love, by reason of the songs that William made, saying that he had set his love on my Lady Marguerite, and so indiscriminately did they talk that the matter came to the ears of my Lord Raymond. Then he was sorely pained and grievously sad, first that he must lose his familiar squire, whom he loved so well, and more still for his wife's shame.

"One day it happened that William went out to hunt with his hawks and a single squire; and my Lord Raymond made inquiry where he was; and a groom answered him

---

[1] i.e. to compose.

[2] He made up both the airs and the words.

[3] *A far all' amore.*

that he had gone out to hawk, and one who knew added that it was in such-and-such a spot. Immediately Raymond took arms, which he hid, and had his horse brought to him, and all alone took his way towards the spot whither William had gone: by dint of hard riding he found him. When William saw him approach he was greatly astonished, and at once evil thoughts came to him, and he advanced to meet him and said: 'My lord, welcome. Why are you thus alone?' My Lord Raymond answered: 'William, because I have come to find you to enjoy myself with you. Have you caught anything?' — 'I have caught nothing, my lord, because I have found nothing; and he who finds little will not catch much, as the saying goes.' — 'Enough of this talk,' said my Lord Raymond, 'and by the faith you owe me, tell me the truth on all the questions that I may wish to ask.' — 'By God, my lord,' said William, 'if there is aught to say, certainly to you shall I say it.' Then said my Lord Raymond: 'I wish for no subtleties here, but you must answer me in all fullness on everything that I shall ask you.' — 'My lord, as it shall please you to ask,' said William, 'so shall I tell you the truth.' And my Lord Raymond asked: 'William, as you value God and the holy faith, have you a mistress for whom you sing and for whom Love constrains you?' William answered: 'My lord, and how else should I be singing, if Love did not urge me on? Know the truth, my lord, that Love has me wholly in his power.' Raymond answered: 'I can well believe it, for otherwise you could not sing so well; but I wish to know, if you please, who is your lady.' — 'Ah, my lord, in God's name,' said William, 'see what you ask me. You know too well that a man must not name his lady, and that Bernard of Ventadour says: —

> " ' In one thing my reason serves me,[1]
> That never man has asked me of my joy,
> But I have lied to him thereof willingly.
> For this does not seem to me good doctrine,
> But rather folly or a child's act,

[1] Word for word translation of the Provençal verses quoted by William.

That whoever is well treated in love
Should wish to open his heart thereon to another man,
Unless he can serve him or help him.'

"My Lord Raymond answered: 'And I give you my word
that I will serve you according to my power.' So said Raymond, and William answered him: 'My lord, you must
know that I love the sister of my Lady Marguerite, your
wife, and that I believe I have exchange with her of love.
Now that you know it, I beg you to come to my aid and at
least not to prejudice me.' — 'Take my word,' said Raymond, 'for I swear to you and engage myself to you that I
will use all my power for you.' And then he gave his word,
and when he had given it to him Raymond said to him:
'I wish us to go to her castle, for it is near by.' — 'And I beg
we may do so, in God's name,' said William. And so they
took their road towards the castle of Liet. And when they
came to the castle they were well received by *En*[1] Robert
of Tarascon, who was the husband of my Lady Agnes, the
sister of my Lady Marguerite, and by my Lady Agnes herself. And my Lord Raymond took my Lady Agnes by the
hand and led her into her chamber, and they sat down on
the bed. And my Lord Raymond said: 'Now tell me, my
sister-in-law, by the faith that you owe me, are you in love
with Love?' And she said: 'Yes, my lord.' — 'And whose?'
said he. 'Oh, that I do not tell you,' answered she; 'what
means this parleying?'

"In the end, so insistently did he demand that she said
that she loved William of Cabstaing; this she said because
she saw William sad and pensive and she knew well that he
loved her sister; and so she feared that Raymond might have
had evil thoughts of William. Such a reply gave great joy
to Raymond. Agnes related it all to her husband, and her
husband answered her that she had done well and gave her
his word that she was at liberty to do and say anything that
could save William. Agnes was not wanting to him. She
called William all alone into her chamber, and remained

[1] *En*, a form of speech among the Provençals, which we would translate by *Sir*.

so long with him that Raymond thought he must have had
the pleasures of love with her; and all this pleased him, and
he began to think that what he had been told of William
was untrue and random talk. Agnes and William came out
of her chamber, supper was prepared and they supped with
great gaiety. And after supper Agnes had the bed of her
two neighbors prepared by the door of her chamber, and so
well did the Lady and William act their parts that Raymond believed he was with her.

"And the next day they dined in the castle with great joy,
and after dinner they set out with all the honors of a noble
leave-taking, and came to Roussillon. And as soon as Raymond could, he separated from William and went away to
his wife, and related to her all that he had seen of William
and her sister, for which his wife was sorely grieved all night.
And the next day she had William summoned to her and
received him ill, calling him false friend and traitor. And
William cried to her for pity, as a man who had done nought
of that with which she charged him, and related to her all
that had passed, word for word. And the lady sent for her
sister and from her she learned that William had done no
wrong. And therefore she called him and bade him make a
song by which he should show that he loved no woman but
her, and then he made the song which says: —

> "The sweet thoughts
> That Love often gives me.

"And when Raymond of Roussillon heard the song that
William had made for his wife, he made him come to speak
with him some way from the castle, and cut off his head,
which he put in a bag; he drew out the heart from the body
and put it with the head. He went back to the castle; he had
the heart roasted and brought to his wife at table and made
her eat it without her knowing. When she had eaten it,
Raymond rose up and told his wife that what she had just
eaten was the heart of Lord William of Cabstaing, and
showed her his head and asked her if the heart had been
good to eat. And she heard what he said, and saw and recog-

nized the head of Lord William. She answered him and said that the heart had been so good and savory, that never other meat or other drink could take away from her mouth the taste that the heart of Lord William had left there. And Raymond ran at her with a sword. She took to flight, threw herself down from a balcony and broke her head.

"This became known through all Catalonia and through all the lands of the King of Aragon. King Alphonse and all the barons of these countries had great grief and sorrow for the death of Lord William and of the woman whom Raymond had so basely done to death. They made war on him with fire and sword. King Alphonse of Aragon having taken Raymond's castle, had William and his lady laid in a monument before the door of a church in a borough named Perpignac. All perfect lovers of either sex prayed God for their souls. The King of Aragon took Raymond and let him die in prison, and gave all his goods to the relatives of William and to the relatives of the woman who died for him."

Arabia

'TIS beneath the dusky tent of the Bedouin Arab that we seek the model and the home of true love. There, as elsewhere, solitude and a fine climate have kindled the noblest passion of the human heart — that passion which must give as much happiness as it feels, in order to be happy itself.

In order that love may be seen in all the fullness of its power over the human heart, equality must be established as far as possible between the mistress and her lover. It does not exist, this equality, in our poor West; a woman deserted is unhappy or dishonored. Under the Arab's tent faith once plighted cannot be broken. Contempt and death immediately follow that crime.

Generosity is held so sacred by this people, that you may

steal, in order to give. For the rest, every day danger stares them in the face, and life flows on ever, so to speak, in a passionate solitude. Even in company the Arabs speak little.

Nothing changes for the inhabitant of the desert; there everything is eternal and motionless. This singular mode of life, of which, owing to my ignorance, I can give but a poor sketch, has probably existed since the time of Homer.[1] It is described for the first time about the year 600 of our era, two centuries before Charlemagne.

Clearly it is we who were the barbarians in the eyes of the East, when we went to trouble them with our crusades.[2] Also we owe all that is in our manners to these crusades and to the Moors of Spain. If we compare ourselves with the Arab, that proud, prosaic man will smile with pity. Our arts are very much superior to theirs, our systems of law to all appearance still more superior. But I doubt if we beat them in the art of domestic happiness — we have always lacked loyalty and simplicity. In family relations the deceiver is the first to suffer. For him the feeling of safety is departed; always unjust, he is always afraid.

In the earliest of their oldest historical monuments we can see the Arabs divided from all antiquity into a large number of independent tribes, wandering about the desert. As soon as these tribes were able to supply, with more or less ease, the simplest human wants, their way of life was already more or less refined. Generosity was the same on every side; only according to the tribe's degree of wealth it found expression, now in the quarter of goat's flesh necessary for the support of life, now in the gift of a hundred camels, occasioned by some family connection or reasons of hospitality.

The heroic age of the Arabs, that in which these generous hearts burned unsullied by any affectation of fine wit or refined sentiment, was that which preceded Mohammed; it corresponds to the fifth century of our era, to the founda-

[1] Nine hundred years before Jesus Christ.

[2] 1095.

tions of Venice and to the reign of Clovis. I beg European pride to compare the Arab love-songs, which have come down to us, and the noble system of life revealed in the *Thousand and One Nights*, with the disgusting horrors that stain every page of Gregory of Tours, the historian of Clovis, and of Eginhard, the historian of Charlemagne.

Mohammed was a puritan; he wished to proscribe pleasures which do no one any harm; he has killed love in those countries which have accepted Islamism.[1] It is for this reason that his religion has always been less observed in Arabia, its cradle, than in all the other Mohammedan countries.

The French brought away from Egypt four folio volumes, entitled *The Book of Songs*. These volumes contain: —

1. Biographies of the poets who composed the songs.

2. The songs themselves. In them the poet sings of everything that interests him; when he has spoken of his mistress he praises his swift coursers and his bow. These songs were often love-letters from their author, giving the object of his love a faithful picture of all that passed in his heart. Sometimes they tell of cold nights when he has been obliged to burn his bow and arrows. The Arabs are a nation without houses.

3. Biographies of the musicians who have composed the music for these songs.

4. Finally, the notation of the musical setting; for us these settings are hieroglyphics. The music will be for ever unknown, and anyhow, it would not please us.

There is another collection entitled *The History of those Arabs who have died for Love*.

In order to feel at home in the midst of remains which owe so much of their interest to their antiquity, and to appreciate the singular beauty of the manners of which they let us catch a glimpse, we must go to history for enlightenment on certain points.

From all time, and especially before Mohammed, the

---

[1] Morals of Constantinople. The one way of killing passion-love is to prevent all crystallization by facility.

Arabs betook themselves to Mecca in order to make the tour of the Caaba or house of Abraham. I have seen at London a very exact model of the Holy City. There are seven or eight hundred houses with terraces on the roofs, set in the midst of a sandy desert devoured by the sun. At one extremity of the city is found an immense building, in form almost a square; this building surrounds the Caaba. It is composed of a long course of colonnades, necessary under an Arabian sun for the performance of the sacred procession. This colonnade is very important in the history of the manners and poetry of the Arabs; it was apparently for centuries the one place where men and women met together. Pell-mell, with slow steps, and reciting in chorus their sacred songs, they walked round the Caaba — it is a walk of three-quarters of an hour. The procession was repeated many times in the same day; this was the sacred rite for which men and women came forth from all parts of the desert. It is under the colonnade of the Caaba that Arab manners became polished. A contest between the father and the lover soon came to be established — in love-lyrics the lover discovered his passion to the girl, jealously guarded by brothers and father, as at her side he walked in the sacred procession. The generous and sentimental habits of this people existed already in the camp; but Arab gallantry seems to me to have been born in the shadow of the Caaba, which is also the home of their literature. At first, passion was expressed with simplicity and vehemence, just as the poet felt it; later the poet, instead of seeking to touch his mistress, aimed at fine writing; then followed that affectation which the Moors introduced into Spain and which still to-day spoils the books of that people.[1]

I find a touching proof of the Arab's respect for the weaker sex in his ceremony of divorce. The woman, during the absence of her husband from whom she wished to separate, opened the tent and drew it up, taking care to

[1] There are a large number of Arabic manuscripts at Paris. Those of a later date show some affectation, but no imitation of the Greeks or Romans; it is this that makes scholars despise them.

place the opening on the opposite side to that which she had formerly occupied. This simple ceremony separated husband and wife for ever.

FRAGMENTS

Gathered and translated from an Arabic Collection entitled:

THE DIVAN OF LOVE

Compiled by Ebn-Abi-Hadglat

(Manuscripts of the King's Library, Nos. 1461 and 1462)

MOHAMMED, son of Djaafar Elahouazadi, relates that Djamil being sick of the illness of which he died, Elabas, son of Sohail, visited him and found him ready to give up the ghost. "O son of Sohail," said Djamil to him, "what do you think of a man who has never drunk wine, who has never made illicit gain, who has never unrighteously given death to any living creature that God has forbidden us to kill, and who confesses that there is no other God but Allah and that Mohammed is his prophet?" "I think," answered Ben Sohail, "that such a man will be saved and will gain Paradise; but who is he, this man of whom you talk?" "'Tis I," answered Djamil. "I did not think that you professed the faith," returned Ben Sohail, "and moreover, for twenty years now you have been making love to Bothaina, and celebrating her in your verses." "Here I am," answered Djamil, "at my first day in the other world and at my last in this, and I pray that the mercy of our Master Mohammed may not be extended to me at the day of judgment, if ever I have laid hands on Bothaina for anything reprehensible."

This Djamil and Bothaina, his mistress, both belonged to the Benou-Azra, who are a tribe famous in love among all the tribes of the Arabs. Also their manner of loving has passed into a proverb, and God has made no other creatures as tender in love as they.

Sahid, son of Agba, one day asked an Arab: "Of what people are you?" "I am of the people that die when they love," replied the Arab. "Then you are of the tribe of

Azra," added Sahid. "Yes, by the Master of the Caaba," replied the Arab. "Whence comes it that you love in this manner?" Sahid asked next. "Our women are beautiful and our young men are chaste," answered the Arab.

One day someone asked Aroua-Ben-Hezam:[1] "Is it really true what people tell of you, that you of all mankind have the heart most tender in love?" "Yes, by Allah, it is true," answered Aroua, "and I have known in my tribe thirty young men whom death has carried off and who had no other sickness but love."

An Arab of the Benou-Fazarat said one day to an Arab of the Benou-Azra: "You, Benou-Azra, you think it a sweet and noble death to die of love; but therein is a manifest weakness and stupidity; and those whom you take for men of great heart are only madmen and soft creatures." "You would not talk like that," the Arab of the tribe of Azra answered him, "if you had seen the great black eyes of our women darting fire from beneath the veil of their long lashes, if you had seen them smile and their teeth gleaming between their brown lips!"

Abou-el-Hassan, Ali, son of Abdalla, Elzagouni, relates the following story: A Mussulman loved to distraction the daughter of a Christian. He was obliged to make a journey to a foreign country with a friend, to whom he had confided his love. His business prolonged his stay in this country, and being attacked there by a mortal sickness, he said to his friend: "Behold, my time approaches; no more in the world shall I meet her whom I love, and I fear, if I die a Mussulman, that I shall not meet her again in the other life." He turned Christian and died. His friend betook himself to the young Christian woman, whom he found sick. She said to him: "I shall not see my friend any more in this world, but I want to be with him in the other; therefore I confess that there is no other God but Allah, and that Mohammed is

---

[1] This Aroua-Ben-Hezam was of the tribe of Azra, of which mention has just been made. He is celebrated as a poet, and still more celebrated as one of the numerous martyrs to love whom the Arabs enumerate.

the prophet of God." Thereupon she died, and may God's mercy be upon her.

Eltemimi relates that there was in the tribe of the Arabs of Tagleb a Christian girl of great riches who was in love with a young Mussulman. She offered him her fortune and all her treasures without succeeding in making him love her. When she had lost all hope she gave an artist a hundred dinars, to make her a statue of the young man she loved. The artist made the statue, and when the girl got it, she placed it in a certain spot where she went every day. There she would begin by kissing this statue, and then sat down beside it and spent the rest of the day in weeping. When the evening came she would bow to the statue and retire. This she did for a long time. The young man chanced to die; she desired to see him and to embrace him dead, after which she returned to her statue, bowed to it, kissed it as usual, and lay down beside it. When day came, they found her dead, stretching out her hand towards some lines of writing, which she had written before she died.

Oueddah, of the land of Yamen, was renowned among the Arabs for his beauty. He and Om-el-Bonain, daughter of Abd-el-Aziz, son of Merouan, while still only children, were even then so much in love that they could not bear to be parted from each other for a moment. When Om-el-Bonain became the wife of Oualid-Ben-Abd-el-Malek, Oueddah became mad for grief. After remaining a long time in a state of distraction and suffering, he betook himself to Syria and began every day to prowl around the house of Oualid, son of Malek, without at first finding the means to attain his desire. In the end, he made the acquaintance of a girl, whom he succeeded in attaching to himself by dint of his perseverance and his pains. When he thought he could rely on her, he asked her if she knew Om-el-Bonain. "To be sure I do," answered the girl, "seeing she is my mistress." "Listen," continued Oueddah, "your mistress is my cousin, and if you care to tell her about me, you will certainly give her pleasure." "I'll tell her willingly," answered the girl.

And thereupon she ran straight to Om-el-Bonain to tell her about Oueddah. "Take care what you say," cried Om-el-Bonain. "What? Oueddah is alive?" "Certainly he is," said the girl. Om-el-Bonain went on, "Go and tell him, on no account to depart until a messenger comes to him from me." Then she took measures to get Oueddah brought to her, where she kept him hidden in a coffer. She let him come out to be with her when she thought it safe; but if someone arrived who might have seen him, she made him get inside the coffer again.

It happened one day that a pearl was brought to Oualid and he said to one of his attendants: "Take this pearl and give it to Om-el-Bonain." The attendant took the pearl and gave it to Om-el-Bonain. As he was not announced, he entered where she dwelt at a time when she was with Oueddah, and thus he was able to throw a glance into Om-el-Bonain's apartment without her noticing him. Oulaid's attendant fulfilled his mission and asked something of Om-el-Bonain for the jewel he had brought her. She refused him with severity and reprimanded him. The attendant went out incensed against her, and went to tell Oualid what he had seen, describing the coffer into which he had seen Oueddah enter. "You lie, bastard slave! You lie," said Oualid. And he ran in haste to Om-el-Bonain. There were several coffers in her apartment; he sat down on the one in which Oueddah was hid and which the slave had described, saying: "Give me one of these coffers." "They are all yours, as much as I myself," answered Om-el-Bonain. "Then," continued Oualid, "I would like to have the one on which I am seated." "There are some things in it that only a woman needs," said Om-el-Bonain. "It is not them, it is the coffer I desire," added Oualid. "It is yours," she answered. Oualid had the coffer taken away at once, and summoned two slaves, whom he ordered to dig a pit in the earth down to the depth where they would find water. Then placing his mouth against the coffer: "I have heard something of you," he cried. "If I have heard the truth, may all trace of you be lost, may all memory of you be buried. If they have told me false I do no harm by entombing a coffer: it is only the funeral of a box." Then he had the coffer pushed into the pit and covered with the stones and the earth which had been dug up. From that time Om-el-Bonain never ceased to frequent this spot and to weep, until one day they found her there lifeless, her face pressed towards the earth.[1]

Of the Education of Women

IN the actual education of girls, which is the fruit of chance and the most idiotic pride, we allow their most shining faculties, and those most fertile in happiness for themselves and for us, to lie fallow. But what man is there, who at least once in his life has not exclaimed: —

> ... a woman always knows enough
> If but her range of understanding reaches
> To telling one from t'other, coat and breeches.
> (*Les Femmes Savantes*, Act II, Scene VII)

At Paris, this is the highest praise for a young girl of a marriageable age: "There is so much that's sweet in her character, and she's as gentle as a lamb." Nothing has more effect on the idiots looking out for wives. But see them two years later, lunching *tête-à-tête* with their wives some dull day, hats on and surrounded by three great lackeys!

We have seen a law carried in the United States, in 1818, which condemns to thirty-four strokes of the cat anyone teaching a Virginian negro to read.[2] Nothing could be more consequent and more reasonable than a law of this kind.

Were the United States of America themselves more use-

---

[1] These fragments are taken from different chapters of the collection which I have mentioned.

[2] I regret to be unable to find in the Italian manuscript the quotation of an official source for this fact; I hope it may be found possible to deny it.

ful to the motherland when they were her slaves or since they have become her equals? If the work of a free man is worth two or three times that of a man reduced to slavery, why should not the same be true of that man's thought?

If we dared, we would give girls the education of a slave; and the proof of this is that if they know anything useful, it is against our wish we teach it them.

"But they turn against us the little education which unhappily they get hold of," some husbands might say. No doubt; and Napoleon was also quite right not to give arms to the National Guard; and the reactionaries are also quite right to proscribe the monitorial system. Arm a man, and then continue to oppress him, and you will see that he can be so perverse as to turn his arms against you, as soon as he can.

Even if it were permissible to bring girls up like idiots, on *Ave Marias* and lewd songs, as they did in the convents of 1770, there would still be several little objections: —

1. In the case of the husband's death, they are called upon to manage the young family.

2. As mothers, they give their male children, the young tyrants of the future, their first education, that education which forms the character, and accustoms the soul to seek happiness by this route rather than by that — and the choice is always an accomplished fact by four or five.

3. In spite of all our pride, the advice of the inevitable partner of our whole life has great influence on those domestic affairs on which our happiness depends so particularly; for, in the absence of passion, happiness is based on the absence of small everyday vexations. Not that we would willingly accord this advice the least influence, but she may repeat the same thing to us for twenty years together. Whose is the spirit of such Roman fortitude as to resist the same idea repeated throughout a whole lifetime? The world is full of husbands who let themselves be led, but it is from weakness and not from a feeling for justice and equality. As they yield perforce, the wife is always tempted to abuse

her power, and it is sometimes necessary to abuse power in order to keep it.

4. Finally, in love, and during a period which, in southern countries, often comprises twelve or fifteen years, and those the fairest of our life, our happiness is entirely in the hands of the woman we love. One moment of untimely pride can make us for ever miserable, and how should a slave raised up to a throne not be tempted to abuse her power? This is the origin of women's false refinement and pride. Of course, there is nothing more useless than these pleas: men are despots and we see what respect other despots show to the wisest counsels. A man who is all-powerful relishes only one sort of advice, the advice of those that tell him to increase his power. Where are poor young girls to find a Quiroga or a Riego to give the despots, who oppress them, and degrade them the better to oppress them, that salutary advice, whose just recompense are favors and orders instead of Porlier's gallows?

If a revolution of this kind needs several centuries, it is because, by a most unlucky chance, all our first experiences must necessarily contradict the truth. Illuminate a girl's mind, form her character, give her, in short, a good education in the true sense of the word — remarking sooner or later her own superiority over other women, she becomes a pedant, that is to say, the most unpleasant and the most degraded creature that there is in the world. There isn't one of us who wouldn't prefer a servant to a *savante*, if we had to pass our life with her.

Plant a young tree in the midst of a dense forest, deprived of air and sun by the closeness of the neighboring trees: its leaves will be blighted, and it will get an overgrown and ridiculous shape — *not* its natural shape. We ought to plant the whole forest at once. What woman is there who is proud of knowing how to read?

Pedants have repeated to us for two thousand years that women were more quick and men more judicious, women more remarkable for delicacy of expression and men for stronger powers of concentration. A Parisian simpleton, who used once upon a time to take his walk in the gardens of Versailles, similarly concluded from all he saw that trees grow ready clipped.

I will allow that little girls have less physical strength than little boys: this must be conclusive as regards intellect; for everyone knows that Voltaire and d'Alembert were the first boxers of their age! Everyone agrees, that a little girl of ten is twenty times as refined as a little boy of the same age. Why, at twenty, is she a great idiot, awkward, timid, and afraid of a spider, while the little boy is a man of intellect?

Women only learn the things we do not wish to teach them, and only read the lessons taught them by experience of life. Hence the extreme disadvantage it is for them to be born in a very rich family; instead of coming into contact with beings who behave naturally to them, they find themselves surrounded by maidservants and governesses, who are already corrupted and blighted by wealth.[1] There is nothing so foolish as a prince.

Young girls soon see that they are slaves and begin to look about them very early; they see everything, but they are too ignorant to see properly. A woman of thirty in France has not the acquired knowledge of a small boy of fifteen, a woman of fifty has not the reason of a man of twenty-five. Look at Madame de Sévigné admiring Louis XIV's most ridiculous actions. Look at the puerility of Madame d'Epinay's reasonings.[2]

"Women ought to nurse and look after their children." I deny the first proposition, I allow the second. "They ought, moreover, to keep their kitchen accounts." — And so have not time to equal a small boy of fifteen in acquired knowledge! Men must be judges, bankers, barristers, merchants, doctors, clergymen, etc., and yet they find time to read Fox's speeches and the *Lusiad* of Camoëns.

[1] Memoirs of Madame de Staël, Collé, Duclos, the Margrave of Bayreuth.
[2] The first volume.

The Pekin magistrate, who hastens at an early hour to the law courts in order to find the means of imprisoning and ruining, in perfect good faith, a poor journalist who has incurred the displeasure of an Under-Secretary of State, with whom he had the honor of dining the day before, is surely as busy as his wife, who keeps her kitchen accounts, gets stockings made for her little daughter, sees her through her dancing and piano lessons, receives a visit from the vicar of the parish who brings her the *Quotidienne*, and then goes to choose a hat in the Rue de Richelieu and take a turn in the Tuileries.

In the midst of his noble occupations this magistrate still finds time to think of this walk his wife is taking in the Tuileries, and, if he were in as good odor with the Power that rules the universe as with that which rules the State, he would pray Heaven to grant women, for their own good, eight or ten hours more sleep. In the present condition of society, leisure, which for man is the source of all his happiness and all his riches, is for women so far from being an advantage as to rank among those baneful liberties, from which the worthy magistrate would wish to help deliver us.

Objections to the Education of Women

"BUT women are charged with the petty labors of the household." The Colonel of my regiment, M. S——, has four daughters, brought up on the best principles, which means that they work all day. When I come, they sing the music of Rossini, that I brought them from Naples. For the rest, they read the Bible of Royaumont, they learn what's most foolish in history, that is to say, chronological tables and the verses of Le Ragois; they know a great deal of geography, embroider admirably — and I expect that each of these pretty little girls could earn, by her work, eight sous a day. Taking three hundred days, that means four hundred and eighty francs a year, which is less than is given to one of their masters. It is for four hundred and eighty francs a year that they lose for ever the time, during which it is granted to the human machine to acquire ideas.

"If women read with pleasure the ten or twelve good volumes that appear every year in Europe, they will soon give up the care of their children." — 'Tis as if we feared, by planting the shore of the ocean with trees, to stop the motion of the waves. It is not in this sense that education is all-powerful. Besides, for four hundred years the same objection has been offered to every sort of education. And yet a Parisian woman has more good qualities in 1820 than she ever had in 1720, the age of Law's system and the Regency, and at that time the daughter of the richest farmer-general had a less good education than the daughter of the pettiest attorney gets to-day. Are her household duties less well performed as a result? Certainly not. And why? Because poverty, illness, shame, instinct, all force her to fulfil them. It is as if you said of an officer who is becoming too sociable, that he will forget how to handle his horse; you have to remember that he'll break his arm the first time he's slack in the saddle.

Knowledge, where it produces any bad effects at all, does as much mischief to one sex as to the other. We shall never lack vanity, even in the completest absence of any reason for having it — look at the middle class in a small town. Why not force it at least to repose on real merit, on merit useful or agreeable to society?

Demi-fools, carried away by the revolution that is changing everything in France, began twenty years ago to allow that women are capable of something. But they must give themselves up to occupations becoming their sex: *educate flowers, make friendships with birds, and pick up plants.* These are called innocent amusements.

These innocent pleasures are better than idleness. Well! let's leave them to stupid women; just as we leave to stupid men the glory of composing verses for the birthday of the master of the house. But do men in good faith really mean

to suggest to Madame Roland or to Mistress Hutchinson[1] that they should spend their time in tending a little Bengal rose-bush?

All such reasoning can be reduced to this: a man likes to be able to say of his slave: "She's too big a fool to be a knave."

But owing to a certain law called *sympathy* — a law of nature which, in truth, vulgar eyes never perceive — the defects in the companion of your life are not destructive of your happiness by reason only of the direct ill they can occasion you. I would almost prefer that my wife should, in a moment of anger, attempt to stab me once a year, than that she should welcome me every evening with bad spirits.

Finally, happiness is contagious among people who live together.

Let your mistress have passed the morning, while you were on parade or at the House of Commons, in painting a rose after a masterpiece of Redouté, or in reading a volume of Shakespeare, her pleasure therein will have been equally innocent. Only, with the ideas that she has got from her rose she will soon bore you on your return, and, indeed, she will crave to go out in the evening among people to seek sensations a little more lively.

Suppose, on the contrary, she has read Shakespeare, she is as tired as you are, she has had as much pleasure, and she will be happier to give you her arm for a solitary walk in the Bois de Vincennes than to appear at the smartest party. The pleasures of the fashionable world are not meant for happy women.

Women have, of course, all ignorant men for enemies to their instruction. To-day they spend their time with them, they make love to them and are well received by them; what would become of them if women began to get tired of Boston? When we return from America or the West Indies with a tanned skin and manners that for six months remain somewhat coarse, how would these fellows answer

[1] See the Memoirs of these admirable women. I could find other names to quote, but they are unknown to the public, and moreover one cannot even point to living merit.

our stories, if they had not this phrase: "As for us, the women are on our side. While you were at New York the color of tilburies has changed; it's grey-black that's fashionable at present." And we listen attentively, for such knowledge is useful. Such and such a pretty woman will not look at us if our carriage is in bad taste.

These same fools, who think themselves obliged, in virtue of the pre-eminence of their sex, to have more knowledge than women, would be ruined past all hope, if women had the audacity to learn something. A fool of thirty says to himself, as he looks at some little girls of twelve at the country house of one of his friends: "It's in their company that I shall spend my life ten years from now." We can imagine his exclamations and his terror, if he saw them studying something useful.

Instead of the society and conversation of effeminate men, an educated woman, if she has acquired ideas without losing the graces of her sex, can always be sure of finding among the most distinguished men of her age a consideration verging on enthusiasm.

"Women would become the rivals instead of the companions of man." Yes, as soon as you have suppressed love by edict. While we are waiting for this fine law, love will redouble its charms and its ecstasy. These are the plain facts: the basis on which crystallization rests will be widened; a man will be able to take pleasure in all his ideas in company of the woman he loves; nature in all its entirety will in their eyes receive new charms; and as ideas always reflect some of the refinements of character, they will understand each other better and will be guilty of fewer imprudent acts — love will be less blind and will produce less unhappiness.

The *desire of pleasing secures all that delicacy and reserve which are of such inestimable value to women* from the influence of any scheme of education. 'Tis as though you feared teaching the nightingales not to sing in the spring-time.

The graces of women do not depend on their ignorance; look at the worthy spouses of our village bourgeois, look at the wives of the opulent merchants in England. Affectation is a kind of pedantry; for I call pedantry the affectation of letting myself talk out of season of a dress by Leroy or a novel by Romagnesi, just as much as the affectation of quoting Fra Paolo and the Council of Trent *à propos* of a discussion on our own mild missionaries. It is the pedantry of dress and good form, it is the necessity of saying exactly the conventional phrase about Rossini, which kills the graces of Parisian women. Nevertheless, in spite of the terrible effects of this contagious malady, is it not in Paris that exist the most delightful women in France? Would not the reason be that chance filled their heads with the most just and interesting ideas? Well, it is these very ideas that I expect from books. I shall not, of course, suggest that they read Grotius of Puffendorf, now that we have Tracy's commentary on Montesquieu.

Woman's delicacy depends on the hazardous position in which she finds herself so early placed, on the necessity of spending her life in the midst of cruel and fascinating enemies.

There are, perhaps, fifty thousand females in Great Britain who are exempted by circumstances from all necessary labor: but without work there is no happiness. Passion forces itself to work, and to work of an exceedingly rough kind — work that employs the whole activity of one's being.

A woman with four children and ten thousand francs income works by making stockings or a frock for her daughter. But it cannot be allowed that a woman who has her own carriage is working when she does her embroidery or a piece of tapestry. Apart from some faint glow of vanity, she cannot possibly have any interest in what she is doing. She does not work.

And thus her happiness runs a grave risk.

And what is more, so does the happiness of her lord and master, for a woman whose heart for two months has been enlivened by no other interest than that of her needlework, may be so insolent as to imagine that gallant-love, vanity-love, or, in fine, even physical love, is a very great happiness in comparison with her habitual condition.

"A woman ought not to make people speak about her." To which I answer once more: "Is any woman specially mentioned as being able to read?"

And what is to prevent women, while awaiting a revolution in their destiny, from hiding a study which forms their habitual occupation and furnishes them every day with an honorable share of happiness. I will reveal a secret to them by the way. When you have given yourself a task — for example, to get a clear idea about the conspiracy of Fiescho, at Genoa in 1547 — the most insipid book becomes interesting. The same is true, in love, of meeting someone quite indifferent, who has just seen the person whom you love. This interest is doubled every month, until you give up the conspiracy of Fiescho.

"The true theatre for a woman is the sick-chamber." But you must be careful to secure that the divine goodness redoubles the frequency of illnesses, in order to give occupation to our women. This is arguing from the exceptional.

Moreover, I maintain that a woman ought to spend three or four hours of leisure every day, just as men of sense spend their hours of leisure.

A young mother, whose little son has the measles, could not, even if she would, find pleasure in reading Volney's *Travels in Syria,* any more than her husband, a rich banker, could get pleasure out of meditating on Malthus in the midst of bankruptcy.

There is one, and only one, way for rich women to distinguish themselves from the vulgar: moral superiority. For in this there is a natural distinction of feeling.[1]

"We do not wish a lady to write books." No, but does giving your daughter a singing-master engage you to make

[1] See Mistress Hutchinson refusing to be of use to her family and her husband, whom she adored, by betraying certain of the regicides to the ministers of the perjured Charles II. (Vol. II, p. 284)

her into an opera-singer? If you like, I'll say that a woman ought only to write, like Madame de Staël (de Launay), posthumous works to be published after her death. For a woman of less than fifty to publish is to risk her happiness in the most terrible lottery: if she has the good fortune to have a lover, she will begin by losing him.

I know but one exception: it is that of a woman who writes books in order to keep or bring up her family. In that case she ought always to confine herself to their money-value when talking of her own works, and say, for example, to a cavalry major: "Your rank gives you four thousand francs a year, and I, with my two translations from the English, was able last year to devote an extra three thousand five hundred francs to the education of my two boys."

Otherwise, a woman should publish as Baron d'Holbach or Madame de la Fayette did; their best friends knew nothing of it. To print a book can only be without inconvenience for a courtesan; the vulgar, who can despise her at their will for her condition, will exalt her to the heavens for her talent, and even make a cult of it.

Many men in France, among those who have an income of six thousand francs, find their habitual source of happiness in literature, without thinking of publishing anything; to read a good book is for them one of the greatest pleasures. At the end of ten years they find that their mind is enlarged twofold, and no one will deny that, in general, the larger the mind the fewer will be its passions incompatible with the happiness of others.[1] I don't suppose anyone will still deny that the sons of a woman who reads Gibbon and Schiller will have more genius than the children of one who tells her beads and reads Madame de Genlis.

A young barrister, a merchant, an engineer can be launched on life without any education; they pick it up themselves every day by practicing their profession. But what resources have their wives for acquiring estimable or

[1] It is this that gives me great hopes for the rising generation among the privileged classes. I also hope that any husbands who read this chapter will be milder despots for three days.

necessary qualities? Hidden in the solitude of their house-hold, for them the great book of life necessarily remains shut. They spend always in the same way, after discussing the accounts with their cook, the three *louis* they get every Monday from their husbands.

I say this in the interest of the tyrant: the least of men, if he is twenty and has nice rosy cheeks, is a danger to a woman with no knowledge, because she is wholly a creature of instinct. In the eyes of a woman of intellect he will pro-duce as much effect as a handsome lackey.

The amusing thing in present-day education is that you teach young girls nothing that they won't have to forget as soon as they are married. It needs four hours a day, for six years, to learn to play the harp well; to paint well in minia-ture or water-colors needs half that time. Most young girls do not attain even to a tolerable mediocrity — hence the very true saying: "Amateur means smatterer."[1]

And even supposing a young girl has some talent; three years after she is married she won't take up her harp or her brushes once a month. These objects of so much study now only bore her — unless chance has given her the soul of an artist, and this is always a rarity and scarcely helpful in the management of a household.

And thus under the vain pretext of decency you teach young girls nothing that can give them guidance in the cir-cumstances they will encounter in their lives. You do more — you hide and deny these circumstances in order to add to their strength, through the effect (i) of surprise, and (ii) of mistrust; for education, once found deceitful, must bring mistrust on education as a whole.[2] I maintain that one ought to talk of love to girls who have been well brought up. Who will dare suggest in good faith that, in the actual state of our manners, girls of sixteen do not know of the existence of love? From whom do they get this idea so important and

---

[1] The contrary of this proverb is true in Italy, where the loveliest voices are heard among amateurs who have no connection with the theatre.

[2] The education given to Madame d'Epinay. (*Memoirs*, Vol. I)

so difficult to give properly? Think of Julie d'Etanges deploring the knowledge that she owes to la Chaillot, one of the maidservants. One must thank Rousseau for having dared be a true painter in an age of false decency.

The present-day education of women being perhaps the most delightful absurdity in modern Europe, strictly speaking the less education they have, the better they are.[1] It is for this reason perhaps that in Italy and Spain they are so superior to the men, and I will even say so superior to the women of other countries.

More Objections

IN France all our ideas about women are got from a twopence-halfpenny catechism. The delightful part of it is that many people, who would not allow the authority of this book to regulate a matter of fifty francs, foolishly follow it word for word in that which bears most nearly on their happiness. Such is the vanity of nineteenth-century ways!

There must be no divorce because marriage is a mystery — and what mystery? The emblem of the union of Jesus Christ with the Church. And what had become of this mystery, if the Church had been given a name of the masculine gender?[2] But let us pass over prejudices already giving way,[3]

---

[1] I make an exception as regards education in manners: a woman enters a drawing-room better in Rue Verte than in Rue St. Martin.

[2] Tu es Petrus, and super hanc petram
Ædificabo Ecclesiam meam.
(See M. de Potter, *Histoire de l'Eglise*)

[3] Religion is a matter between each man and the Divinity. By what right do you come and place yourself between my God and me? I accept a proctor appointed by the social contract only in those matters which I cannot do myself.

Why should not a Frenchman pay his priest like his baker? If we have good bread in Paris, the reason is that the State has not yet ventured to declare the provision of bread gratuitous and put all the bakers at the charge of the Treasury.

In the United States every man pays his own priest. These gentry are compelled to have some merit, and my neighbor does not see good to make his happiness depend on submitting me to his priest. (Letters of Birkbeck) and let us merely observe this singular spectacle: the root of the tree sapped by the axe of ridicule, but the branches continuing to flower.

Now to return to the observation of facts and their consequences.

In both sexes it is on the manner in which youth has been employed that depends the fate of extreme old age — this is true for women earlier than for men. How is a woman of forty-five received in society? Severely, or more often in a way that is below her dignity. Women are flattered at twenty and abandoned at forty.

A woman of forty-five is of importance only by reason of her children or her lover.

A mother who excels in the fine arts can communicate her talent to her son only in the extremely rare case, where he has received from nature precisely the soul for this talent. But a mother of intellect and culture will give her young son a grasp not only of all merely agreeable talents, but also of all talents that are useful to man in society; and he will be able to make his own choice. The barbarism of the Turks depends in great part on the state of moral degradation among the beautiful Georgians. The young men born at Paris owe to their mothers the incontestable superiority that they show at sixteen over the young provincials of their age. It is from sixteen to twenty-five that the luck turns.

The men who invented gunpowder, printing, the art of weaving, contribute every day to our happiness, and the same is true of the Montesquieus, the Racines and the La Fontaines. Now the number of geniuses produced by a nation is in proportion to the number of men receiving sufficient culture,[1] and there is nothing to prove to me that my bootmaker has not the soul to write like Corneille. He

What will happen if I have the conviction, as our fathers did, that my priest is the intimate ally of my bishop? Without a Luther, there will be no more Catholicism in France in 1850. That religion could only be saved in 1820 by M. Grégoire: see how he is treated.

[1] See the Generals of 1795.

lacks the education necessary to develop his feelings and teach him to communicate them to the public.[1]

Owing to the present system of girls' education, all geniuses who are born women are lost to the public good. So soon as chance gives them the means of displaying themselves, you see them attain to talents the most difficult to acquire. In our own days you see a Catherine II, who had no other education but danger and ... ; a Madame Roland; an Alessandra Mari, who raised a regiment in Arezzo and sent it against the French; a Caroline, Queen of Naples, who knew how to put a stop to the contagion of liberalism better than all our Castlereaghs and our Pitts. As for what stands in the way of women's superiority in works of art, see the chapter on Modesty, article 9. What might Miss Edgeworth not have done, if the circumspection necessary to a young English girl had not forced her at the outset of her career to carry the pulpit into her novel?

What man is there, in love or in marriage, who has the good fortune to be able to communicate his thoughts, just as they occur to him, to the woman with whom he passes his life? He may find a good heart that will share his sorrows, but he is always obliged to turn his thoughts into small change if he wishes to be understood, and it would be ridiculous to expect reasonable counsel from an intellect that has need of such a method in order to seize the facts. The most perfect woman, according to the ideas of present-day education, leaves her partner isolated amid the dangers of life and soon runs the risk of wearying him.

What an excellent counsellor would a man not find in a wife, if only she could think — a counsellor, after all, whose interests, apart from one single object, and one which does not last beyond the morning of life, are exactly identical with his own!

183

[1] As regards the arts, here we have the great defect of a reasonable government as well as the sole reasonable eulogy of monarchy *à la* Louis XIV. Look at the literary sterility of America. Not a single romance like those of Robert Burns or the Spaniards of the thirteenth century. See the admirable romances of the modern Greeks, those of the Spaniards and Danes of the thirteenth century, and still better, the Arabic poetry of the seventh century.

One of the finest prerogatives of the mind is that it provides old age with consideration. See how the arrival of Voltaire in Paris makes the Royal majesty pale. But poor women! so soon as they have no longer the brilliance of youth, their one sad happiness is to be able to delude themselves on the part they take in society.

The ruins of youthful talents become merely ridiculous, and it were a happiness for our women, such as they actually are, to die at fifty. As for a higher morality — the clearer the mind, the surer the conviction that justice is the only road to happiness. Genius is a power; but still more is it a torch, to light the way to the great art of being happy.

Most men have a moment in their life when they are capable of great things — that moment when nothing seems impossible to them. The ignorance of women causes this magnificent chance to be lost to the human race. Love, nowadays, at the very most will make a man a good horseman or teach him to choose his tailor.

I have no time to defend myself against the advances of criticism. If my word could set up systems, I should give girls, as far as possible, exactly the same education as boys. As I have no intention of writing a book about everything and nothing, I shall be excused from explaining in what regards the present education of men is absurd. But taking it such as it is (they are not taught the two premier sciences, logic and ethics), it is better, I say, to give this education to girls than merely to teach them to play the piano, to paint in water-colors and to do needlework.

Teach girls, therefore, reading, writing and arithmetic by the monitorial system in the central convent schools, in which the presence of any man, except the masters, should be severely punished. The great advantage of bringing children together is that, however narrow the masters may be, in spite of them the children learn from their little comrades the art of living in the world and of managing conflicting interests. A sensible master would explain their little quarrels and friendships to the children, and begin his course of ethics in this way rather than with the story of the Golden Calf.[1]

No doubt some years hence the monitorial system will be applied to everything that is learned; but, taking things as they actually are, I would have girls learn Latin like boys. Latin is a good subject because it accustoms one to be bored; with Latin should go history, mathematics, a knowledge of the plants useful as nourishment or medicine; then logic and the moral sciences, etc. Dancing, music and drawing ought to begin at five.

At sixteen a girl ought to think about finding a husband, and get from her mother right ideas on love, marriage, and the want of honesty that exists among men.[2]

On Marriage

THE fidelity of married women, where love is absent, is probably something contrary to nature.[3]

Men have attempted to obtain this unnatural result by the fear of hell and sentiments of religion; the example of Spain and Italy shows how far they have succeeded.

In France they have attempted to obtain it by public opinion — the one dike capable of resistance, yet it has been

---

[1] My dear pupil, your father loves you; this makes him give me forty francs a month to teach you mathematics, drawing — in a word, how to earn your living. If you were cold, because your overcoat was too small, your father would be unhappy. He would be unhappy because he would sympathize, etc., etc. But when you are eighteen, you yourself will have to earn the money needed to buy your overcoat. Your father, I have heard, has an income of twenty-five thousand francs, but there are four of you children; therefore you will have to accustom yourself to do without the carriage you enjoy while you live with your father, etc., etc.

[2] Yesterday evening I listened to two charming little girls of four years old singing very gay love-songs in a swing which I was pushing. The maidservants teach them these songs and their mother tells them that "love" and "lover" are words without any meaning.

[3] Not probably — but certainly. With love there, one has no taste for any water but that of the beloved fount. So far fidelity is natural.

In the case of marriage without love, in less than two years the water of this fountain becomes bitter. Now the desire for water always exists in nature. Habits may conquer nature, but only when it can be conquered in an instant: the Indian wife who burns herself (October 21st, 1821), after the death of the old husband whom she hated; the European girl who barbarously murders the innocent child to whom she has just given life. But for a very high wall the monks would soon leave the monastery.

badly built. It is absurd to tell a young girl: "You must be faithful to the husband of your choice," and then to marry her by force to a boring old dotard.[1]

"But girls are pleased to get married." Because, under the narrow system of present-day education, the slavery that they undergo in their mother's house is intolerably tedious; further, they lack enlightenment; and, lastly, there are the demands of nature. There is but one way to obtain more fidelity among married women: it is to give freedom to girls and divorce to married people.

A woman always loses the fairest days of her youth in her first marriage, and by divorce she gives fools the chance of talking against her.

Young women who have plenty of lovers have nothing to get from divorce, and women of a certain age, who have already had them, hope to repair their reputation — in France they always succeed in doing so — by showing themselves extremely severe against the errors which have left them behind. It is generally some wretched young woman, virtuous and desperately in love, who seeks a divorce, and gets her good name blackened at the hands of women who have had fifty different men.

Of Virtue, So Called

MYSELF, I honor with the name of virtue the habit of doing painful actions which are of use to others.

St. Simon Stylites, who sits twenty-two years on the top of a column beating himself with a strap, is in my eyes, I

[1] Even down to details, with us everything that regards the education of women is comic. For example, in 1820, under the rule of these very nobles who have proscribed divorce, the Home Office sends to the town of Lâon a bust and a statue of Gabrielle d'Estrées. The statue is to be set up in the public square, apparently to spread love of the Bourbons among the young girls and to exhort them, in case of need, not to be cruel to amorous kings and to give scions to this illustrious family.

But, in return, the same office refuses the town of Lâon a bust of Marshal Serrurier, a brave man who was no gallant, and moreover had been so vulgar as to begin his career by the trade of private soldier. (Speech of General Foy, *Courrier* of 17th June, 1820. Dulaure, in his curious *History of Paris*, Amours of Henry IV)

confess, not at all virtuous; and it is this that gives this essay a tone only too unprincipled.

I esteem not a bit more the Chartreux monk who eats nothing but fish and allows himself to talk only on Thursday. I own I prefer General Carnot, who, at an advanced age, puts up with the rigors of exile in a little northern town rather than do a base action.

I have some hope that this extremely vulgar declaration will lead the reader to skip the rest of this chapter.

This morning, a holiday, at Pesaro (May 7th, 1819), being obliged to go to Mass, I got hold of a Missal and fell upon these words: —

Joanna, Alphonsi quinti Lusitaniæ regis filia, tanta divini amoris flamma præventa fuit, ut ab ipsa pueritia rerum caducarum pertæsa, solo cœlestis patriæ desiderio flagraret.

The virtue so touchingly preached by the very beautiful words of the *Génie du Christianisme* is thus reduced to not eating truffles for fear of a stomach-ache. It is quite a reasonable calculation, if you believe in hell; but it is a self-interested calculation, the most personal and prosaic possible. That philosophic virtue, which so well explains the return of Regulus to Carthage, and which was responsible for some similar incidents in our own Revolution,[1] proves, on the contrary, generosity of soul.

It is merely in order not to be burned in the next world, in a great cauldron of boiling oil, that Madame de Tourvel resists Valmont. I cannot imagine how the idea, with all its ignominy, of being the rival of a cauldron of boiling oil does not drive Valmont away.

How much more touching is Julie d'Etanges, respecting her vows and the happiness of M. de Wolmar.

What I say of Madame de Tourvel, I find applicable to the lofty virtue of Mistress Hutchinson. What a soul did Puritanism steal away from love!

---

[1] Memoirs of Madame Roland. M. Grangeneuve, who goes out for a walk at eight o'clock in a certain street, in order to be killed by the Capuchin Chabot. A death was thought expedient in the cause of liberty.

One of the oddest peculiarities of this world is that men always think they know whatever it is clearly necessary for them to know.

188

Hear them talk about politics, that very complicated science; hear them talk of marriage and morals.

State of Marriage in Europe

S O FAR we have only treated the question of marriage according to theory;[1] we are now to treat it according to the facts.

Which of all countries is that in which there are the most happy marriages? Without dispute, Protestant Germany.

I extract the following fragment from the diary of Captain Salviati, without changing a single word in it: —

"Halberstadt, *June 23rd, 1807....* Nevertheless, M. de Bülow is absolutely and openly in love with Mademoiselle de Feltheim; he follows her about everywhere, always, talks to her unceasingly, and very often keeps her yards away from us. Such open marks of affection shock society, break it up — and on the banks of the Seine would pass for the height of indecency. The Germans think much less than we do about what breaks up society; indecency is little more than a conventional evil. For five years M. de Bülow has been paying court in this may to Mina, whom he has been unable to marry owing to the war. All the young ladies in society have their lover, and he is known to everyone. Among all the German acquaintances of my friend M. de Mermann there is not a single one who has not married for love.

"Mermann, his brother George, M. de Voigt, M. de Lazing, etc. He has just given me the names of a dozen of them.

---

[1] The author had read a chapter called "Dell' amore," in the Italian translation of the *Idéologie* of M. de Tracy. In that chapter the reader will find ideas incomparable, in philosophical importance, with anything he can find here.

"The open and passionate way in which these lovers pay their court to their mistresses would be the height of indecency, absurdity and shame in France.

"Mermann told me this evening, as we were returning from the *Chasseur Vert*, that, among all the women of his very numerous family, he did not suppose there was a single one who had deceived her husband. Allowing that he is wrong about half of them, it is still a singular country.

"His shady proposal to his sister-in-law, Madame de Munichow, whose family is about to die out for want of male heirs, and its very considerable possessions revert to the crown, coldly received, but merely with: 'Let's hear no more of that.'

"He tells the divine Philippine (who has just obtained a divorce from her husband, who only wanted to sell her to his Sovereign) something about it in very covert terms. Unfeigned indignation, toned down in its expression instead of being exaggerated: 'Have you, then, no longer any respect for our sex? I prefer to think, for the sake of your honor, that you're joking.'

"During a journey to the Brocken with this really beautiful woman, she reclined on his shoulder while asleep or pretending to sleep; a jolt threw her somewhat on to the top of him, and he put his arm round her waist; she threw herself into the other corner of the carriage. He doesn't think that she is incorruptible, but he believes that she would kill herself the day after her mistake. What is certain is that he loved her passionately and that he was similarly loved by her, that they saw each other continually and that she is without reproach. But the sun is very pale at Halberstadt, the Government very meddling, and these two persons very cold. In their most passionate interviews Kant and Klopstock were always of the party.

"Mermann told me that a married man, convicted of adultery, could be condemned by the courts of Brunswick to ten years' imprisonment; the law has fallen into disuse, but at least ensures that people do not joke about this sort of affair. The distinction of being a man with a past is very far from being such an advantage here as it is in France, where you can scarcely refuse it a married man in his presence without insulting him.

"Anyone who told my Colonel or Ch . . . that they no longer have women since their marriage would get a very poor reception.

"Some years ago a woman of this country, in a fit of religious fervor, told her husband, a gentleman of the Court of Brunswick, that she had deceived him for six years together. The husband, as big a fool as his wife, went to tell the news to the Duke; the gallant was obliged to resign all his employments and to leave the country in twenty-four hours, under a threat from the Duke to put the laws in motion."

"HALBERSTADT, *July 7th, 1807*

"Husbands are not deceived here, 'tis true — but ye gods, what women! Statues, masses scarcely organic! Before marriage they are exceedingly attractive, graceful as gazelles, with quick tender eyes that always understand the least hint of love. The reason is that they are on the look out for a husband. So soon as the husband is found, they become absolutely nothing but getters of children, in a state of perpetual adoration before the begetter. In a family of four or five children there must always be one of them ill, since half the children die before seven, and in this country, immediately one of the babies is ill, the mother goes out no more. I can see that they find an indescribable pleasure in being caressed by their children. Little by little they lose all their ideas. It is the same at Philadelphia. There girls of the wildest and most innocent gaiety become, in less than a year, the most boring of women. To have done with the marriages of Protestant Germany — a wife's dowry is almost nil because of the fiefs. Mademoiselle de Diesdorff, daughter of a man with an income of forty thousand francs, will have a dowry of perhaps two thousand crowns (seven thousand five hundred francs).

"M. de Mermann got four thousand crowns with his wife.

"The rest of the dowry is payable in vanity at the Court. 'One could find among the middle class,' Mermann told me, 'matches with a hundred or a hundred and fifty thousand crowns (six hundred thousand francs instead of fifteen). But one could no longer be presented at Court; one would be barred all society in which a prince or princess appeared: *it's terrible.*' These were his words, and they came from the heart.

"A German woman with the soul of Phi . . ., her intellect, her noble and sensitive face, the fire she must have had at eighteen (she is now twenty-seven), a woman such as this country produces, with her virtue, naturalness and no more than a useful little dose of religion — such a woman would no doubt make her husband very happy. But how flatter oneself that one would remain true to such insipid matrons?

" 'But he was married,' she answered me this morning when I blamed the four years' silence of Corinne's lover, Lord Oswald. She sat up till three o'clock to read *Corinne.* The novel gave her profound emotion, and now she answers me with touching candor: 'But he was married.'

"Phi . . . is so natural, with so naïve a sensibility, that even in this land of the natural, she seems a prude to the petty heads that govern petty hearts; their witticisms make her sick, and she in no way hides it.

"When she is in good company, she laughs like mad at the most lively jokes. It was she who told me the story of the young princess of sixteen, later on so well known, who often managed to make the officer on guard at her door come up into her rooms."

SWITZERLAND

I know few families happier than those of the Oberland, the part of Switzerland that lies round Berne; and it is a fact of public notoriety (1816) that the girls there spend Saturday to Sunday nights with their lovers.

The fools who know the world, after a voyage from Paris to Saint Cloud, will cry out; happily I find in a Swiss writer confirmation of what I myself saw during four months.[1]

"An honest peasant complained of certain losses he had sustained in his orchard; I asked him why he didn't keep a dog: 'My daughters would never get married.' I did not understand his answer; he told me he had had such a bad-tempered dog that none of the young men dared climb up to the windows any longer.

"Another peasant, mayor of his village, told me in praise of his wife, that when she was a girl no one had had more *Kilter* or *Wächterer* — that is, had had more young men come to spend the night with her.

"A Colonel, widely esteemed, was forced, while crossing the mountains, to spend the night at the bottom of one of the most lonely and picturesque valleys in the country. He lodged with the first magistrate in the valley, a man rich and of good repute. On entering, the stranger noticed a young girl of sixteen, a model of gracefulness, freshness and simplicity: she was the daughter of the master of the house. That night there was a village ball; the stranger paid court to the girl, who was really strikingly beautiful. At last, screwing up courage, he ventured to ask her whether he couldn't 'keep watch' with her. 'No,' answered the girl, 'I share a room with my cousin, but I'll come myself to yours.' You can judge of the confusion this answer gave him. They had supper, the stranger got up, the girl took a torch and followed him into his room; he imagined the moment was at hand. 'Oh no,' she said simply, 'I must first ask Mamma's permission.' He would have been less staggered by a thunderbolt! She went out; his courage revived; he slipped into these good folks' parlor, and listened to the girl begging her mother in a caressing tone to grant her the desired permission; in the end she got it. 'Eh, old man,' said the mother to her husband who was already in bed, 'd'you allow Trineli to spend the night with the Colonel?' 'With all my heart,'

192

[1] *Principes philosophiques du Colonel Weiss*, 7 ed., Vol. II, p. 245.

answers the father, 'I think I'd lend even my wife to such a man.' 'Right then, go,' says the mother to Trineli; 'but be a good girl, and don't take off your petticoat . . .' At daybreak, Trineli, respected by the stranger, rose still virgin. She arranged the bedclothes, prepared coffee and cream for her partner and, after she had breakfasted with him, seated on his bed, cut off a little piece of her *broustpletz* (a piece of velvet going over the breast). 'Here,' she said, 'keep this souvenir of a happy night; I shall never forget it. — Why are you a Colonel?' And giving him a last kiss, she ran away; he didn't manage to see her again.[1] Here you have the absolute opposite of French morals, and I am far from approving them."

Were I a legislator, I would have people adopt in France, as in Germany, the custom of evening dances. Three times a week girls would go with their mothers to a ball, beginning at seven and ending at midnight, and demanding no other outlay but a violin and a few glasses of water. In a neighboring room the mothers, maybe a little jealous of their daughters' happy education, would play Boston; in a third, the fathers would find papers and could talk politics. Between midnight and one o'clock all the families would collect together and return to the paternal roof. Girls would get to know young men; they would soon come to loathe fatuity and the indiscretions it is responsible for — in fact they would choose themselves husbands. Some girls would have unhappy love-affairs, but the number of deceived husbands and unhappy matches would diminish to an immense degree. It would then be less absurd to attempt to punish infidelity with dishonor. The law could say to young women: "You have chosen your husband — be faithful to him." In those circumstances I would allow the indictment and punishment by the courts of what the English call criminal conversation. The courts could impose, to the

[1] I am fortunate to be able to describe in the words of another some extraordinary facts that I have had occasion to observe. Certainly, but for M. de Weiss, I shouldn't have related this glimpse of foreign customs. I have omitted others equally characteristic of Valencia and Vienna.

profit of prisons and hospitals, a fine equal to two-thirds of the seducer's fortune and imprisonment for several years.

A woman could be indicted for adultery before a jury. The jury should first declare that the husband's conduct had been irreproachable.

A woman, if convicted, could be condemned to imprisonment for life. If the husband had been absent more than two years, the woman could not be condemned to more than some years' imprisonment. Public morals would soon model themselves on these laws and would perfect them.[1]

And then the nobles and the priests, still regretting bitterly the proper times of Madame de Montespan or Madame du Barry, would be forced to allow divorce.[2]

There would be in a village within sight of Paris an asylum for unfortunate women, a house of refuge into which, under pain of the galleys, no man besides the doctor and the almoner should enter. A woman who wished to get a divorce would be bound, first of all, to go and place herself as prisoner in this asylum; there she would spend two years without going out once. She could write, but never receive an answer.

A council composed of peers of France and certain magistrates of repute would direct, in the woman's name, the proceedings for a divorce and would regulate the pension

[1] *The Examiner*, an English paper, when giving a report of the Queen's case (No. 662, September 3rd, 1820), adds: —

"We have a system of sexual morality, under which thousands of women become mercenary prostitutes whom virtuous women are taught to scorn, while virtuous men retain the privilege of frequenting these very women, without its being regarded as anything more than a venial offence."

In the land of Cant there is something noble in the courage that dares speak the truth on this subject, however trivial and obvious it be; it is all the more meritorious in a poor paper, which can only hope for success if bought by the rich — and they look on the bishops and the Bible as the one safeguard of their fine feathers.

[2] Madame de Sévigné wrote to her daughter, December 23rd, 1671: "I don't know if you have heard that Villarceaux, when talking to the king of a post for his son, adroitly took the occasion to tell him, that there were people busy telling his niece (Mademoiselle de Rouxel) that his Majesty had designs on her; that if it were so, he begged his Majesty to make use of him; said that the affair would be better in his hands than in others, and that he would discharge it with success. The King began to laugh and said: 'Villarceaux, we are too old, you and I, to attack young ladies of fifteen.' And like a gallant man, he laughed at him and told the ladies what he had said." See Memoirs of Lauzun, Bezenval, Madame d'Epinay, etc., etc. I beg my readers not to condemn me altogether without re-reading these Memoirs.

to be paid to the institution by the husband. A woman who failed in her plea before the courts would be allowed to spend the rest of her life in the asylum. The Government would compensate the administration of the asylum with a sum of two thousand francs for each woman who sought its refuge. To be received in the asylum, a woman must have had a dowry of over twenty thousand francs. The moral *régime* would be one of extreme severity.

After two years of complete seclusion from the world, a divorced woman could marry again.

Once arrived at this point, Parliament could consider whether, in order to infuse in girls a spirit of emulation, it would not be advisable to allow the sons a share of the paternal heritage double that of their sisters. The daughters who did not find husbands would have a share equal to that of the male children. It may be remarked, by the way, that this system would, little by little, destroy the only too inconvenient custom of marriages of convenience. The possibility of divorce would render useless such outrageous meanness.

At various points in France, and in certain poor villages, thirty abbeys for old maids should be established. The Government should endeavor to surround these establishments with consideration, in order to console a little the sorrows of the poor women who were to end their lives there. They should be given all the toys of dignity.

But enough of such chimeras!

Werther and Don Juan

AMONG young people, when they have done with mocking at some poor lover, and he has left the room, the conversation generally ends by discussing the question, whether it is better to deal with women like Mozart's Don Juan or like Werther. The contrast would be more exact, if I had said Saint-Preux, but he is so dull a personage, that in making him their representative, I should be wronging feeling hearts.

Don Juan's character requires the greater number of useful and generally esteemed virtues — admirable daring, resourcefulness, vivacity, a cool head, a witty mind, etc.

The Don Juans have great moments of bitterness and a very miserable old age — but then most men do not reach old age.

The lover plays a poor rôle in the drawing-room in the evening, because to be a success and a power among women a man must show just as much keenness on winning them as on a game of billiards. As everybody knows that the lover has a great interest in life, he exposes himself, for all his cleverness, to mockery. Only, next morning he wakes, not to be in a bad temper until something piquant or something nasty turns up to revive him, but to dream of her he loves and build castles in the air for love to dwell in.

Love à la Werther opens the soul to all the arts, to all sweet and romantic impressions, to the moonlight, to the beauty of the forest, to the beauty of pictures — in a word, to the feeling and enjoyment of the beautiful, under whatever form it be found, even under the coarsest cloak. It causes man to find happiness even without riches.[1] Such souls, instead of growing weary like Mielhan, Bezenval, etc., go mad, like Rousseau, from an excess of sensibility. Women endowed with a certain elevation of soul, who, after their first youth, know how to recognize love, both where it is and what it is, generally escape the Don Juan — he is remarkable in their eyes rather by the number than the quality of his conquests. Observe, to the prejudice of

[1] See the first volume of the *Nouvelle Héloïse*. I should say every volume, if Saint-Preux had happened to have the ghost of a character, but he was a real poet, a babbler without resolution, who had no courage until he had made a peroration — yes, a very dull man. Such men have an immense advantage, in not upsetting feminine pride, and in never giving their mistress a fright. Weigh the word well; it contains perhaps the whole secret of the success of dull men with distinguished women. Nevertheless love is only a passion in so far as it makes one forget one's self-love. Thus they do not completely know love, these women, who, like L., ask of it the pleasures of pride. Unconsciously, they are on the same level as the prosaic man, the object of their contempt, who in love seeks love plus vanity. And they too, they want love and pride; but love goes out with flaming cheeks; he is the proudest of despots; he will be all, or nothing.

tender hearts, that publicity is as necessary to Don Juan's triumph as secrecy is to Werther's. Most of the men who make women the business of their life are born in the lap of luxury; that is to say, they are, as a result of their education and the example set by everything that surrounded them in youth, hardened egoists.[1]

The real Don Juan even ends by looking on women as the enemy, and rejoicing in their misfortunes of every sort.

On the other hand, the charming Duke delle Pignatelle showed us the proper way to find happiness in pleasures, even without passion. "I know that I like a woman," he told me one evening, "when I find myself completely confused in her company, and don't know what to say to her." So far from letting his self-esteem be put to shame or take its revenge for these embarrassing moments, he cultivated them lovingly as the source of his happiness. With this charming young man gallant-love was quite free from the corroding influence of vanity; his was a shade of true love, pale, but innocent and unmixed; and he respected all women, as charming beings, towards whom we are far from just. (February 20, 1820)

As a man does not choose himself a temperament, that is to say, a soul, he cannot play a part above him. J. J. Rousseau and the Duc de Richelieu might have tried in vain; for all their cleverness, they could never have exchanged their fortunes with respect to women. I could well believe that the Duke never had moments such as those that Rousseau experienced in the Parc de la Chevrette with Madame d'Houdetot; at Venice, when listening to the music of the *scuole;* and at Turin at the feet of Madame Bazile. But then he never had to blush at the ridicule that overwhelmed Rousseau in his affair with Madame de Larnage, remorse for which pursued him during the rest of his life.

A Saint-Preux's part is sweeter and fills up every moment

---

[1] See a certain page of André Chénier (Works, p. 370); or rather look at life, though that's much harder. "In general, those whom we call patricians are much further than other men from loving anything," says the Emperor Marcus Aurelius. (*Meditations*)

of existence, but it must be owned that that of a Don Juan is far more brilliant. Saint-Preux's tastes may change at middle age: solitary and retired, and of pensive habits, he takes a back place on the stage of life, while Don Juan realizes the magnificence of his reputation among men, and could yet perhaps please a woman of feeling by making sincerely the sacrifice of his libertine's tastes.

After all the reasons offered so far, on both sides of the question, the balance still seems to be even. What makes me think that the Werthers are the happier, is that Don Juan reduces love to the level of an ordinary affair. Instead of being able, like Werther, to shape realities to his desires, he finds, in love, desires which are imperfectly satisfied by cold reality, just as in ambition, avarice or other passions. Instead of losing himself in the enchanting reveries of crystallization, he thinks, like a general, of the success of his manœuvres[1] and, in a word, he kills love, instead of enjoying it more keenly than other men, as ordinary people imagine.

This seems to me unanswerable. And there is another reason, which is no less so in my eyes, though, thanks to the malignity of Providence, we must pardon men for not recognizing it. The habit of justice is, to my thinking, apart from accidents, the most assured way of arriving at happiness — and a Werther is no villain.[2]

To be happy in crime, it is absolutely necessary to have no remorse. I do not know whether such a creature can exist;[3] I have never seen him. I would bet that the affair of Madame Michelin disturbed the Duc de Richelieu's nights.

---

[1] Compare Lovelace and Tom Jones.

[2] See the *Vie privée du duc de Richelieu,* nine volumes in 8vo. Why, at the moment that an assassin kills a man, does he not fall dead at his victim's feet? Why is there illness? And, if there is illness, why does not a Troistaillons die of the colic? Why does Henry IV reign twenty-one years and Louis XV fifty-nine? Why is not the length of life in exact proportion to the degree of virtue in each man? These and other "infamous questions," English philosophers will say there is certainly no merit in posing; but there would be some merit in answering them otherwise than with insults and "cant."

[3] Note Nero after the murder of his mother, in Suetonius, and yet with what a fine lot of flattery was he surrounded.

One ought either to have absolutely no sympathy or be able to put the human race to death — which is impossible.[1]

People who only know love from novels will experience a natural repugnance in reading these words in favor of virtue in love. The reason is that, by the laws of the novel, the portraiture of a virtuous love is essentially tiresome and uninteresting. Thus the sentiment of virtue seems from a distance to neutralize that of love, and the words "a virtuous love" seem synonymous with a feeble love. But all this comes from weakness in the art of painting, and has nothing to do with passion such as it exists in nature.[2]

I beg to be allowed to draw a picture of my most intimate friend.

Don Juan renounces all the duties which bind him to the rest of men. In the great market of life he is a dishonest merchant, who is always buying and never paying. The idea of equality inspires the same rage in him as water in a man with hydrophobia; it is for this reason that pride of birth goes so well with the character of Don Juan. With the idea of the equality of rights disappears that of justice, or, rather, if Don Juan is sprung from an illustrious family, such common ideas have never come to him. I could easily believe that a man with an historic name is sooner disposed than another to set fire to the town in order to get his egg cooked.[3] We must excuse him; he is so possessed with self-love that he comes to the point of losing all idea of the evil

---

[1] Cruelty is only a morbid kind of sympathy. Power is, after love, the first source of happiness, only because one believes oneself to be in a position to command sympathy.

[2] If you offer the spectator a picture of the sentiment of virtue side by side with the sentiment of love, you will find that you have represented a heart divided between two sentiments. In novels the only good of virtue is to be sacrificed; *vide* Julie d'Etanges.

[3] *Vide* Saint-Simon, *fausse couche* of the Duchesse de Bourgoyne; and Madame de Motteville, *passim:* That princess, who was surprised to find that other women had five fingers on their hands like herself; that Gaston, Duke of Orleans, brother of Louis XIII, who found it quite easy to understand why his favorites went to the scaffold just to please him. Note, in 1820, these fine gentlemen putting forward an electoral law that may bring back your Robespierres into France, etc., etc. And observe Naples in 1799. (I leave this note written in 1820. A list of the great nobles in 1778, with notes on their morals, compiled by General Laclos, seen at Naples in the library of the Marchese Berio — very scandalous manuscript of more than three hundred pages.)

he causes, and of seeing no longer anything in the universe capable of joy or sorrow except himself. In the fire of youth, when passion fills our own hearts with the pulse of life and keeps us from mistrust of others, Don Juan, all senses and apparent happiness, applauds himself for thinking only of himself, while he sees other men pay their sacrifices to duty. He imagines that he has found out the great art of living. But, in the midst of his triumph, while still scarcely thirty years of age, he perceives to his astonishment that life is wanting, and feels a growing disgust for what were all his pleasures. Don Juan told me at Thorn, in an access of melancholy: "There are not twenty different sorts of women, and once you have had two or three of each sort, satiety sets in.

I answered: "It is only imagination that can for ever escape satiety. Each woman inspires a different interest, and, what is more, if chance throws the same woman in your way two or three years earlier or later in the course of life, and if chance means you to love, you can love the same woman in different manners. But a woman of gentle heart, even when she loved you, would produce in you, because of her pretensions to equality, only irritation to your pride. Your way of having women kills all the other pleasures of life; Werther's increases them a hundredfold."

This sad tragedy reaches the last act. You see Don Juan in old age, turning on this and that, never on himself, as the cause of his own satiety. You see him, tormented by a consuming poison, flying from this to that in a continual change of purpose. But, however brilliant the appearances may be, in the end he only changes one misery for another. He tries the boredom of inaction, he tries the boredom of excitement — there is nothing else for him to choose.

At last he discovers the fatal truth and confesses it to himself; henceforward he is reduced for all his enjoyment to making display of his power, and openly doing evil for evil's sake. In short, 'tis the last degree of settled gloom; no poet has dared give us a faithful picture of it — the picture, if true, would strike horror. But one may hope that a man, above the ordinary, will retrace his steps along his fatal path; for at the bottom of Don Juan's character there is a contradiction. I have supposed him a man of great intellect, and great intellect leads us to the discovery of virtue by the road that runs to the temple of glory.[1]

La Rochefoucauld, who, however, was a master of self-love, and who in real life was nothing but a silly man of letters,[2] says: "The pleasure of love consists in loving, and a man gets more happiness from the passion he feels than from the passion he inspires."

Don Juan's happiness consists in vanity, based, it is true, on circumstances brought about by great intelligence and activity; but he must feel that the most inconsiderable general who wins a battle, the most inconsiderable prefect who keeps his department in order, realizes a more signal enjoyment than his own. The Duc de Nemours' happiness when Madame de Clèves tells him that she loves him, is, I imagine, above Napoleon's happiness at Marengo.

Love *à la* Don Juan is a sentiment of the same kind as a taste for hunting. It is a desire for activity which must be kept alive by divers objects and by putting a man's talents continually to the test.

Love *à la* Werther is like the feeling of a schoolboy writing a tragedy—and a thousand times better; it is a new goal, to which everything in life is referred and which changes the face of everything. Passion-love casts all nature in its sublimer aspects before the eyes of a man, as a novelty invented but yesterday. He is amazed that he has never seen the singular spectacle that is now discovered to his soul. Everything is new, everything is alive, everything breathes the most passionate interest.[3] A lover sees the woman he loves on the horizon of every landscape he comes across,

[1] The character of the young man of the privileged classes in 1820 is pretty correctly represented by the brave Bothwell of *Old Mortality*.

[2] See Memoirs of de Retz and the unpleasant minute he gave the coadjutor at the Parliament between two doors.

[3] Vol. 1819. Honeysuckle on the slopes.

and, while he travels a hundred miles to go and catch a glimpse of her for an instant, each tree, each rock speaks to him of her in a different manner and tells him something new about her. Instead of the tumult of this magic spectacle, Don Juan finds that external objects have for him no value apart from their degree of utility, and must be made amusing by some new intrigue.

Love *à la* Werther has strange pleasures; after a year or two, the lover has now, so to speak, but one heart with her he loves; and this, strange to say, even independent of his success in love — even under a cruel mistress. Whatever he does, whatever he sees, he asks himself: "What would she say if she were with me? What would I say to her about this view of Casa-Lecchio?" He speaks to her, he hears her answer, he smiles at her fun. A hundred miles from her, and under the weight of her anger, he surprises himself, reflecting: "Léonore was very gay that night." Then he wakes up: "Good God!" he says to himself with a sigh, "there are madmen in Bedlam less mad than I."

"You make me quite impatient," said a friend of mine, to whom I read out this remark:" you are continually opposing the passionate man to the Don Juan, and that is not the point in dispute. You would be right, if a man could provide himself with passion at will. But what about indifference — what is to be done then?" — Gallant-love without horrors. Its horrors always come from a little soul, that needs to be reassured as to its own merit.

To continue. — The Don Juans must find great difficulty in agreeing with what I was saying just now of this state of the soul. Besides the fact that they can neither see nor feel this state, it gives too great a blow to their vanity. The error of their life is expecting to win in a fortnight what a timid lover can scarcely obtain in six months. They base their reckoning on experience got at the expense of those poor devils, who have neither the soul to please a woman of feeling by revealing its ingenuous workings, nor the necessary wit for the part of a Don Juan. They refuse to see that the same prize, though granted by the same woman, is not the same thing.

> L'homme prudent sans cesse se méfie.
> C'est pour cela que des amants trompeurs
> Le nombre est grand. Les dames que l'on prie
> Font soupirer longtemps des serviteurs
> Qui n'ont jamais été faux de leur vie.
> Mais du trésor qu'elles donnent enfin
> Le prix n'est su que du cœur qui le goûte;
> Plus on l'achète et plus il est divin:
> Le los d'amour ne vaut pas ce qu'il coûte.[1]
> (Nievernais, *La Troubadour
> Guillaume de la Tour*, 111, 342)

Passion-love in the eyes of a Don Juan may be compared to a strange road, steep and toilsome, that begins, 'tis true, amidst delicious copses, but is soon lost among sheer rocks, whose aspect is anything but inviting to the eyes of the vulgar. Little by little the road penetrates into the mountain-heights, in the midst of a dark forest, where the huge trees, intercepting the daylight with their shaggy tops that seem to touch the sky, throw a kind of horror into souls untempered by dangers.

After wandering with difficulty, as in an endless maze, whose multiple turnings try the patience of our self-love, on a sudden we turn a corner and find ourselves in a new world, in the delicious valley of Cashmire of Lalla Rookh. How can the Don Juans, who never venture along this road, or at most take but a few steps along it, judge of the views that it offers at the end of the journey? ...

.   .   .   .   .   .

So you see inconstancy is good:

"Il me faut du nouveau, n'en fût-il plus au monde."[2]

---

[1] [A prudent man continually mistrusts himself. 'Tis the reason why the number of false lovers is great. The women whom men worship, make their servants, who have never been false in their life, sigh a long time. But the value of the prize that they give them in the end, can only be known to the heart that tastes it; the greater the cost, the more divine it is. The praises of love are not worth its pains.]

[2] [I must have novelty, even if there were none left in the world.]

Very well, I reply, you make light of oaths and justice, and what can you look for in inconstancy? Pleasure apparently.

But the pleasure to be got from a pretty woman, desired a fortnight and loved three months, is different from the pleasure to be found in a mistress, desired three years and loved ten.

If I do not insert the word "always" the reason is that I have been told old age, by altering our organs, renders us incapable of loving; myself, I don't believe it. When your mistress has become your intimate friend, she can give you new pleasures, the pleasures of old age. 'Tis a flower that, after it has been a rose in the morning — the season of flowers — becomes a delicious fruit in the evening, when the roses are no longer in season.[1]

A mistress desired three years is really a mistress in every sense of the word; you cannot approach her without trembling; and let me tell the Don Juans that a man who trembles is not bored. The pleasures of love are always in proportion to our fear.

The evil of inconstancy is weariness; the evil of passion is despair and death. The cases of despair are noted and become legend. No one pays attention to the weary old libertines dying of boredom, with whom the streets of Paris are lined.

"Love blows out more brains than boredom." I have no doubt of it: boredom robs a man of everything, even the courage to kill himself.

There is a certain type of character which can find pleasure only in variety. A man who cries up Champagne at the expense of Bordeaux is only saying, with more or less eloquence: "I prefer Champagne."

Each of these wines has its partisans, and they are all right, so long as they quite understand themselves, and run after the kind of happiness best suited to their organs[2] and

[1] See the Memoirs of Collé — his wife.

[2] Physiologists, who understand our organs, tell you: "Injustice, in the relations of social life, produces harshness, diffidence and misery."

their habits. What ruins the case for inconstancy is that all fools range themselves on that side from lack of courage.

But after all, everyone, if he will take the trouble to look into himself, has his ideal, and there always seems to me something a little ridiculous in wanting to convert your neighbor.

BOOK THE THIRD

Scattered Fragments

UNDER this title, which I would willingly have made still more modest, I have brought together, without excessive severity, a selection made from three or four hundred playing cards, on which I found a few lines scrawled in pencil.

That which, I suppose, must be called the original manuscript, for want of a simpler name, was in many places made up of pieces of paper of all sizes, written on in pencil, and joined together by Lisio with sealing-wax, to save him the trouble of copying them afresh. He told me once that nothing he ever noted down seemed to him worth the trouble of recopying an hour later. I have entered so fully into all this in the hope that it may serve as an excuse for repetitions.

1. Everything can be acquired in solitude, except character.

2. 1821. Hatred, love and avarice, the three ruling passions at Rome, and with gambling added, almost the only ones.

At first sight the Romans seem ill-natured, but they are only very much on their guard and blessed with an imagination which flares up at the least suggestion.

If they give a gratuitous proof of ill-nature, it is the case of a man, gnawed by fear, and testing his gun to reassure himself.

3. If I were to say, as I believe, that good-nature is the key-note of the Parisian's character, I should be very frightened of having offended him. — "I won't be good!"

4. A proof of love comes to light, when all the pleasures and all the pains, which all the other passions and wants of man can produce, in a moment cease working.

5. Prudery is a kind of avarice — the worst of all.

6. To have a solid character is to have a long and tried experience of life's disillusions and misfortunes. Then it is a question of desiring constantly or not at all.

7. Love, such as it exists in smart society, is the love of battle, the love of gambling.

8. Nothing kills gallant love like gusts of passion-love from the other side. (Contessina L. Forlì — 1819)

9. A great fault in women, and the most offensive of all to a man a little worthy of that name: The public, in matters of feeling, never soars above mean ideas, and women make the public the supreme judge of their lives — even the most distinguished women, I maintain, often unconsciously, and even while believing and saying the contrary. (Brescia, 1819)

10. Prosaic is a new word, which once I thought absurd, for nothing could be colder than our poetry. If there has been any warmth in France for the last fifty years, it is assuredly to be found in its prose. But anyhow, the little Countess L—— used the word and I like writing it.

The definition of prosaic is to be got from *Don Quixote*, and "the complete contrast of Knight and Squire." The Knight tall and pale; the Squire fat and fresh. The former all heroism and courtesy; the latter all selfishness and ser- vility. The former always full of romantic and touching fancies; the latter a model of worldly wisdom, a compen- dium of wise saws. The one always feeding his soul on dreams of heroism and daring; the other ruminating some really sensible scheme in which, never fear, he will take into strict account all the shameful, selfish little movements the human heart is prone to.

At the very moment when the former should be brought to his senses by the non-success of yesterday's dreams, he is already busy on his castles in Spain for to-day.

You ought to have a prosaic husband and to choose a romantic lover.

Marlborough had a prosaic soul: Henry IV, in love at fifty-five with a young princess, who could not forget his age, a romantic heart.[1]

There are fewer prosaic beings among the nobility than in the middle-class.

This is the fault of trade, it makes people prosaic.

11. Nothing so interesting as passion: for there everything is unforeseen, and the principal is the victim. Nothing so flat as gallantry, where everything is a matter of calculation, as in all the prosaic affairs of life.

12. At the end of a visit you always finish by treating a lover better than you meant to. (L., *November 2nd*, 1818)

[1] Dulaure, *History of Paris*. Silent episode in the Queen's apartment the eve- ning of the flight of the Princess de Condé: the ministers transfixed to the wall and mute, the King striding up and down.

13. In spite of genius in an upstart, the influence of rank always makes itself felt. Think of Rousseau losing his heart to all the "ladies" he met, and weeping tears of rapture because the Duke of L——, one of the dullest courtiers of the period, deigns to take the right side rather than the left in a walk with a certain M. Coindet, friend of Rousseau! (L., *May 3rd,* 1820)

14. Women's only educator is the world. A mother in love does not hesitate to appear in the seventh heaven of delight, or in the depth of despair, before her daughters aged fourteen or fifteen. Remember that, under these happy skies, plenty of women are quite nice-looking till forty-five, and the majority are married at eighteen.

Think of La Valchiusa saying yesterday of Lampugnani: "Ah, that man was made for me, he could love, . . . etc., etc," and so on in this strain to a friend — all before her daughter, a little thing of fourteen or fifteen, very much on the alert, and whom she also took with her on the more than friendly walks with the lover in question.

Sometimes girls get hold of sound rules of conduct. For example, take Madame Guarnacci, addressing her two daughters and two men, who have never called on her before. For an hour and a half she treats them to profound maxims, based on examples within their own knowledge (that of La Cercara in Hungary), on the precise point at which it is right to punish with infidelity a lover who misbehaves himself. (Ravenna, *January 23rd,* 1820)

15. The sanguine man, the true Frenchman (Colonel M——) instead of being tormented by excess of feeling, like Rousseau, if he has a rendezvous for the next evening at seven, sees everything, right up to the blessed moment, through rosy spectacles. People of this kind are not in the least susceptible to passion-love; it would upset their sweet tranquillity. I will go so far as to say that perhaps they would find its transports a nuisance, or at all events be humiliated by the timidity it produces.

16. Most men of the world, through vanity, caution or disaster, let themselves love a woman freely only after intimate intercourse.

17. With very gentle souls a woman needs to be easy-going in order to encourage crystallization.

18. A woman imagines that the voice of the public is speaking through the mouth of the first fool or the first treacherous friend who claims to be its faithful interpreter to her.

19. There is a delicious pleasure in clasping in your arms a woman who has wronged you grievously. who has been your bitter enemy for many a day, and is ready to be so again. Good fortune of the French officers in Spain, 1812.

20. Solitude is what one wants, to relish one's own heart and to love; but to succeed one must go amongst men, here, there and everywhere.

21. "All the observations of the French on love are well written, carefully and without exaggeration, but they bear only on light affections," said that delightful person, Cardinal Lante.

22. In Goldoni's comedy, the *Innamorati*, all the workings of passion are excellent; it is the very repulsive meanness of style and thought which revolts one. The contrary is true of a French comedy.

23. The youth of 1822: To say "serious turn of mind, active disposition" means "sacrifice of the present to the future." Nothing develops the soul like the power and the habit of making such sacrifices. I foresee the probability of more great passions in 1832 than in 1772.

24. The choleric temperament, when it does not display itself in too repulsive a form, is one perhaps most apt of all

to strike and keep alive the imagination of women. If the choleric temperament does not fall among propitious surroundings, as Lauzun in Saint-Simon (Memoirs), the difficulty is to grow used to it. But once grasped by a woman, this character must fascinate her: yes, even the savage and fanatic Balfour (*Old Mortality*). For women it is the antithesis of the prosaic.

25. In love one often doubts what one believes most strongly (La R., 355). In every other passion, what once we have proved, we no longer doubt.

26. Verse was invented to assist the memory. Later it was kept to increase the pleasure of reading by the sight of the difficulty overcome. Its survival nowadays in dramatic art is a relic of barbarity. Example: the Cavalry Regulations put into verse by M. de Bonnay.

27. While this jealous slave feeds his soul on boredom, avarice, hatred and other such poisonous, cold passions, I spend a night of happiness dreaming of her — of her who, through mistrust, treats me badly.

28. It needs a great soul to dare have a simple style. That is why Rousseau put so much rhetoric into the *Nouvelle Héloïse* — which makes it unreadable for anyone over thirty.

29. "The greatest reproach we could possibly make against ourselves is, certainly, to have let fade, like the shadowy phantoms produced by sleep, the ideas of honor and justice, which from time to time well up in our hearts." (*Letter from Jena, March, 1819*)

30. A respectable woman is in the country and passes an hour in the hot-house with her gardener. Certain people, whose views she has upset, accuse her of having found a lover in this gardner. What answer is there?

Speaking absolutely, the thing is possible. She could say: "My character speaks for me, look at my behavior throughout life" — only all this is equally invisible to the eyes of the ill-natured who won't see, and the fools who can't. (Salviati, Rome, *July 23rd, 1819*)

31. I have known a man find out that his rival's love was returned, and yet the rival himself remain blinded to the fact by his passion.

32. The more desperately he is in love, the more violent the pressure a man is forced to put upon himself, in order to risk annoying the woman he loves by taking her hand.

33. Ludicrous rhetoric but, unlike that of Rousseau, inspired by true passion. (Memoirs of M. de Mau . . ., *Letter of S——*)

34. I saw, or I thought I saw, this evening the triumph of naturalness in a young woman, who certainly seems to me to possess a great character. She adores, obviously, I think, one of her cousins and must have confessed to herself the state of her heart. The cousin is in love with her, but as she is very serious with him, thinks she does not like him, and lets himself be fascinated by the marks of preference shown him by Clara, a young widow and friend of Mélanie. I think he will marry her. Mélanie sees it and suffers all that a proud heart, struggling involuntarily with a violent passion, is capable of suffering. She has only to alter her ways a little; but she would look upon it as a piece of meanness, the consequences of which would affect her whole life, to depart one instant from her natural self.

35. Sappho saw in love only sensual intoxication or physical pleasure made sublime by crystallization. Anacreon looked for sensual and intellectual amusement. There was too little security in Antiquity for people to find leisure for passion-love.

36. The foregoing fact fully justifies me in rather laughing at people who think Homer superior to Tasso. Passion-love did exist in the time of Homer, and at no great distance from Greece.

37. Woman with a heart, if you wish to know whether the man you adore loves you with passion-love, study your lover's early youth. Every man of distinction in the early days of his life is either a ridiculous enthusiast or an unfortunate. A man easy to please, of gay and cheerful humor, can never love with the passion your heart requires.

Passion I call only that which has gone through long misfortunes, misfortunes which novels take good care not to depict — what's more they can't!

38. A bold resolution can change in an instant the most extreme misfortune into quite a tolerable state of things. The evening of a defeat, a man is retreating in hot haste, his charger already spent. He can hear distinctly the troop of cavalry galloping in pursuit. Suddenly he stops, dismounts, recharges his carbine and pistols, and makes up his mind to defend himself. Straightway, instead of having death, he has a cross of the Legion of Honor before his eyes.

39. Basis of English habits. About 1730, while we already had Voltaire and Fontenelle, a machine was invented in England to separate the grain, after threshing, from the chaff. It worked by means of a wheel, which gave the air enough movement to blow away the bits of chaff. But in that biblical country the peasants pretended that it was wicked to go against the will of Divine Providence, and to produce an artificial wind like this, instead of begging Heaven with an ardent prayer for enough wind to thresh the corn and waiting for the moment appointed by the God of Israel. Compare this with French peasants.[1]

[1] For the actual state of English habits, see the Life of Mr. Beattie, written by an intimate friend. The reader will be edified by the profound humility of Mr. Beattie, when he receives ten guineas from an old Marchioness in order to slander Hume. The trembling aristocracy relies on the bishops with incomes of

40. No doubt about it — 'tis a form of madness to expose oneself to passion-love. In some cases, however, the cure works too energetically. American girls in the United States are so saturated and fortified with reasonable ideas, that in that country love, the flower of life, has deserted youth. At Boston a girl can be left perfectly safely alone with a handsome stranger — in all probability she's thinking of nothing but her marriage settlement.

41. In France men who have lost their wives are melancholy; widows on the contrary, merry and light-hearted. There is a proverb current among women on the felicity of this state. So there must be some inequality in the articles of union.

42. People who are happy in their love have an air of profound pre-occupation, which, for a Frenchman, is the same as saying an air of profound gloom. (Dresden, 1818)

43. The more generally a man pleases, the less deeply can he please.

44. As a result of imitation in the early years of life, we contract the passions of our parents, even when these very passions poison our life. (L.'s pride.)

45. The most honorable source of feminine pride is a woman's fear of degrading herself in her lover's eyes by some hasty step or some action that he may think unwomanly.

46. Real love renders the thought of death frequent, agreeable, unterrifying, a mere subject of comparison, the price we are willing to pay for many a thing.

£200,000, and pays in money and honor so-called liberal writers to throw mud at Chénier. (*Edinburgh Review*, 1821)

The most disgusting cant leaks through on all sides. Everything except the portrayal of primitive and energetic feelings is stifled by it: impossible to write a joyous page in English.

47. How often have I exclaimed for all my bravery: "If anyone would blow out my brains, I'd thank him before I
expired, if there were time." A man can only be brave, with
the woman he loves, by loving her a little less. (S., *February,
1820*)

48. "I could never love!" a young woman said to me. "Mirabeau and his letters to Sophie have given me a disgust for
great souls. Those fatal letters impressed me like a personal
experience."

Try a plan which you never read of in novels; let two
years' constancy assure you, before intimate intercourse, of
your lover's heart.

49. Ridicule scares love. Ridicule is impossible in Italy:
what's good form in Venice is odd at Naples — consequently
nothing's odd in Italy. Besides, nothing that gives pleasure
is found fault with. 'Tis this that does away with the fool's
honor and half the farce.

50. Children command by tears, and if people do not at-
tend to their wishes, they hurt themselves on purpose.
Young women are piqued from a sense of honor.

51. 'Tis a common reflection, but one for that reason easily
forgotten, that every day sensitive souls become rarer, cul-
tured minds commoner.

52. I have just witnessed a striking example—but on mature
consideration I should need fifteen pages to give a proper
idea of it. If I dared, I would much rather note the consequences; my eyes have convinced me beyond the possibility
of doubt. But, no, it is a conviction I must give up all idea
of communicating, there are too many little details. Such
pride is the opposite of French vanity. So far as I can remember, the only work, in which I have seen a sketch of it,
is that part of Madame Roland's Memoirs, where she re-
counts the petty reasonings she made as a girl. (Bologna,
*April 18*th, 2 a.m.)

53. In France, most women make no account of a young man until they have turned him into a coxcomb. It is only then that he can flatter their vanity. (Duclos)

54. Zilietti said to me at midnight (at the charming Marchesina R . . . 's): "I'm not going to dine at San Michele (an inn). Yesterday I said some smart things — I was joking with Cl...; it might make me conspicuous."

Don't go and think that Zilietti is either a fool or a coward. He is a prudent and very rich man in this happy land. (Modena, 1820)

55. What is admirable in America is the government, not society. Elsewhere government does the harm. At Boston they have changed parts, and government plays the hypocrite, in order not to shock society.

56. Italian girls, if they love, are entirely given over to natural inspiration. At the very most all that can aid them is a handful of excellent maxims, which they have picked up by listening at the keyhole. As if fate had decreed that everything here should combine to preserve naturalness, they read no novels — and for this reason, that there are none. At Geneva or in France, on the contrary, a girl falls in love at sixteen in order to be a heroine, and at each step, almost at each tear, she asks herself: "Am I not just like Julie d'Etanges?"

57. The husband of a young woman adored by a lover, whom she treats unkindly and scarcely allows to kiss her hand, has, at the very most, only the grossest physical pleasure, where the lover would find the charms and transports of the keenest happiness that exists on earth.

58. The laws of the imagination are still so little understood, that I include the following estimate, though perhaps it is all quite wrong.

I seem to distinguish two sorts of imagination: —

1. Imagination like Fabio's, ardent, impetuous, inconsiderate, leading straight to action, consuming itself, and already languishing at a delay of twenty-four hours. Impatience is its prime characteristic; it becomes enraged against that which it cannot obtain. It sees all exterior objects, but they only serve to inflame it. It assimilates them to its own substance, and converts them straight away to the profit of passion.

2. Imagination which takes fire slowly and little by little, but which loses in time the perception of exterior objects, and comes to find occupation and nourishment in nothing but its own passion. This last sort of imagination goes quite easily with slowness, or even scarcity, of ideas. It is favorable to constancy. It is the imagination of the greater part of those poor German girls, who are dying of love and consumption. That sad spectacle, so frequent beyond the Rhine, is never met with in Italy.

59. Imaginative habits. A Frenchman is really shocked by eight changes of scenery in one act of a tragedy. Such a man is incapable of pleasure in seeing Macbeth. He consoles himself by damning Shakespeare.

60. In France the provinces are forty years behind Paris in all that regards women. A. C., a married woman, tells me that she only liked to read certain parts of Lanzi's Memoirs. Such stupidity is too much for me; I can no longer find a word to say to her. As if that were a book one *could* put down!

Want of naturalness — the great failing in provincial women. Their effusive and gracious gestures; those who play the first fiddle in the town are worse than the others.

61. Goethe, or any other German genius, esteems money at what it's worth. Until he has got an income of six thousand francs, he must think of nothing but his banking-account. After that he must never think of it again. The fool, on his side, does not understand the advantage there is of feeling

and thinking like Goethe. All his life he feels in terms of money and thinks of sums of money. It is owing to this support from both sides, that the prosaic in this world seem to come off so much better than the high-minded.

62. In Europe, desire is inflamed by constraint; in America it is dulled by liberty.

63. A mania for discussion has got hold of the younger generation and stolen it from love. While they are considering whether Napoleon was of service to France, they let the age of love speed past. Even with those who mean to be young, it is all affectation — a tie, a spur, their martial swagger, their all-absorbing self—and they forget to cast a glance at the girl who passes by so modestly and cannot go out more than once a week through want of means.

64. I have suppressed a chapter on Prudery, and others as well. I am happy to find the following passage in Horace Walpole's Memoirs:

The Two Elizabeths. Let us compare the daughters of two ferocious men, and see which was sovereign of a civilized nation, which of a barbarous one. Both were Elizabeths. The daughter of Peter (of Russia) was absolute, yet spared a competitor and a rival; and thought the person of an empress had sufficient allurements for as many of her subjects as she chose to honor with the communication. Elizabeth of England could neither forgive the claim of Mary Stuart nor her charms, but ungenerously imprisoned her (as George IV did Napoleon[1]) when imploring protection, and, without the sanction of either despotism or law, sacrificed many to her great and little jealousy. Yet this Elizabeth piqued herself on chastity; and while she practiced every ridiculous art of coquetry to be admired at an unseemly age, kept off lovers whom she encouraged, and neither gratified her own desires nor their ambition. Who

---

[1] [Added, of course, by Stendhal.]

can help preferring the honest, open-hearted barbarian empress? (Lord Orford's Memoirs)

65. Extreme familiarity may destroy crystallization. A charming girl of sixteen fell in love with a handsome youth of the same age, who never failed one evening to pass under her window at nightfall. Her mother invites him to spend a week with them in the country — a desperate remedy, I agree. But the girl was romantic, and the youth rather dull: after three days she despised him.

66. Ave Maria — twilight in Italy, the hour of tenderness, of the soul's pleasures and of melancholy — sensation intensified by the sound of those lovely bells.

Hours of pleasure, which only in memory touch the senses.... (Bologna, *April 17th, 1817*)

67. A young man's first love-affair on entering society is ordinarily one of ambition. He rarely declares his love for a sweet, amiable and innocent young girl. How tremble before her, adore her, feel oneself in the presence of a divinity? Youth must love a being whose qualities lift him up in his own eyes. It is in the decline of life that we sadly come back to love the simple and the innocent, despairing of the sublime. Between the two comes true love, which thinks of nothing but itself.

68. The existence of great souls is not suspected. They hide away; all that is seen is a little originality. There are **more** great souls than one would think.

69. The first clasp of the beloved's hand — what a moment that is! The only joy to be compared to it is the ravishing joy of power — which statesmen and kings make pretense of despising. This joy also has its crystallization, though it demands a colder and more reasonable imagination. Think of a man whom, a quarter of an hour ago, Napoleon has called to be a minister.

70. The celebrated Johannes von Muller said to me at Cassel in 1808 — Nature has given strength to the north and wit to the South.

71. Nothing more untrue than the maxim: No man is a hero before his valet. Or, rather, nothing truer in the monarchic sense of the word hero — the affected hero, like Hippolytus in *Phèdre*. Desaix, for example, would have been a hero even before his valet (it's true I don't know if he had one), and a still greater hero for his valet than for anyone else. Turenne and Fénelon might each have been a Desaix, but for "good form" and the necessary amount of force.

72. Here is blasphemy. I, a Dutchman, dare say this: the French possess neither the true pleasures of conversation nor the true pleasures of the theatre; instead of relaxation and complete unrestraint, they mean hard labor. Among the sources of fatigue which hastened on the death of Mme. de Staël I have heard counted the strain of conversation during her last winter.[1]

73. The degree of tension of the nerves in the ear, necessary to hear each note, explains well enough the physical part of one's pleasure in music.

74. What degrades rakish women is the opinion, which they share with the public, that they are guilty of a great sin.

75. In an army in retreat, warn an Italian soldier of a danger which it is no use running — he'll almost thank you and he'll carefully avoid it. If, from kindness, you point out the same danger to a French soldier, he'll think you're defying him — his sense of honor is piqued, and he runs his head straight against it. If he dared, he'd like to jeer at you. (Gyat, 1812)

[1] Memoirs of Marmontel, Montesquieu's conversation.

76. In France, any idea that can be explained only in the very simplest terms is sure to be despised, even the most useful. The Monitorial system, invented by a Frenchman, could never catch on. It is exactly the opposite in Italy.

77. Suppose you are passionately in love with a woman and that your imagination has not run dry. One evening she is tactless enough to say, looking at you tenderly and abashed: "Er — yes — come to-morrow at midday; I shall be in to no one but you." You cannot sleep; you cannot think of anything; the morning is torture. At last twelve o'clock strikes, and every stroke of the clock seems to clash and clang on your heart.

78. In love, to share money is to increase love, to give it is to kill love. You are putting off the present difficulty, and the odious fear of want in the future; or rather you are sowing the seeds of policy, of the feeling of being two. — You destroy sympathy.

79. Court ceremonies involuntarily call to mind scenes from Aretine — the way the women display their bare shoulders, like officers their uniform, and, for all their charms, make no more sensation!

There you see what in a mercenary way all will do to win a man's approval; there you see a whole world acting without morality and, what's more, without passion. All this added to the presence of the women with their very low dresses and their expression of malice, greeting with a sardonic smile everything but selfish advantage payable in the hard cash of solid pleasures — why! it gives the idea of scenes from the Bagno. It drives far away all doubts suggested by virtue or the conscious satisfaction of a heart at peace with itself. Yet I have seen the feeling of isolation amidst all this dispose gentle hearts to love. (*Mars at the Tuileries, 1811*)

80. A soul taken up with bashfulness and the effort to suppress it, is incapable of pleasure. Pleasure is a luxury — to enjoy it, security is essential and must run no risks.

81. A test of love in which mercenary women cannot disguise their feelings — "Do you feel real delight in reconciliation or is it only the thought of what you'll gain by it?"

82. The poor things who fill La Trappe are wretches who have not had quite enough courage to kill themselves. I expect, of course, the heads, who find pleasure in being heads.

83. It is a misfortune to have known Italian beauty: you lose your sensibility. Out of Italy, you prefer the conversation of men.

84. Italian prudence looks to the preservation of life, and this allows free play to the imagination. (Cf. a version of the death of Pertica the famous comic actor, December 24th, 1821.) On the other hand, English prudence, wholly relative to the gain and safe-keeping of just enough money to cover expenses, demands detailed and everyday exactitude, and this habit paralyzes the imagination. Notice also how enormously it strengthens the conception of duty.

85. The immense respect for money, which is the first and foremost vice of Englishmen and Italians, is less felt in France and reduced to perfectly rational limits in Germany.

86. French women, having never known the happiness of true passion, are anything but exacting over internal domestic happiness and the everyday side of life. (*Compiègne*)

87. "You talk to me of ambition for driving away boredom," said Kamensky: "but all the time I used to gallop a couple of leagues every evening, for the pleasure of seeing the Princess at Kolich, I was on terms of intimacy with a despot whom I respected, who had my whole good fortune in his power and the satisfaction of all my possible desires."

88. Pretty contrast! On the one hand — perfection in the little niceties of worldly wisdom and of dress, great kindli-

ness, want of genius, daily cult of a thousand and one petty observances, and incapacity for three days' attention to the same event: on the other — puritan severity, biblical cruelty, strict probity, timid, morbid self-love and universal cant! And yet these are the two foremost nations of the world.

89. As among princesses there has been an Empress Catherine II, why should not a female Samuel Bernard, or a Lagrange, appear among the middle-class?

90. Alviza calls this an unpardonable want of refinement — to dare to make love by letter to a woman you adore and who looks at you tenderly, but declares that she can never love you.

91. It was a mistake of the greatest philosopher that France has had, not to have stayed in some Alpine solitude, in some remote abode, thence to launch his book on Paris without ever coming there himself. Seeing Helvétius so simple and straightforward, unnatural, hot-house people like Suard, Marmontel or Diderot could never imagine they had a great philosopher before them. They were perfectly honest in their contempt for his profound reason. First of all, it was simple — a fault unpardonable in France; secondly, the author, not, of course, his book, was lowered in value by this weakness — the extreme importance he attached to getting what in France is called glory, to being, like Balzac, Voiture or Fontenelle, the fashion among his contemporaries.

Rousseau had too much feeling and too little logic, Buffon, in his Botanical Garden, was too hypocritical, and Voltaire too paltry to be able to judge the principle of Helvétius. Helvétius was guilty of a little slip in calling this principle *interest*, instead of giving it a pretty name like *Pleasure*,[1] but what are we to think of a nation's litera-

---

[1] Torva leoena lupum sequitur, lupus ipse capellam;
Florentem cytisum sequitur lasciva capella.
.... Trahit sua quemque voluptas. (Virgil, Eclogue II)

ture, which shows its sense by letting itself be led astray by a fault so slight?

The ordinary clever man, Prince Eugene of Savoy for example, finding himself in the position of Regulus, would have stayed quietly at Rome, and even laughed at the stupidity of the Carthaginian Senate. Regulus goes back to Carthage. Prince Eugene would have been prosecuting his own interest, and in exactly the same way Regulus was prosecuting his.

All through life a noble spirit is seeing possibilities of action, of which a common spirit can form no idea. The very second the possibility of that action becomes visible to the noble spirit, it is its interest thus to act.

If this noble spirit did not perform the action, which it has just perceived, it would despise itself — it would be unhappy. Man's duties are in the ratio of his moral range. The principle of Helvétius holds good, even in the wildest exaltations of love, even in suicide. It is contrary to his nature, it is an impossibility for a man not to do, always and at any moment you choose to take, that which is possible and which gives him most pleasure at that moment to do.

92. To have firmness of character means to have experienced the influence of others on oneself. Therefore others are necessary.

ANCIENT LOVE

93. No posthumous love-letters of Roman ladies have been printed. Petronius has written a charming book, but it is only debauch that he has painted.

For love at Rome, apart from Virgil's story of Dido[1] and his second Eclogue, we have no evidence more precise than the writings of the three great poets, Ovid, Tibullus and Propertius.

Now, Parny's *Elegies* or Colardeau's *Letter of Héloïse to Abelard* are pictures of a very imperfect and vague kind,

---

[1] Mark Dido's look in the superb sketch by M. Gúerin at the Luxembourg.

if you compare them to some of the letters in the *Nouvelle Héloïse*, to those of the Portuguese Nun, of Mademoiselle de Lespinasse, of Mirabeau's Sophie, of Werther, etc., etc.

Poetry, with its obligatory comparisons, its mythology in which the poet doesn't believe, its dignity of style *à la* Louis XIV, and all its superfluous stock of ornaments called poetical, is very inferior to prose when it comes to a question of giving a clear and precise idea of the working of the heart. And, in this class of writing, clearness alone is effective.

Tibullus, Ovid and Propertius had better taste than our poets; they have painted love such as it was to be found among the proud citizens of Rome: moreover, they lived under Augustus, who, having shut the temple of Janus, sought to debase these citizens to the condition of the loyal subjects of a monarchy.

The mistresses of these three great poets were coquettes, faithless and venal women; in their company the poets only sought physical pleasure, and never, I should think, caught a glimpse of the sublime sentiments[1] which, thirteen centuries later, stirred the heart of the gentle Héloïse.

I borrow the following passage from a distinguished man of letters,[2] and one who knows the Latin poets much better than I do: —

The brilliant genius of Ovid, the rich imagination of Propertius, the impressionable heart of Tibullus, doubtless inspired them with verses of a different flavor, but all, in the same manner, they loved women of much the same kind. They desire, they triumph, they have fortunate rivals, they are jealous, they quarrel and make it up; they are faithless in their turn, they are forgiven; and they recover their happiness only to be ruffled by the return of the same mischances.

Corinna is married. The first lessons that Ovid gives her are to teach her the address with which to deceive her husband: the signs they are to make each other before him and in society, so that they

---

[1] Everything that is beautiful in the world having become a part of the beauty of the woman you love, you find yourself inclined to do everything in the world that is beautiful.

[2] Guinguené's *Histoire littéraire de l'Italie* (Vol. II, p. 490)

can understand each other and be understood only by themselves. Enjoyment quickly follows; afterwards quarrels, and, what you wouldn't expect from so gallant a man as Ovid, insults and blows; then excuses, tears and forgiveness. Sometimes he addresses himself to subordinates — to the servants, to his mistress' porter, who is to open to him at night, to a cursed old beldam who corrupts her and teaches her to sell herself for gold, to an old eunuch who keeps watch over her, to a slave-girl who is to convey the tablets in which he begs for a rendezvous. The rendezvous is refused: he curses his tablets, that have had such sorry fortune. Fortune shines brighter: he adjures the dawn not to come to interrupt his happiness.

Soon he accuses himself of numberless infidelities, of his indiscriminate taste for women. A moment after, Corinna is herself faithless; he cannot bear the idea that he has given her lessons from which she reaps the profit with someone else. Corinna in her turn is jealous; she abuses him like a fury rather than a gentle woman; she accuses him of loving a slave-girl. He swears that there is nothing in it and writes to the slave — yet everything that made Corinna angry was true. But how did she get to know of it? What clue had led to their betrayal? He asks the slave-girl for another rendezvous. If she refuse him, he threatens to confess everything to Corinna. He jokes with a friend about his two loves and the trouble and pleasure they give him. Soon after, it is Corinna alone that fills his thoughts. She is everything to him. He sings his triumph, as if it were his first victory.

After certain incidents, which for more than one reason we must leave in Ovid, and others, which it would be too long to recount, he discovers that Corinna's husband has become too lax. He is no longer jealous; our lover does not like this, and threatens to leave the wife, if the husband does not resume his jealousy. The husband obeys him but too well; he has Corinna watched so closely, that Ovid can no longer come to her. He complains of this close watch, which he had himself provoked — but he will find a way to get round it. Unfortunately, he is not the only one to succeed therein. Corinna's infidelities begin again and multiply; her intrigues become so public, that the only boon that Ovid can crave of her, is that she will take some trouble to deceive him, and show a little less obviously what she really is. Such were the morals of Ovid and his mistress, such is the character of their love.

Cynthia is the first love of Propertius, and she will be his last. No sooner is he happy, but he is jealous. Cynthia is too fond of dress; he begs her to shun luxury and to love simplicity. He himself is given up to more than one kind of debauch. Cynthia expects him;

he only comes to her at dawn, leaving a banquet in his cups. He finds her asleep; it is a long time before she wakes, in spite of the noise he makes and even of his kisses; at last she opens her eyes and reproaches him as he deserves. A friend tries to detach him from Cynthia; he gives his friend a eulogy of her beauty and talents. He is threatened with losing her; she goes off with a soldier; she means to follow the army; she will expose herself to every danger in order to follow her soldier. Propertius does not storm; he weeps and prays heaven for her happiness. He will never leave the house she has deserted; he will look out for strangers who have seen her, and will never leave off asking them for news of Cynthia. She is touched by love so great. She deserts the soldier and stays with the poet. He gives thanks to Apollo and the Muses; he is drunk with his happiness. This happiness is soon troubled by a new access of jealousy, interrupted by separation and by absence. Far from Cynthia, he can only think of her. Her past infidelities make him fear for news. Death does not frighten him, he only fears to lose Cynthia; let him be but certain that she will be faithful and he will go down without regret to the grave.

After more treachery, he fancies he is delivered from his love; but soon he is again in its bonds. He paints the most ravishing portrait of his mistress, her beauty, the elegance of her dress, her talents in singing, poetry and dancing; everything redoubles and justifies his love. But Cynthia, as perverse as she is captivating, dishonors herself before the whole town by such scandalous adventures that Propertius can no longer love her without shame. He blushes, but he cannot shake her off. He will be her lover, her husband; he will never love any but Cynthia. They part and come together again. Cynthia is jealous, he reassures her. He will never love any other woman. But in fact it is never one woman he loves — it is all women. He never has enough of them, he is insatiable of pleasure. To recall him to himself, Cynthia has to desert him yet again. Then his complaints are as vigorous as if he had never been faithless himself. He tries to escape. He seeks distraction in debauch. — Is he drunk as usual? He pretends that a troupe of loves meets him and brings him back to Cynthia's feet. Reconciliation is followed by more storms. Cynthia, at one of their supper parties, gets heated with wine like himself, upsets the table and hits him over the head. Propertius thinks this charming. More perfidy forces him at last to break his chains; he tries to go away; he means to travel in Greece; he completes all his plans for the journey, but he renounces the project — and all in order to see himself once more the butt of new outrages. Cynthia does not confine herself to betraying him; she makes him the laughing-stock of his rivals. But illness seizes her and she dies. She reproaches him with his faithlessness, his caprices and his desertion of her in her last moments, and swears that she herself, in spite of appearances, was always faithful.

Such are the morals and adventures of Propertius and his mistress; such in abstract is the history of their love. Such was the woman that a soul like Propertius was reduced to loving.

Ovid and Propertius were often faithless, but never inconstant. Confirmed libertines, they distribute their homage far and wide, but always return to take up the same chains again. Corinna and Cynthia have womankind for rivals, but no woman in particular. The Muse of these two poets is faithful, if their love is not, and no other names besides those of Corinna and of Cynthia figure in their verses.

Tibullus, a tender lover and tender poet, less lively and less headlong in his tastes, has not their constancy. Three beauties are one after the other the objects of his love and of his verses. Delia is the first, the most celebrated and also the best beloved. Tibullus has lost his fortune, but he still has the country and Delia. To enjoy her amid the peaceful fields; to be able, at his ease, to press Delia's hand in his; to have her for his only mourner at his funeral — he makes no other prayers. Delia is kept shut up by a jealous husband; he will penetrate into her prison, in spite of any Argus and triple bolts. He will forget all his troubles in her arms. He falls ill and Delia alone fills his thoughts. He exhorts her to be always chaste, to despise gold, and to grant none but him the love she has granted him. But Delia does not follow his advice. He thought he could put up with her infidelity; but it is too much for him and he begs Delia and Venus for pity. He seeks in wine a remedy and does not find it; he can neither soften his regret nor cure himself of his love. He turns to Delia's husband, deceived like himself, and reveals to him all the tricks she uses to attract and see her lovers. If the husband does not know how to keep watch over her, let her be trusted to himself; he will manage right enough to ward the lovers off and to keep from their toils the author of their common wrongs. He is appeased and returns to her; he remembers Delia's mother who favored their love; the memory of this good woman opens his heart once more to tender thoughts, and all Delia's wrongs are forgotten. But she is soon guilty of others more serious. She lets herself be corrupted by gold and presents; she gives herself to another, to others. At length Tibullus breaks his shameful chains and says good-bye to her for ever.

He passes under the sway of Nemesis and is no happier; she loves only gold and cares little for poetry and the gifts of genius. Nemesis is a greedy woman who sells herself to the highest bidder; he curses her avarice, but he loves her and cannot live unless she loves him. He tries to move her with touching images. She has lost her young sister; he will go and weep on her tomb and confide his grief to her dumb ashes. The shade of her sister will take offence at the tears that Nemesis causes to flow. She must not despise her anger. The sad image of her sister might come at night to trouble her sleep.... But these sad memories force tears from Nemesis — and at that price he could not buy even happiness. Neæra is his third mistress. He has long enjoyed her love; he only prays the gods that he may live and die with her; but she leaves him, she is gone; he can only think of her, she is his only prayer; he has seen in a dream Apollo, who announces to him that Neæra is unfaithful. He refuses to believe this dream; he could not survive his misfortune, and none the less the misfortune is there. Neæra is faithless; once more Tibullus is deserted. Such was his character and fortune, such is the triple and all unhappy story of his loves.

In him particularly there is a sweet, all-pervading melancholy, that gives even to his pleasures the tone of dreaminess and sadness which constitutes his charm. If any poet of antiquity introduced moral sensibility into love, it was Tibullus; but these fine shades of feeling which he expresses so well, are in himself; he expects no more than the other two to find them or engender them in his mistresses. Their grace, their beauty is all that inflames him; their favors all he desires or regrets; their perfidy, their venality, their loss, all that torments him. Of all these women, celebrated in the verses of three great poets, Cynthia seems the most lovable. The attraction of talent is joined to all the others; she cultivates singing and poetry; and yet all these talents, which were found not infrequently in courtesans of a certain standing, were of no avail — it was none the less pleasure, gold and wine which ruled her. And Propertius, who boasts only once or twice of her artistic tastes, in his passion for her is none the less seduced by a very different power!

These great poets are apparently to be numbered among the most tender and refined souls of their century — well! this is how they loved and whom. We must here put literary considerations on one side. I only ask of them evidence concerning their century; and in two thousand years a novel by Ducray-Duminil will be evidence concerning the annals of ours.

93b. One of my great regrets is not to have been able to see Venice in 1760.[1] A run of happy chances had apparently united, in so small a space, both the political institutions and the public opinion that are most favorable to the happiness of mankind. A soft spirit of luxury gave everyone an easy access to happiness. There were no domestic struggles and no crimes. Serenity was seen on every face; no one thought about seeming richer than he was; hypocrisy had no point. I imagine it must have been the direct contrary to London in 1822.

94. If in the place of the want of personal security you put the natural fear of economic want, you will see that the United States of America bears a considerable resemblance to the ancient world as regards that passion, on which we are attempting to write a monograph.

In speaking of the more or less imperfect sketches of passion-love which the ancients have left us, I see that I have forgotten the Loves of Medea in the *Argonautica*. Virgil copied them in his picture of Dido. Compare that with love as seen in a modern novel — *Le Doyen de Killerine*, for example.

95. The Roman feels the beauties of Nature and Art with amazing strength, depth and justice; but if he sets out to try and reason on what he feels so forcibly, it is pitiful.

The reason may be that his feelings come to him from Nature, but his logic from government.

You can see at once why the fine arts, outside Italy, are only a farce; men reason better, but the public has no feeling.

London, *November 20th, 1821*

96. A very sensible man, who arrived yesterday from Madras, told me in a two hours' conversation what I reduce to the following few lines: —

[1] *Travels in Italy* of the President de Brosses, Travels of Eustace, Sharp, Smollett.

This gloom, which from an unknown cause depresses the English character, penetrates so deeply into their hearts, that at the end of the world, at Madras, no sooner does an Englishman get a few days' holiday, than he quickly leaves rich and flourishing Madras and comes to revive his spirits in the little French town of Pondicherry, which, without wealth and almost without commerce, flourishes under the paternal administration of M. Dupuy. At Madras you drink Burgundy that costs thirty-six francs a bottle; the poverty of the French in Pondicherry is such that, in the most distinguished circles, the refreshments consist of large glasses of water. But in Pondicherry they laugh.

At present there is more liberty in England than in Prussia. The climate is the same as that of Koenigsberg, Berlin or Warsaw, cities which are far from being famous for their gloom. The working classes in these towns have less security and drink quite as little wine as in England; and they are much worse clothed.

The aristocracies of Venice and Vienna are not gloomy.

I can see only one point of difference: in gay countries the Bible is little read, and there is gallantry. I am sorry to have to come back so often to a demonstration with which I am unsatisfied. I suppress a score of facts pointing in the same direction.

97. I have just seen, in a fine country-house near Paris, a very good-looking, very clever, and very rich young man of less than twenty; he has been left there by chance almost alone, for a long time too, with a most beautiful girl of eighteen, full of talent, of a most distinguished mind, and also very rich. Who wouldn't have expected a passionate love-affair? Not a bit of it — such was the affectation of these two charming creatures that both were occupied solely with themselves and the effect they were to produce.

98. I am ready to agree that on the morrow of a great action a savage pride has made this people fall into all the faults and follies that lay open to it. But you will see what prevents me from effacing my previous praises of this representative of the Middle Ages.

The prettiest woman in Narbonne is a young Spaniard, scarcely twenty years old, who lives there very retired with her husband, a Spaniard also, and an officer on half-pay. Some time ago there was a fool whom this officer was obliged to insult. The next day, on the field of combat, the fool sees the young Spanish woman arrive. He begins a renewed flow of affected nothings: —

"No, indeed, it's shocking! How could you tell your wife about it? You see, she has come to prevent us fighting!"

"I have come to bury you," she answered.

Happy the husband who can tell his wife everything! The result did not belie this woman's haughty words. Her action would have been considered hardly the thing in England. Thus does false decency diminish the little happiness that exists here below.

99. The delightful Domézan said yesterday: "In my youth, and well on in my career — for I was fifty in '89 — women wore powder in their hair.

"I own that a woman without powder gives me a feeling of repugnance; the first impression is always that of a chamber-maid who hasn't had time to get dressed."

Here we have the one argument against Shakespeare and in favor of the dramatic unities.

While young men read nothing but Le Harpe, the taste for great powdered *toupées,* such as the late Queen Marie Antoinette used to wear, can still last some years. I know people too, who despise Correggio and Michael Angelo, and, to be sure, M. Donézan was extremely clever.

100. Cold, brave, calculating, suspicious, contentious, for ever afraid of being attracted by anyone who might possibly be laughing at them in secret, absolutely devoid of enthusiasm, and a little jealous of people who saw great events with Napoleon, such was the youth of that age, estimable rather than lovable. They forced on the country that Right-Centre form of government-to-the-lowest-bidder. This

temper in the younger generation was to be found even among the conscripts, each of whom only longed to finish his time.

All systems of education, whether given expressly or by chance, form men for a certain period in their life. The education of the age of Louis XV made twenty-five the finest moment in the lives of its pupils.[1]

It is at forty that the young men of this period will be at their best; they will have lost their suspiciousness and pretensions, and have gained ease and gaiety.

DISCUSSION BETWEEN AN HONEST MAN AND AN ACADEMIC

101. "In this discussion, the academic always saved himself by fixing on little dates and other similar errors of small importance; but the consequences and natural qualifications of things, these he always denied, or seemed not to understand: for example, that Nero was a cruel Emperor or Charles II a perjurer. Now, how are you to prove things of this kind, or, even if you do, manage not to put a stop to the general discussion or lose the thread of it?

"This, I have always remarked, is the method of discussion between such folk, one of whom seeks only the truth and advancement thereto, the other the favor of his master or his party and the glory of talking well. And I always consider it great folly and waste of time for an honest man to stop and talk with the said academics." (*Œuvres badines* of Guy Allard de Voiron)

102. Only a small part of the art of being happy is an exact science, a sort of ladder up which one can be sure of climbing a rung per century — and that is the part which depends on government. (Still, this is only theory. I find the Venetians of 1770 happier than the people of Philadelphia to-day.)

For the rest, the art of being happy is like poetry; in spite of the perfecting of all things, Homer, two thousand seven hundred years ago, had more talent than Lord Byron.

[1] M. de Francueil with too much powder: Memoirs of Madame d'Epinay.

Reading Plutarch with attention, I think I can see that men were happier in Sicily in the time of Dion than we manage to be to-day, although they had no printing and no iced punch!

I would rather be an Arab of the fifth century than a Frenchman of the nineteenth.

103. People go to the theatre, never for that kind of illusion which is lost one minute and found again the next, but for an opportunity of convincing their neighbor, or at least themselves, that they have read their La Harpe and are people who know what's good. It is an old pedant's pleasure that the younger generation indulges in.

104. A woman belongs by right to the man who loves her and is dearer to her than life.

105. Crystallization cannot be excited by an understudy, and your most dangerous rivals are those most unlike you.

106. In a very advanced state of society passion-love is as natural as physical love among savages. (M)

107. But for an infinite number of shades of feeling, to have a woman you adore would be no happiness and scarcely a possibility. (L., *October 7th*)

108. Whence comes the intolerance of Stoic philosophers? From the same source as that of religious fanatics. They are put out because they are struggling against nature, because they deny themselves, and because it hurts them. If they would question themselves honestly on the hatred they bear towards those who profess a code of morals less severe, they would have to own that it springs from a secret jealousy of a bliss which they envy and have renounced, without believing in the rewards which would make up for this sacrifice. (Diderot)

109. Women who are always taking offence might well ask themselves whether they are following a line of conduct, which they think really and truly is the road to happiness. Is there not a little lack of courage, mixed with a little mean revenge, at the bottom of a prude's heart? Consider the ill-humor of Madame de Deshoulières in her last day. (Note by M. Lemontey)

110. Nothing more indulgent than virtue without hypocrisy — because nothing happier; yet even Mistress Hutchinson might well be more indulgent.

111. Immediately below this kind of happiness comes that of a young, pretty and easy-going woman, with a conscience that does not reproach her. At Messina people used to talk scandal about the Contessina Vicenzella. "Well, well!" she would say, "I'm young, free, rich and perhaps not ugly. I wish the same to all the ladies of Messina!" It was this charming woman, who would never be more than a friend to me, who introduced me to the Abbé Melli's sweet poems in Sicilian dialect. His poetry is delicious, though still disfigured by mythology. (Delfante)

112. The public of Paris has a fixed capacity for attention — three days: after which, bring to its notice the death of Napoleon or M. Béranger sent to prison for two months — the news is just as sensational, and to bring it up on the fourth day just as tactless. Must every great capital be like this, or has it to do with the good nature and light heart of the Parisian? Thanks to aristocratic pride and morbid reserve, London is nothing but a numerous collection of hermits; it is not a capital. Vienna is nothing but an oligarchy of two hundred families surrounded by a hundred and fifty thousand workpeople and servants who wait on them. No more is that a capital. — Naples and Paris, the only two capitals. (Extract from Birkbeck's *Travels*, p. 371)

113. According to common ideas, or reasonable ideas, as they are called by ordinary people, if any period of imprisonment could possibly be tolerable, it would be after several years' confinement, when at last the poor prisoner is only separated by a month or two from the moment of his release. But the ways of crystallization are otherwise. The last month is more painful than the last three years. In the gaol at Melum, M. d'Hotelans has seen several prisoners die of impatience within a few months of the day of release.

114. I cannot resist the pleasure of copying out a letter written in bad English by a young German woman. It proves that, after all, constant love exists, and that not every man of genius is a Mirabeau. Klopstock, the great poet, passes at Hamburg for having been an attractive person. Read what his young wife wrote to an intimate friend:

"After having seen him two hours, I was obliged to pass the evening in a company, which never had been so wearisome to me. I could not speak, I could not play; I thought I saw nothing but Klopstock; I saw him the next day and the following and we were very seriously friends. But the fourth day he departed. It was a strong hour the hour of his departure! He wrote soon after; from that time our correspondence began to be a very diligent one. I sincerely believed my love to be friendship. I spoke with my friends of nothing but Klopstock, and showed his letters. They raillied at me and said I was in love. I raillied then again, and said that they must have a very friendshipless heart, if they had no idea of friendship to a man as well as to a woman. Thus it continued eight months, in which time my friends found as much love in Klopstock's letters as in me. I perceived it likewise, but I would not believe it. At the last Klopstock said plainly that he loved; and I startled as for a wrong thing; I answered that it was no love, but friendship, as it was what I felt for him; we had not seen one another enough to love (as if love must have more time than friendship). This was sincerely my meaning, and I had this meaning till Klopstock came again to Hamburg. This he did a year after we had seen one another the first time. We saw, we were friends, we loved; and a short time after, I could even tell Klopstock that I loved. But we were obliged to part again, and wait two years for our wedding. My mother would not let me marry a stranger. I could marry then without her consent, as by the death of my father my fortune depended not on her; but this was a horrible idea for me; and thank heaven that I have prevailed by prayers! At this time knowing Klopstock, she loves him as her lifely son, and thanks God that she has not persisted. We married and I am the happiest wife in the world. In some few months it will be four years that I am so happy. . . ." (*Correspondence of Richardson*, Vol. III, p. 147)

115. The only unions legitimate for all time are those that answer to a real passion.

116. To be happy with laxity of morals, one wants the simplicity of character that is found in Germany and Italy, but never in France. (The Duchess de C——)

117. It is their pride that makes the Turks deprive their women of everything that can nourish crystallization. I have been living for the last three months in a country where the titled folk will soon be carried just as far by theirs.

Modesty is the name given here by men to the exactions of aristocratic pride run mad. Who would risk a lapse of modesty? Here also, as at Athens, the intellectuals show a marked tendency to take refuge with courtesans — that is to say, with the women whom a scandal shelters from the need to affect modesty. (*Life of Fox*)

118. In the case of love blighted by too prompt a victory, I have seen in very tender characters crystallization trying to form later. "I don't love you a bit," she says, but laughing.

119. The present-day education of women — that odd mix-ture of works of charity and risqué songs ("Di piecer mi balza il cor," in *La Gazza Ladra*) — is the one thing in the world best calculated to keep off happiness. This form of educa-tion produces minds completely inconsequent. Madame de R——, who was afraid of dying, has just met her death through thinking it funny to throw her medicines out of the window. Poor little women like her take inconsequence for gaiety, because, in appearance, gaiety is often inconse-quent. 'Tis like the German, who threw himself out of the window in order to be sprightly.

120. Vulgarity, by stifling imagination, instantly produces in me a deadly boredom. Charming Countess K——, show-ing me this evening her lovers' letters, which to my mind were in bad taste. (Forlì, *March 17th*, Henri)

Imagination was not stifled: it was only deranged, and very soon from mere repugnance ceased to picture the un-pleasantness of these dull lovers.

METAPHYSICAL REVERIE

121. Real passion has only to be crossed for it to produce apparently more unhappiness than happiness. This thought may not be true in the case of gentle souls, but it is abso-lutely proved in the case of the majority of men, and par-ticularly of cold philosophers, who, as regards passion, live, one might say, only on curiosity and self-love.

I said all this to the Contessina Fulvia yesterday evening, as we were walking together near the great pine on the eastern terrace of Isola Bella. She answered: "Unhappiness makes a much stronger impression on a man's life than pleasure.

"The prime virtue in anything which claims to give us pleasure, is that it strikes hard.

"Might we not say that life itself being made up only of sensation, there is a universal taste in all living beings for the consciousness that the sensations of their life are the keenest that can be? In the North people are hardly alive — look at the slowness of their movements. The Italian's *dolce far niente* is the pleasure of relishing one's soul and one's emotions, softly reclining on a divan. Such pleasure is impossible, if you are racing all day on horseback or in a drosky, like the Englishman or the Russian. Such people would die of boredom on a divan. There is no reason to look into their souls.

"Love gives the keenest possible of all sensations — and the proof is that in these moments of 'inflammation,' as physiologists would say, the heart is open to those 'complex sensations' which Helvétius, Buffon and other philosophers think so absurd. The other day, as you know, Luizina fell into the lake; you see, her eye was following a laurel leaf that had fallen from a tree on Isola-Madre (one of the Borromean Islands). The poor woman owned to me that one day her lover, while talking to her, threw into the lake the leaves of a laurel branch he was stripping, and said: 'Your cruelty and the calumnies of your friend are preventing me from turning my life to account and winning a little glory.'

"It is a peculiar and incomprehensible fact that, when some great passion has brought upon the soul moments of torture and extreme unhappiness, the soul comes to despise the happiness of a peaceful life, where everything seems framed to our desires. A fine country-house in a picturesque position, substantial means, a good wife, three pretty children, and friends charming and numerous — this is but a mere outline of all our host, General C——, possesses. And yet he said, as you know, he felt tempted to go to Naples and take the command of a guerilla band. A soul made for passion soon finds this happy life monotonous, and feels, perhaps, that it only offers him commonplace ideas. 'I wish,' C. said to you, 'that I had never known the fever of high passion. I wish I could rest content with the apparent happiness on which people pay me every day such stupid compliments, which, to put the finishing touch to, I have to answer politely.'"

I, a philosopher, rejoin: "Do you want the thousandth proof that we are not created by a good Being? It is the fact that pleasure does not make perhaps half as much impression on human life as pain. . . ."[1] The Contessina interrupted me. "In life there are few mental pains that are not rendered sweet by the emotion they themselves excite, and, if there is a spark of magnanimity in the soul, this pleasure is increased a hundred-fold. The man condemned to death in 1815 and saved by chance (M. de Lavalette, for example), if he was going courageously to his doom, must recall that moment ten times a month. But the coward, who was going to die crying and yelling (the exciseman, Morris thrown into the lake, *Rob Roy*) — suppose him also saved by chance —can at most recall that instant with pleasure because he was *saved*, not for the treasures of magnanimity that he discovered within him, and that take away for the future all his fears."

I: "Love, even unhappy love, gives a gentle soul, for whom a thing imagined is a thing existent, treasures of this kind of enjoyment. He weaves sublime visions of happiness and beauty about himself and his beloved. How often has Salviati heard Léonore, with her enchanting smile, say, like Mademoiselle Mars in *Les Fausses Confidences*: 'Well, yes, I do love you!' No, these are never the illusions of a prudent mind."

Fulvia (raising her eyes to heaven): "Yes, for you and me, love, even unhappy love, if only our admiration for the beloved knows no limit, is the supreme happiness."

(Fulvia is twenty-three, — the most celebrated beauty of . . . . Her eyes were heavenly as she talked like this at midnight and raised them towards the glorious sky above the Borromean Islands. The stars seemed to answer her. I looked down and could find no more philosophical arguments to meet her. She continued:)

---

[1] See the analysis of the ascetic principle in Bentham, *Principles of Morals and Legislation*.

By giving oneself pain one pleases a *good* Being.

"And all that the world calls happiness is not worth the trouble. Only contempt, I think, can cure this passion; not contempt too violent, for that is torture. For you men it is enough to see the object of your adoration love some gross, prosaic creature, or sacrifice you in order to enjoy pleasures of luxurious comfort with a woman friend." (Belgirate, *26th October, 1816*)

122. *To will* means to have the courage to expose onself to troubles; to expose oneself is to take risks — to gamble. You find military men who cannot exist without such gambling — that's what makes them intolerable in home-life.

123. General Teulié told me this evening that he had found out why, as soon as there were affected women in a drawing-room, he became so horribly dry and floored for ideas. It was because he was sure to be bitterly ashamed of having exposed his feelings with warmth before such creatures. General Teulié had to speak from his heart, though the talk were only of Punch and Judy; otherwise he had nothing to say. Moreover, I could see he never knew the conventional phrase about anything nor what was the right thing to say. That is really where he made himself so monstrously ridiculous in the eyes of affected women. Heaven had not made him for elegant society.

124. Irreligion is bad form at Court, because it is calculated to be contrary to the interests of princes: irreligion is also bad form in the presence of girls, for it would prevent their finding husbands. It must be owned that, if God exists, it must be nice for Him to be honored from motives like these.

125. For the soul of a great painter or a great poet, love is divine in that it increases a hundredfold the empire and the delight of his art, and the beauties of art are his soul's daily bread. How many great artists are unconscious both

of their soul and of their genius! Often they reckon as mediocre their talent for the thing they adore, because they cannot agree with the eunuchs of the harem, La Harpe and such-like. For them even unhappy love is happiness.

126. The picture of first love is taken generally as the most touching. Why? Because it is the same in all countries and in all characters. But for this reason first love is not the most passionate.

127. Reason! Reason! Reason! That is what the world is always shouting at poor lovers. In 1760, at the most thrilling moment in the Seven Years' War, Grimm wrote: " . . . It is indubitable that the King of Russia, by yielding Silesia, could have prevented the war from ever breaking out. In so doing he would have done a very wise thing. How many evils would he have prevented! And what can there be in common between the possession of a province and the happiness of a king? Was not the great Elector a very happy and highly respected prince without possessing Silesia? It is also quite clear that a king might have taken this course in obedience to the precepts of the soundest reason, and yet — I know not how — that king would inevitably have been the object of universal contempt, while Frederick, sacrificing everything to the *necessity* of keeping Silesia, has invested himself with immortal glory.

"Without any doubt the action of Cromwell's son was the wisest a man could take: he preferred obscurity and repose to the bother and danger of ruling over a people sombre, fiery and proud. This wise man won the contempt of his own time and posterity; while his father, to this day, has been held a great man by the wisdom of nations.

"The *Fair Penitent* is a sublime subject on the Spanish[1] stage, but spoiled by Otway and Colardeau in England and France. Calista has been dishonored by a man she adores; he is odious from the violence of his inborn pride, but tal-

---

[1] See the Spanish and Danish romances of the thirteenth century. French taste would find them dull and coarse.

ent, wit and a handsome face — everything, in fact — combine to make him seductive. Indeed, Lothario would have been too charming could he have moderated these criminal outbursts. Moreover, an hereditary and bitter feud separates his family from that of the woman he loves. These families are at the head of two factions dividing a Spanish town during the horrors of the Middle Age. Sciolto, Calista's father, is the chief of the faction, which at the moment has the upper hand; he knows that Lothario has had the insolence to try to seduce his daughter. The weak Calista is weighed down by the torment of shame and passion. Her father has succeeded in getting his enemy appointed to the command of a naval armament that is setting out on a distant and perilous expedition, where Lothario will probably meet his death. In Colardeau's tragedy, he has just told his daughter this news. At his words Calista can no longer hide her passion:

> O dieux!
> Il part! . . . Vous l'ordonnez! . . . Il a pu s'y résoudre?[1]

"Think of the danger she is placed in. Another word, and Sciolto will learn the secret of his daughter's passion for Lothario. The father is confounded and cries: —

> Qu'entends-je? Me trompê-je? Où s'égarent tes voeux?[2]

"At this Calista recovers herself and answers: —

> Ce n'est pas son exile, c'est sa mort que je veux,
> Qu'il périsse![3]

"By these words Calista stifles her father's rising suspicions; yet there is no deceit, for the sentiment she utters is true. The existence of a man, who has succeeded after winning her love in dishonoring her, must poison her life, were he even at the ends of the earth. His death alone could

---

[1] ["My God!
He is gone. . . . . You have sent him. . . . And he had the heart?"]

[2] ["What do I hear? I am deceived? Where now are all your vows?"]

[3] ["It is not his banishment I desire; it is his death. Let him die!"]

restore her peace of mind, if for unfortunate lovers peace of mind existed. . . . Soon after Lothario is killed and, happily for her, Calista dies.

"'There's a lot of crying and moaning over nothing!' say the chilly folk who plume themselves on being philosophers. 'Somebody with an enterprising and violent nature abuses a woman's weakness for him — that is nothing to tear our hair over, or at least there is nothing in Calista's troubles to concern us. She must console herself with having satisfied her lover, and she will not be the first woman of merit who has made the best of her misfortune in that way.'"[1]

Richard Cromwell, the King of Prussia, and Calista, with the souls given them by Heaven, could only find peace and happiness by acting as they did. The conduct of the two last is eminently unreasonable and yet it is those two that we admire. (Sagan, 1813)

128. The likelihood of constancy when desire is satisfied can only be foretold from the constancy displayed, in spite of cruel doubts and jealousy and ridicule, in the days before intimate intercourse.

129. A woman is in despair at the death of her lover, who has been killed in the wars — of course she means to follow him. Now first make quite sure that it is not the best thing for her to do; then, if you decide it is not, attack her on the side of a very primitive habit of the human kind — the desire to survive. If the woman has an enemy, one may persuade her that her enemy has obtained a warrant for her imprisonment. Unless that threat only increases her desire of death, she may think about hiding herself in order to escape imprisonment. For three weeks she will lie low, escaping from refuge to refuge. She must be caught, but must get away after three days.

Then people must arrange for her to withdraw under a false name to some very remote town, as unlike as possible

[1] Grimm, Vol. III, p. 107.

the one in which she was so desperately unhappy. But who is going to devote himself to the consolation of a being so unfortunate and so lost to friendship? (Warsaw, 1808)

130. Academical wise-heads can see a people's habits in its language. In Italy, of all the countries in the world, the word love is least often spoken — always "amicizia" and "avvicinar" (*amicizia* or friendship, for love; *avvicinar*, to approach, for courtship that succeeds).

131. A dictionary of music has never been achieved, nor even begun. It is only by chance that you find the phrase for: "I am angry" or "I love you," and the subtler feelings involved therein. The composer finds them only when passion, present in his heart or memory, dictates them to him. Well! that is why people, who spend the fire of youth studying instead of feeling, cannot be artists — the way *that* works is perfectly simple.

132. In France far too much power is given to Women, far too little to Woman.

133. The most flattering thing that the most exalted imagination could find to say to the generation now arising among us to take possession of life, of public opinion and of power, happens to be a piece of truth plainer than the light of day. This generation has nothing to *continue*, it has everything to *create*. Napoleon's great merit is to have left the road clear.

134. I should like to be able to say something on consolation. Enough is not done to console.

The main principle is that you try to form a kind of crystallization as remote as possible from the source of present suffering.

In order to discover an unknown principle, we must bravely face a little anatomy.

If the reader will consult Chapter II of M. Villermé's work on prisons (Paris, 1820), he will see that the prisoners "si maritano fra di loro" (it is the expression in the prisoner's language). The women also "si maritano fra di loro," and in these unions, generally speaking, much fidelity is shown. That is an outcome of the principle of modesty, and is not observed among the men.

"At Saint-Lazare," says M. Villermé, page 96, "a woman, seeing a new-comer preferred to her, gave herself several wounds with a knife. (*October, 1818*)

"Usually it is the younger woman who is more fond than the other."

135. Vivacità, leggerezza, soggettisima a prendere puntiglio, occupazione di ogni momento delle apparenze della propria esistenza agli occhi altrui: Ecco i tre gran caratteri di questa pianta che risveglia Europa nell 1808.[1]

Of Italians, those are preferable who still preserve a little savagery and taste for blood — the people of the Romagna, Calabria, and, among the more civilized, the Brescians, Piedmontese and Corsicans.

The Florentine bourgeois has more sheepish docility than the Parisian. Leopold's spies have degraded him. See M. Courier's letter on the Librarian Furia and the Chamberlain Puccini.

136. I smile when I see earnest people never able to agree, saying quite unconcernedly the most abusive things of each other — and thinking still worse. To live is to feel life — to have strong feelings. But strength must be rated for each individual, and what is painful — that is, too strong — for one man is exactly enough to stir another's interest. Take, for example, the feeling of just being spared by the cannon shot in the line of fire, the feeling of penetrating into Russia in pursuit of Parthian hordes. . . . And it is the same with the tragedies of Shakespeare and those of Racine, etc., etc. . . . (Orcha, *August 13, 1812*)

---

[1] ["Vivacity, levity, very subject to pique, and unflagging preoccupation with other people's views of its own existence — these are the three distinguishing points in the stock which is stirring the life of Europe in 1808."]

137. Pleasure does not produce half so strong an impression as pain — that is the first point. Then, besides this disadvantage in the quantity of emotion, it is certainly not half as easy to excite sympathy by the picture of happiness as by that of misfortune. Hence poets cannot depict unhappiness too forcibly. They have only one shoal to fear, namely, things that disgust. Here again, the force of feeling must be rated differently for monarchies and republics. A Louis XIV increases a hundredfold the number of disgusting things. (Crabbe's Poems.)

By the mere fact of its existence a monarchy à la Louis XIV, with its circle of nobles, makes everything simple in Art become coarse. The noble personage for whom the thing is exposed feels insulted; the feeling is sincere — and in so far worthy.

See what the gentle Racine has been able to make of the heroic friendship, so sacred to antiquity, of Orestes and Pylades. Orestes addresses Pylades with the familiar *"tu."* Pylades answers him *"Seigneur."* And then people pretend Racine is our most touching writer! If they won't give in after this example, we must change the subject.

138. Directly the hope of revenge is possible, the feeling of hatred returns. Until the last weeks of my imprisonment it never entered my head to run away and break the solemn oath I had sworn to my friend. Two confidences these — made this morning in my presence by a gentleman cut-throat who favored us with the history of his life. (Faenza, 1817)

139. All Europe, put together, could never make one French book of the really good type — the *Lettres Persanes,* for example.

140. I call pleasure every impression which the soul would rather receive than not receive.[1]

[1] Maupertius.

I call pain every impression which the soul would rather not receive than receive.

If I want to go to sleep rather than be conscious of my feelings, they are undoubtedly pain. Hence the desire of love is not pain, for the lover will leave the most agreeable society in order to day-dream in peace.

Time weakens pleasures of the body and aggravates its pains.

As for spiritual pleasures — they grow weaker or stronger according to the passion. For example, after six months passed in the study of astronomy you like astronomy all the more, and after a year of avarice money is still sweeter.

Spiritual pains are softened by time — how many widows, really inconsolable, console themselves with time! — *Vide* Lady Waldegrave — Horace Walpole.

Given a man in a state of indifference — now let him have a pleasure;

Given another man in a state of poignant suffering — suddenly let the suffering cease;

Now is the pleasure this man feels of the same nature as that of the other? M. Verri says Yes, but, to my mind — No.

Not all pleasures come from cessation of pain.

A man had lived for a long time on an income of six thousand francs — he wins five hundred thousand in the lottery. He had got out of the way of having desires which wealth alone can satisfy. — And that, by the bye, is one of my objections to Paris — it is so easy to lose this habit there.

The latest invention is a machine for cutting quills. I bought one this morning and it's a great joy to me, as I cannot stand cutting them myself. But yesterday I was certainly not unhappy for not knowing of this machine. Or was Petrarch unhappy for not taking coffee?

What is the use of defining happiness? Everyone knows it — the first partridge you kill on the wing at twelve, the first battle you come through safely at seventeen. . . .

Pleasure which is only the cessation of pain passes very quickly, and its memory, after some years, is even distasteful. One of my friends was wounded in the side by a bursting shell at the battle of Moscow, and a few days later mortification threatened. After a delay of some hours they managed to get together M. Béclar, M. Larrey and some surgeons of repute, and the result of their consultation was that my friend was informed that mortification had not set in. At the moment I could see his happiness — it was a great happiness, but not unalloyed. In the secret depth of his heart he could not believe that it was really all over, he kept reconsidering the surgeons' words and debating whether he could rely on them entirely. He never lost sight completely of the possibility of mortification. Nowadays, after eight years, if you speak to him of that consultation, it gives him pain — it brings to mind unexpectedly a passed unhappiness.

Pleasure caused by the cessation of pain consists in: —

1. Defeating the continual succession of one's own misgivings:
2. Reviewing all the advantages one was on the point of losing.

Pleasure caused by winning five hundred thousand francs consists in foreseeing all the new and unusual pleasures one is going to indulge in.

There is this peculiar reservation to be made. You have to take into account whether a man is too used, or not used enough, to wishing for wealth. If he is not used enough, if his mind is closely circumscribed, for two or three days together he will feel embarrassed; while if he is inclined very often to wish for great riches, he will find he has used up their enjoyments in advance by too frequently foretasting them.

This misfortune is unknown to passion-love.

A soul on fire pictures to itself not the last favor, but the nearest — perhaps just her hand to press, if, for example, your mistress is unkind to you. Imagination does not pass beyond that of its own accord; you may force it, but a moment later it is gone — for fear of profaning its idol.

When pleasure has run through the length of its career, we fall again, of course, into indifference, but this is not the same indifference as we felt before. The second state differs from the first in that we are no longer in a position to relish with such delight the pleasure that we have just tasted. The organs we use for plucking pleasures are worn out. The imagination is no longer so inclined to offer fancies for the enjoyment of desire — desire is satisfied.

In the midst of enjoyment to be torn from pleasure produces pain.

141. With regard to physical love and, in fact, physical pleasure, the disposition of the two sexes is not the same. Unlike men, practically all women are at least susceptible in secret to one kind of love. Ever after opening her first novel at fifteen, a woman is silently waiting for the coming of passion-love, and towards twenty, when she is just over the irresponsibility of life's first flush, the suspense redoubles. As for men, they think love impossible or ridiculous, almost before they are thirty.

142. From the age of six we grow used to run after pleasure in our parents' footsteps.

The pride of Contessina Nella's mother was the starting-point of that charming woman's troubles, and by the same insane pride she now makes them hopeless. (Venice, 1819)

ROMANTICISM

143. I hear from Paris that there are heaps and heaps of pictures to be seen there (Exhibition of 1822), representing subjects taken from the Bible, painted by artists who hardly believe in it, admired and criticized by people who don't believe, and finally paid for by people who don't believe.

After that — you ask why art is decadent.

The artist who does not believe what he is saying is always afraid of appearing exaggerated or ridiculous. How is he to touch the sublime? Nothing uplifts him. (*Lettera di Roma*, Giugna, 1822)

144. One of the greatest poets the world has seen in modern times is, to my mind, Robert Burns, a Scotch peasant, who died of want. He had a salary of seventy pounds as exciseman — for himself, his wife and four children. One cannot help saying, by the way, that Napoleon was more liberal towards his enemy Chénier. Burns had none of the English prudery about him. His was a Roman genius, without chivalry and without honor. I have no space here to tell of his love-affairs with Mary Campbell and their mournful ending. I shall merely point out that Edinburgh is on the same latitude as Moscow — a fact which perhaps upsets my system of climates a little.

"One of Burns' remarks, when he first came to Edinburgh, was all between the men of rustic life and those of the polite world he observed little difference; that in the former, though unpolished by fashion and unenlightened by science, he had found much observation and much intelligence; but that a refined and accomplished woman was a being almost new to him, and of which he had formed but a very inadequate idea." (London, *November 1st, 1821*, vol. V, p. 69)

145. Love is the only passion that mints the coin to pay its own expenses.

146. The compliments paid to little girls of three furnish exactly the right sort of education to imbue them with the most pernicious vanity. To look pretty is the highest virtue, the greatest advantage on earth. To have a pretty dress is to look pretty.

These idiotic compliments are not current except in the middle class. Happily they are bad form outside the suburbs — being too easy to pay.

Loretto, *September 11th, 1811*

147. I have just seen a very fine battalion composed of natives of this country — the remains, in fact, of four thousand who left for Vienna in 1809. I passed along the ranks

with the Colonel, and asked several of the soldiers to tell me their story. Theirs is the virtue of the republics of the Middle Age, though more or less debased by the Spaniards,[1] the Roman Church,[2] and two centuries of the cruel, treacherous governments, which, one after another, have spoiled the country.

Flashing, chivalrous honor, sublime but senseless, is an exotic plant introduced here only a very few years back.

In 1740 there was no trace of it. *Vide* de Brosses. The officers of Montenotte and of Rivoli had too many chances of showing their comrades true virtue to go and *imitate* a kind of honor unknown to the cottage homes from which the soldiery of 1796 was drawn — indeed, it would have seemed to them highly fantastic.

In 1796 there was no Legion of Honor, no enthusiasm for one man, but plenty of simple truth and virtue *à la* Desaix. We may conclude that honor was imported into Italy by people too reasonable and too virtuous to cut much of a figure. One is sensible of a large gap between the soldiers of '96, often shoeless and coatless, the victors of twenty battles in one year, and the brilliant regiments of Fontenoy, taking off their hats and saying to the English politely: *Messieurs, tirez les premiers* — gentlemen, pray begin.

148. I am ready to agree that one must judge the soundness of a system of life by the perfect representative of its supporters. For example, Richard Cœur-de-Lion is the perfect pattern on the throne of heroism and chivalrous valor, and as a king was a ludicrous failure.

149. Public opinion in 1822: A man of thirty seduces a girl of fifteen — the girl loses her reputation.

[1] The Spaniards abroad, about 1580, were nothing but energetic agents of despotism or serenaders beneath the windows of Italian beauties. In those days Spaniards dropped into Italy just in the way people come nowadays to Paris. For the rest, they prided themselves on nothing but upholding the honor of the king, *their master*. They ruined Italy — ruined and degraded it.
In 1626 the great poet Calderon was an officer at Milan.

[2] See *Life of S. Carlo Borromeo*, who transformed Milan and debased it, emptied its drill halls and filled its chapels. Merveilles kills Castiglione, 1533.

150. Ten years later I met Countess Ottavia again; on seeing me once more she wept bitterly. I reminded her of Okinski. "I can no longer love," she told me. I answered in the poet's words: "How changed, how saddened, yet how elevated was her character!"

151. French morals will be formed between 1815 and 1880, just as English morals were formed between 1668 and 1730. There will be nothing finer, juster or happier than moral France about the year 1900. At the present day it does not exist. What is considered infamous in Rue de Belle-Chasse is an act of heroism in Rue du Mont-Blanc, and, allowing for all exaggeration, people really worthy of contempt escape by a change of residence. One remedy we did have — the freedom of the Press. In the long run the Press gives each man his due, and when this due happens to fall in with public opinion, so it remains. This remedy is now torn from us — and it will somewhat retard the regeneration of morals.

152. The Abbé Rousseau was a poor young man (1784), reduced to running all over the town, from morn till night, giving lessons in history and geography. He fell in love with one of his pupils, like Abelard with Héloïse or Saint-Preux with Julie. Less happy than they, no doubt — yet, probably, pretty nearly so — as full of passion as Saint-Preux, but with a heart more virtuous, more refined and also more courageous, he seems to have sacrificed himself to the object of his passion. After dining in a restaurant at the Palais-Royal with no outward sign of distress or frenzy, this is what he wrote before blowing out his brains. The text of his note is taken from the enquiry held on the spot by the commissary and the police, and is remarkable enough to be preserved.

"The immeasurable contrast that exists between the nobility of my feelings and the meanness of my birth, my love, as violent as it is invincible, for this adorable girl[1] and

[1] The girl in question appears to have been Mademoiselle Gromaire, daughter of M. Gromaire, expeditionary at the Court of Rome.

my fear of causing her dishonor, the necessity of choosing between crime and death — everything has made me decide to say good-bye to life. Born for virtue, I was about to become a criminal; I preferred death." (Grimm, Part III, Vol. II, p. 395)

This is an admirable case of suicide, but would be merely silly according to the morals of 1880.

153. Try as they may, the French, in Art, will never get beyond the pretty.

The comic presupposes "go" in the public, and *brio* in the actor. The delicious foolery of Palomba, played at Naples by Casaccia, is an impossibility at Paris. There we have the pretty — always and only the pretty — cried up sometimes, it is true, as the sublime.

I don't waste much thought, you see, on general considerations of national honor.

154. We are very fond of a beautiful picture, say the French — and quite truly — but we exact, as the essential condition of beauty, that it be produced by a painter standing on one leg the whole time he is working. —Verse in dramatic art.

155. Much less envy in America than in France, and much less intellect.

156. Since 1530 tyranny *à la* Philip II has so degraded men's intellect, has so overshadowed the garden of the world, that the poor Italian writers have not yet plucked up enough courage to *invent* a national novel. Yet, thanks to the naturalness which reigns there, nothing could be simpler. They need only copy faithfully what stares the world in the face. Think of Cardinal Gonzalvi, for three hours gravely looking for flaws in the libretto of an opera-bouffe, and saying uneasily to the composer: "But you're continually repeating this word *Cozzar, cozzar.*"

157. Héloïse speaks of love, a coxcomb of *his* love — don't you see that these things have really nothing but their name

in common! Just so, there is the love of concerts and the love of music: the love of successes that tickle your vanity — successes your harp may bring you in the midst of a brilliant society — or the love of a tender day-dream, solitary and timid.

158. When you have just seen the woman you love, the sight of any other woman spoils your vision, gives your eyes physical pain. I know why.

159. Reply to an objection: —

Perfect naturalness in intimate intercourse can find no place but in passion-love, for in all the other kinds of love a man feels the possibility of a favored rival.

160. In a man who, to be released from life, has taken poison, the moral part of his being is dead. Dazed by what he has done and by what he is about to experience, he no longer attends to anything. There are some rare exceptions.

161. An old sea captain, to whom I respectfully offered my manuscript, thought it the silliest thing in the world to honor with six hundred pages so trivial a thing as love. But, however trivial, love is still the only weapon which can strike strong souls, and strike home.

What was it prevented M. de M——, in 1814, from despatching Napoleon in the forest of Fontainebleau? The contemptuous glance of a pretty woman coming into the Bains-Chinois.[1] What a difference in the destiny of the world if Napoleon and his son had been killed in 1814!

162. I quote the following lines from a French letter received from Znaim, remarking at the same time that there is not a man in the provinces capable of understanding my brilliant lady correspondent: —

[1] *Memoirs*, p. 88. (London edition)

"... Chance means a lot in love. When for a whole year I have read no English, I find the first novel I pick up delicious. One who is used to the love of a prosaic being — slow, shy of all that is refined, and passionately responsive to none but material interests, the love of shekels, the glory of a fine stable and bodily desires, etc. — can easily feel disgust at the behavior of impetuous genius, ardent and uncurbed in fancy, mindful of love, forgetful of all the rest, always active and always headlong, just where the other let himself be led and never acted for himself. The shock, which genius causes, may offend what, last year at Zithau, we used to call feminine pride, *l'orgueil féminin* — (is that French?). With the man of genius comes the startling feeling which with his predecessor was unknown—and, remember, this predecessor came to an untimely end in the wars and remains a synonym for perfection. This feeling may easily be mistaken for repulsion by a soul, lofty but without that assurance which is the fruit of a goodly number of intrigues."

163. "Geoffry Rudel, of Blaye, was a very great lord, prince of Blaye, and he fell in love, without knowing her, with the Princess of Tripoli, for the great goodness and great graciousness, which he heard tell of her from the pilgrims, who came from Antioch. And he made for her many fair songs, with good melodies and suppliant words, and, for the desire he had to see her, he took the cross and set out upon the sea to go to her. And it happened that in the ship a grievous malady took him, in such wise that those that were with him believed him to be dead, but they contrived to bring him to Tripoli into a hostelry, like one dead. They sent word to the countess and she came to his bed and took him in her arms. Then he knew that she was the countess and he recovered his sight and his hearing and he praised God, giving Him thanks that He had sustained his life until he had seen her. And thus he died in the arms of the countess, and she gave him noble burial in the house of the

Temple at Tripoli. And then the same day she took the veil for the sorrow she had for him and for his death."[1]

164. Here is a singular proof of the madness called crystallization, to be found in Mistress Hutchinson's Memoirs:

"He told to M. Hutchinson a very true story of a gentleman who not long before had come for some time to lodge in Richmond, and found all the people he came in company with bewailing the death of a gentlewoman that had lived there. Hearing her so much deplored, he made inquiry after her, and grew so in love with the description, that no other discourse could at first please him nor could he at last endure any other; he grew desperately melancholy and would go to a mount where the print of her foot was cut and lie there pining and kissing it all the day long, till at length death in some months' space concluded his languishment. This story was very true." (Vol. I, p. 83)

165. Lisio Visconti was anything but a great reader. Not to mention what he may have seen while knocking about the world, his essay is based on the Memoirs of some fifteen or twenty persons of note. In case it happens that the reader thinks such trifling points worthy of a moment's attention, I give the books from which Lisio drew his reflections and conclusions: —

The *Autobiography* of Benvenuto Cellini.
The novels of Cervantes and Scarron.
Manon Lescaut and *Le Doyen de Killerine*, by the Abbé Prévôt.
The Latin Letters of Héloïse to Abelard.
Tom Jones.
Letters of a Portuguese Nun.
Two or three stories by Auguste La Fontaine.
Pignotti's *History of Tuscany.*
Werther.
Brantôme.

[1] Translated from a Provençal MS. of the thirteenth century.

Memoirs of Carlo Gozzi (Venice, 1760) — on the eighty
pages on the history of his love affairs.

The *Memoirs* of Lauzun, Saint-Simon, d'Epinay, de
Staël, Marmontel, Bezenval, Roland, Duclos, Horace
Walpole, Evelyn, Hutchinson.

Letters of Mademoiselle Lespinasse.

166. One of the most important persons of our age, one of
the most prominent men in the Church and in the State,
related to us this evening (January, 1822), at Madame de
M——'s, the very real dangers he had gone through under
the Terror.

"I had the misfortune to be one of the most prominent
members of the Constituent Assembly. I stayed in Paris,
trying to hide myself as best I could, so long as there was
any hope of success there for the good cause. At last, as the
danger grew greater and greater, while the foreigner made
no energetic move in our favor, I decided to leave — only
I had to leave without a passport. Everyone was going off
to Coblentz, so I determined to make for Calais. But my
portrait had been so widely circulated eighteen months
before, that I was recognized at the last post. However, I
was allowed to pass and arrived at an inn at Calais, where,
you can imagine, I did not sleep a wink — and very lucky it
was, since at four o'clock in the morning I heard someone
pronounce my name quite distinctly. While I got up and
was dressing in all haste I could clearly distinguish, in spite
of the darkness, the National Guards with their rifles; the
people had opened the main door for them and they were
entering the courtyard of the inn. Fortunately it was raining in torrents — a winter morning, very dark and with a
high wind. The darkness and the noise of the wind enabled
me to escape by the back courtyard and stables. There I
stood in the street at seven o'clock in the morning, utterly
resourceless!

I imagined they were following me from my inn. Hardly
knowing what I was doing, I went down to the port, on to

the jetty. I own I had rather lost my head — everywhere the vision of the guillotine floated before my eyes.

A packet-boat was leaving the port in a very rough sea — it was already a hundred yards from the jetty. Suddenly I heard a shout from out at sea, as if I were being called. I saw a small boat approaching. "Hi! sir, come on! We're waiting for you!" Mechanically I got into the boat. A man was in it. "I saw you walking on the jetty with a scared look," he whispered, "I thought you might be some poor fugitive. I've told them you are a friend I was expecting; pretend to be sea-sick and go and hide below in a dark corner of the cabin."

"Oh, what a fine touch!" cried our hostess. She was almost speechless and had been moved to tears by the Abbé's long and excellently told story of his perils. "How you must have thanked your unknown benefactor! What was his name?"

"I do not know his name," the Abbé answered, a little confused.

And there was a moment of profound silence in the room.

167. THE FATHER AND THE SON (A dialogue of 1787)

The Father (Minister of ——): "I congratulate you, my son; it's a splendid thing for you to be invited to the Duke of ——; it's a distinction for a man of your age. Don't fail to be at the Palace punctually at six o'clock."

The Son: "I believe, sir, you are dining there also."

The Father: "The Duke of —— is always more than kind to our family, and, as he's asking you for the first time, he has been pleased to invite me as well."

The son, a young man of high birth and most distinguished intellect, does not fail to be at the Palace punctually at six o'clock. Dinner was at seven. The son found himself placed opposite his father. Each guest had a naked woman next to him. The dinner was served by a score of lackeys in full livery.[1]

[1] From December 27, 1819, till 3 June, 1820, Mil. [This note is written thus in English by Stendhal.]

168. Never in my life have I been so struck or intimidated by the presence of beauty as to-night, at a concert given by Madame Pasta.

She was surrounded, as she sang, by three rows of young women, so beautiful — of a beauty so pure and heavenly — that I felt myself lower my eyes, out of respect, instead of raising them to admire and enjoy. This has never happened to me in any other land, not even in my beloved Italy.

169. In France one thing is absolutely impossible in the arts, and that is "go." A man really carried away would be too much laughed at — he would look too happy. See a Venetian recite Buratti's satires.